FRONTIERS OF NARRATIVE

Series Editor: David Herman,

North Carolina State University

Handbook of Narrat

Handbook of Narrative Analysis

Written and translated by
Luc Herman
and Bart Vervaeck

University of Nebraska Press
Lincoln and London

 Manufactured in the United States of America. Set in Quadraat by Tseng Information Systems, Inc. Design: R. Eckersley. Printed by Thomson-Shore, Inc.

Library of Congress Cataloging-in-Publication Data
Herman, Luc.
[Vertelduivels. English]
Handbook of narrative analysis / written and translated by Luc Herman and Bart Vervaeck.
p. cm. – (Frontiers of narrative)
Translation of Vertelduivels : handboek verhaalanalyse.
Includes bibliographical references and index.
ISBN 0-8032-2413-3 (cloth : alkaline paper) –
ISBN 0-8032-7349-5 (paperback : alkaline paper)
1. Narration (Rhetoric) I. Vervaeck, Bart. II. Title.
III. Series.
PN212.H4813 2005 808–dc22 2004018004

Contents

Acknowledgments

Many people have helped us along the way. We wish to thank Jürgen Pieters, Hans Vandevoorde, and Jan Vernimmen, who have read earlier versions of this book, for their many comments and Bert Bultinck, Gert Morreel, and Marija Rac for their contributions to the translation from Dutch to English. Special thanks to David Herman for directing us to UNP and to Charlotte Mutsaers and Gerrit Krol for letting us give their stories the full narratological treatment.

Handbook of Narrative Analysis

Introduction

No single period or society can do without narratives. And, a good number of contemporary thinkers hasten to add, whatever you say and think about a certain time or place becomes a narrative in its own right. From the oldest myths and legends to postmodern fabulation, narration has always been central. Postmodern philosophers may submit that there are no longer any grand, encompassing narratives, but they also contend that everything amounts to a narrative, including the world and the self. If that is correct, then the study of narrative is not just a pastime for literary theorists in their ivory towers. Instead it unveils fundamental culture-specific opinions about reality and humankind, which are narrativized in stories and novels.

Theory and practice

Theories of narrative are misconstrued if they insist on abstraction and lose touch with actual stories. This handbook aims to avoid this. It is geared to a concrete illustration of the relevance – and the potential shortcomings – of major narrative theories. This is why we constantly refer to two short stories that we briefly present in this introduction and that we have made available in the appendix to this book: "Pegasian" by Charlotte Mutsaers and "The Map" by Gerrit Krol.[1] Although these short stories have been selected pretty much at random, they can still serve to illustrate several basic problems of narration. In the introduction we only indicate what these problems might be, and we formulate a number of related questions. The rest of the book consists of the various answers to those questions.

Mustsaers and Krol

Obviously we will not restrict ourselves to an analysis of just two stories. When discussing the various theories, we will quote from a number of other narrative texts but always from literary narratives in prose. Literary prose has in fact always been the starting point of the study of narrative, which since its upsurge in the sixties and seventies has come to be known as narratology and which provides the framework for our undertaking. There are many other forms of narration, such as comics and poetry, but we will not be dealing with those. Also, the more general cultural dimensions of narration are only occasionally touched upon – mostly in the final chapter in which we connect stories with their contexts. Limiting ourselves in such a way is a direct consequence of our effort to remain as close to the actual texts as we possibly can.

1. TRADITIONAL QUESTIONS

The narrator problem

Contrary to poetry and drama, a prose story cannot do without a narrator, or so most people seem to think. The first lines of "The Map" seem to feature one of those good old narrators who knows everything and hovers over the universe of the story. He tells about the Christian shops whose shades were rolled down on Sundays. Yet in the second paragraph it becomes clear that this seemingly objective voice is in fact subjective since it belongs to an I-narrator. It seems obvious to imagine that this I-narrator is present already in the first paragraph but that he remains more or less in the background. However, it is not that simple. Let us suppose that the first paragraph is expanded into an entire chapter and the second paragraph into yet another full chapter. In that case, are we speaking of different narrators? Or are we going to think of these two voices as belonging to one and the same narrator who switches back and forth between the relatively impersonal voice of an all-knowing third-person narrator and the very personal voice of a first-person narrator?

The answer to this question may well depend on the size of the passages at hand. The briefer the passage, the more one tends to choose the single-narrator option. The first sentence about the shops with their rolled-down shades could be followed by "But one of these Sundays, on my way to children's church, I saw part of a map." In that case the first sentence would be attributed to the first-person narrator as well. In the case of a paragraph this becomes less obvious, and in the case of a chapter even less so. All this may seem quite irrelevant, but in fact it amounts to a fundamental problem. Is it possible to say that a text is narrated by one specific type of narrator? Or is there a constant change? Would it be correct to suggest that a traditional ninenteenth-century novel, for instance, is narrated by a third-person narrator?

The narrator's scope

Put in more abstract terms, we are dealing here with the demarcation of units for investigation. Does a narrator have to be defined for every unit, or does every unit have to fit into a larger subdivision of the novel or story? A case in point, to which we will return, is the famous monologue by Molly Bloom in the final chapter of *Ulysses*. If you consider this chapter separately, you could say that Molly narrates what is going on in her mind. However, if you consider this chapter in conjunction with the rest of the novel, you could say that there is an omniscient narrator who quotes or recounts Molly's thoughts. Drawing a borderline between narrative units is therefore of paramount importance. If the chapter is a separate unit, then the character is the narrator. If the chapter is part of the larger whole, then the narrator is not a character at all.

Narration and perception

Let us reconsider the first-person narrator of "The Map." The act of seeing seems to be very important for him. One Sunday in his childhood he notices that the shades of one particular shop window have not been fully rolled down, and he goes on to spot a cycling map through the slit that has remained: "Never had I seen such a map, with such minute detail." Is this I-witness the same as the figure who reports the discovery? Or do we have to say that the I-witness is a little boy and that the I-narrator is much older, perhaps the adult who is looking back? In retrospect he does not see in the same way as the child. These two figures are not only separated in time, they also do not share the same view. The story does not explicitly thematize this distinction. It could have been thematized as follows: "Later I would see many more maps, but none of them would entrance me as much as this one." In "The Map," the rift in question is only addressed toward the end of the story. What amounts to an exciting discovery for the child has become routine for the adult. In the last paragraph, a sentence such as "[Later] my dream would fade away" proves that the I-narrator differs from the boy who makes the discovery. Indeed, how could the child know that his dream would fade away later? The narrator knows more than the boy, especially the disenchanting outcome of the story that leads him to throw out the map: "I haven't kept it either."

Narration and interpretation

The reader who puts all the I-figures in this story into the same bag misses out on the thematic essence of the story – the loss of a childlike enchantment. This loss only emerges when the reader realizes the difference between the boy and the narrator. This is just one example of the way in which a narratological analysis can contribute to an interpretation focusing on content. In this case the act of seeing is indeed the main theme. The narrator announces it in the opening sentence with the closed shops, and he develops it in "those two forbidden inches" that enable the boy to see the map, which in its turn enables him to see mapped for the first time the areas he would otherwise have crossed and biked unthinkingly. The real enchantment resides in the graphic representation of reality. The transition from reality to representation on the level of content reflects the narratological development from someone who sees and acts to someone who narrates. We will repeatedly stress that a narratological analysis does not have any value as long as it does not connect with the contents of the story.

Narrator and character in "The Map"

There are a few other problems with the so-called I-narrator in "The Map." The first paragraph features the following sentence: "There was a counter behind which ('he's nice, she's wearing the pants') Mr and Mrs Paalman operated as if it were a grocery store." The brief comment in parentheses describes Mr and Mrs Paalman, but as a reader you never get to know who does the actual talking. Perhaps this view corresponds to the village opinion. In any case, the speaker is not a character in the story. He or she is merely a voice instead of an embodied figure. This abstract and general agency might relate to "one," who is mentioned a little later in the text and becomes a speaker: "One waited one's turn and when it was finally there, one uttered one's wishes, in the manner of 'a light novel for a girl of seventeen' or 'a historical novel, preferably illustrated. . . .' " The narrator quotes impersonal visitors who do appear in the story and who therefore differ from the impersonal village opinion in "he's nice, she's wearing the pants." Quoted figures can apparently hail from inside as well as from outside the story.

Obviously, figures do not only appear in the guise of quotation marks. The narrator can summarize what they think or say in which case these talking and thinking figures actually recede in favor of the summarizing narrator. Take a sentence like "The village contended that Mrs Paalman was the boss at home and that her husband was a mere meek shadow." If the narrator had summarized the village opinion in this way, these different words would also create a different view. In the imaginary summary the wife becomes more threatening while the husband seems to disappear altogether. For a reader it is often very difficult to make a clear distinction between what was originally said and what the narrator made of it.

Narrator and character in "Pegasian"

This certainly applies to the story by Charlotte Mutsaers. Since she does not use any quotation marks, it is often impossible to differentiate between the words of the characters and those of the narrator. "The riding master[2] answers that you catch a very special wind with it," is a summary in indirect speech by the narrator. The original words of the riding master are not directly reproduced, but instead they are paraphrased and presented in a that-clause. It is impossible to decide whether the summary remains close to the original. One might surmise that the riding master said, "You catch a very special wind with it," in which case the summary is extremely true to the original, but there is no way to be sure. Indirect speech always betrays an intervention by the narrator. Less so in the case of direct speech because it quotes the original expression. The fourth paragraph of "Pegasian" might be such a direct quotation, even though there are no quotation marks. "Do they make you go faster?" would then equal the actual question the female character asked her riding master.

Problems, however, are just beginning. Who says "true dressage, just like real life, doesn't have anything to do with racing"? Is it the riding master and is he quoted literally? Or is it the narrator who is speaking here? And if so, is the formulation his, or does he choose an unusual way to represent a statement by the riding master? This strange method of speech representation occurs again and again, as for instance in the following sentence: "Little girls . . . did well not to shoot off their mouths." This is not a direct quotation, otherwise the sentence would read, "Little girls do well not to shoot off their mouths." Neither is it a summary, since in that case the sentence would read, "The riding master thought that little girls did well not to shoot off their mouths." The actual sentence sits somewhere in between the two, which makes it very difficult to decide which words belong to the riding master and which ones to the narrator. That position which belongs to neither of the two traditional methods of speech representation is occupied by free indirect speech. As we will see, this intermediate form has caused many controversies in traditional structuralist narratology.

At the end, "the riding master doesn't feel like explaining anything anymore. Sometimes your patience simply runs out." Who pronounces the latter sentence? The narrator? Or, in the case of free indirect speech, the riding master, who may have sighed, "Sometimes my patience simply runs out"? This is important, since in free indirect speech "your patience" seems to be that of a specific character; that is, the riding master. However, if it is the narrator who says, "Sometimes your patience simply runs out," then "your" is much more general and refers to a general agent outside the story: "People will sometimes run out of patience." The next sentence, "Furthermore, all this questioning ruins the class, notably for the other ladies," is probably a statement by the riding master, represented in free indirect speech. This makes it more probable that the brief sentence about patience is also a statement by the riding master. But one can never be sure.

In the last paragraph another "you" appears: "Whatever. As long as you take off." Either this is an idea of the female character, and in that case the "you" can be a general "one" or a transposition of "I" into free indirect speech; or this is a statement by the narrator, in which case only the general interpretation is possible. The general "one" does not appear in the story as an embodied figure, but the transposed "I" of course does.

Inside or outside the story

In "Pegasian" by Mutsaers, this ambiguity concerning inside or outside the story is present from the beginning. In the first sentence, the main female character might consider that "when horse riding you might best be wearing a real pair of riding breeches." Who is this "you"? Is it the main character to whom the riding master says that she should wear proper riding pants, or is this another general you-figure, a "one" that hovers over the story and is not really addressed? Does this really matter? As we will see, it really does since the difference between elements within the narrative world and those outside it is one of the most fundamental distinctions made by traditional narratology. It has already become clear that stories are somewhat casual with regard to this abstract difference, and we will find this repeatedly in the course of our investigation.

In "The Map," the distinction is mostly easy to make. In "he's nice, she's wearing the pants," we have a general agent, the village opinion, that does not appear as a character. If this agent were to be turned into a customer in the bookshop, then she or he would become a character in the story, for instance someone who would wish to buy "a light novel for a girl of seventeen." Even if the you-figure in "The Map" does not speak, it is relatively easy to decide whether it belongs to the narrative world or not. "On the corner of little Brouwerstreet and Ebbingestreet, for instance, you had the Paalman bookshop." This "you" can be understood as "one," a general and abstract agent who does not assume any concrete form. He or she does not appear as a visitor to the small town, while the "one" who talks does, as a bookshop customer. On the other hand, it could be said that also the I-figure as a young man is contained in the abstract "one" since he too obviously knew the bookshop on the corner. As a result, Krol's general "one" also occupies a position between the I-figure within the narrative world and the abstract agent outside it.

The fact that "Pegasian" often does not allow us to decide the position of the you-figure is highly significant. The reader can connect the form of narration with its content. Maybe the "you" in the story cannot properly be separated from a general "one" because the story has allegorical dimensions. That which holds for the female "you" on the horse does in fact hold for everyone. One could even speak of a moral, which, as happens often, the story reserves for its last few sentences: "Whatever. As long as you take off." In other words, the thing the you-figure learns in this short story resembles that which the reader (and human beings in general) must learn as well. The method of overcoming gravity is not important as long as you take off.

Inside or outside: interpretation

We do not believe it is farfetched to connect the confusion of figures inside and outside of the story with the story's content. This connection is precisely what makes narratology relevant. If narratology becomes a mere formalistic game in which the distinction of various narrators does not go hand-in-hand with a discussion of what they actually tell us, then the contents of a narrative remain mistakingly untouched. Conversely, it would be wrong to forget the narrative aspects of a story and to focus exclusively on content. Whoever insists on doing the latter not only misses out on various thematic and interpretive layers but also reduces a text to its content or message. In fact it is the way in which a story is narrated that turns it into what it is. Those who insist on denying the importance of the method of narration by reducing a story to content might just as well go to the movies or watch television because both of them can offer similar content.

Only a narratology that deals both with the narrated world (content) and also with the way in which this world is represented (form) has any relevance for text interpretation. We consider interpretation precisely as the effort to connect the content of a particular object – in this case a literary text – with its form. This connection works both ways. Form always implies content, and content in its turn clarifies the meaning of form. Such a connection is by no means readily evident. The reader has to discover it, and such a discovery always reveals a certain ideology. Reading and ideology will therefore be addressed momentarily.

2. NEW QUESTIONS

The problems we have dealt with so far all have to do with borders, such as that between the story's various passages; narrating and seeing; then and now; talking and acting; inside and outside the story; and the words of a character and those of the narrator. In general, traditional narratology tries to draw these borders as clearly as possible, while more recent theories of narrative emphasize the transitions and potential confusions. The interest in transitions also explains why recent approaches no longer consider a literary narrative in terms of a closed system. They insist that a text always functions in a context, while traditional theory largely remained blind to this.

Ideology and context

Context always has to do with ideology. We conceive of ideology in its widest sense as the collection of conscious or unconscious views of the world and what it is to be human, which means that for us the term need not have any negative connotations. This view of ideology allows for the study of various elements. In "The Map," one could look for the narrative's religious aspects. Indeed, the story deals with Christian shops whose shades are rolled down "to avoid that man would be seduced on Sunday to buy something on Monday." This ironic formulation suggests that religion wants to hide things but in the process only makes them more attractive. This explains the attraction of the "two forbidden inches" that enable the boy to see the map. Seeing and not seeing do not merely constitute the story's themes or its technical aspects, but they also have a major ideological import. Religion doubtlessly plays a role in the boy's desire, which is not coincidentally described with a word – "prospect" – related to seeing: "The prospect I was going to cover the earth with my body. To be everywhere . . ." The latter is only given to God.

In "Pegasian," ideology could be thought to relate to the currently popular difference between male and female aspects of narrative. The riding master can easily be simplified so as to appear as the representative of male attitudes. He demands submissiveness, imposes rules, and thinks that the heavenly feeling at stake in the story can only be attained by seriousness and study. To the psychoanalytically oriented reader, the riding master might even represent the paternal agent. The female figure, on the contrary, comes across as much more frivolous. In her view study and rules do not matter all that much, and she promotes that which is carefree and unregulated. The unorthodox narration in this story could then be thought to undermine (male) discipline and to promote the free-floating transience of (female) lightness.

Literary context

When extending narratology to the study of the narrative's context, attention must obviously be paid to the literary context as well. In this respect, "Pegasian" might be compared to the story "Up in the Gallery" by Franz Kafka.[3] This story likewise deals with a pupil in a riding school and her ruthless riding master who enjoys cracking the whip. Also in "Up in the Gallery," the male and female perspectives clash. The story consists of only two paragraphs. In the first one we get a description of how the female rider would be bullied by the male character. In the second we get exactly the opposite. The male character adores the female rider. The reader who knows this story will undoubtedly hear echoes of Kafka in the story by Mutsaers, which will affect the narrative. This means that the analysis of a story cannot remain independent of the reader who brings the story to life. While the traditional approach hardly makes any room for the reader, more recent theories give him or her a central position.

Reader and context

The reader and the context – literary as well as ideological – perhaps constitute the most important new ingredients of contemporary narrative theory, but narratology has expanded in other directions as well. In the last two or three decades a number of new approaches have been developed, some of which contain significant revisions of traditional structuralist theory. In the final chapter of this book, we discuss a representative selection of these new approaches, highlighting their potential for interpretation and making sure to show just how they improve narrative theory. However, it is important not to throw out the narrative baby with the structuralist bathwater, and therefore the second chapter of this handbook will provide a sizeable summary of traditional narratology geared to classroom treatment. Starting from a traditional division between story, narrative, and narration – terms we have so far used in their non-technical meaning – we have brought together all narrative elements structuralism can be thought to offer as potentially important for interpretation. Obviously, structuralist narratology did not come into being in a vacuum, which explains why in the first chapter we discuss the early stages of narrative theory and also some important theories that were developed simultaneously with structuralism and that therefore already betray an awareness of its approach. Our overall aim in this handbook is to make narrative theory available to those who are interested in close and ideologically relevant readings of literary prose. We are aware of the ideological dangers inherent in our self-appointed status as facilitators, but we have tried to come up with (con)testable possibilities rather than take-it-or-leave-it solutions.

Chapter 1

Before and Surrounding Structuralism

Structuralism has undoubtedly offered the most popular theory of narrative. It was able to build on an age-old tradition, a lot of which it rejected. Yet structuralism also held on to a number of classical concepts, some of which we will explain in this chapter. In the course of these explanations we will also present a few more recent theories that do not really belong to the structuralist canon but that have made important contributions and have very often led to interesting discussions with structuralism. We do not aim to be exhaustive or, for that matter, to provide a history of narratology. Instead we only mention those theoreticians and concepts that still figure in narratological discussions.

1. STORY AND PLOT

If narratology is the theory of the narrative text, then it should first come up with a definition of narrative. Traditionally a narrative is considered to be a sequence of events. This formulation is highly problematic, and some of the problems it entails seem to defy solution. First of all, this definition simply shifts the problem in defining narrative to the equally problematic concept of "event." What does the event in "Pegasian" consist of? Rather than a narrative, isn't this text perhaps a sketch or a scene?

Secondly, one could ask what kind of sequence of events appears in a narrative. Can we already speak of a narrative when one event follows the other in time? Or does the link between the events have to be stronger? For instance, does there have to be a link of cause and effect? In order to answer this question, the novelist and theoretician E. M. Forster introduced his famous distinction between *story* and *plot*. For the time being we will work with these two terms, but later on in this book we will replace *plot* with a pair of technical terms gleaned from structuralism, *narrative* and *narration*. According to Forster, story is the chronological sequence of events. Plot refers to the causal connection between those *Forster* events. Forster provides the following example of a story: "The king died and then the queen died." This sequence becomes a plot in the following sentence: "The king died and then the queen died of grief."[1]

Unfortunately the distinction between temporal and causal connections is not always easy to make. Apparently human beings tend to interpret events succeeding each other in time as events with a causal connection. Shlomith Rimmon-Kenan quotes the following joke about Milton: "Milton wrote *Paradise Lost*, then his wife died, and then he wrote *Paradise Regained*."[2] The joke resides in the suggestion of an (unspoken) causal connection between the death of the wife and the discovery of paradise. The sequence seems chronological, but it has a causal dimension as well.

This means that the distinction between plot and story is by no means absolute. The example readily shows the importance of the reader, who interprets the sentence about Milton and thus turns the story into a plot. We do not reject the fundamental distinction between the two levels, but we want to make clear from the start that such a distinction comes down to a theoretical construct, which doesn't tie in with concrete interpretations by actual readers. The sequence of events is always the work of the reader, who makes links between the story's several incidents. This provides the plot with its dynamic, and it also gives rise to the idea that something is in fact happening. Just like the sequence of events, the event itself turns out to be dependent on the reader's input. It is impossible to define an event *in abstracto* once and for all. What happens in "Pegasian"? A reader who approaches this text as we have done in our introduction might say that quite a lot is happening here. There is a discussion between teacher and pupil about the correct way to ride a horse, followed by a double space and a resolution in which the question of who is right reveals itself to be less important than the fact that both characters use the horse to defy gravity. In "The Map," the events may seem more easily discernable – the acquisition of a map, the bike rides relative to it, and, more generally, the mapping of ordinary activities – but still, how the events are discerned will depend on the reader.

Events and their connections

One may doubt whether meaningful connections that the reader makes between events can be reduced to causal connections. In "Pegasian," although we do not see all that much cause and effect in the plot development, there is a meaningful transition from the discussion to the conclusion. It is one from dogmatism to relativism, from dressage or submission to freedom and take-off. These connections are not causal, but they are significant and not merely chronological. A plot therefore depends not on causal connections but rather on a wealth of relevant connections that transcend mere chronology and are always introduced by the reader.

If we consider plot as an event sequence meaningful to the reader, then we still have to distinguish the narrative text from other genres. Does a newspaper article constitute a plot-driven narrative? Do non-linguistic sign systems result in such narratives? Do movies, plays, comic strips, and video games all come down to this type of narrative? For us they do. We define plot-driven narrative as the representation of meaningfully related events. Such a representation can use any sign system.

Definition of narrative

This means we use a broad definition of narrative that is even broader than the one proposed by Susana Onega and José Angel García Landa in their narratology reader. They say, "A narrative is the semiotic representation of a series of events meaningfully connected in a temporal and causal way."[3] In our view the last six words of this sentence can be dropped. For us, meaning in meaningfully related events cannot be reduced to temporality and causality. It results from the interaction between reader and text.

Since we extend temporal and causal links to meaningful connections at large, we deviate from the traditional view on the so-called minimal story – with "story" used here, contrary to Forster, in its general meaning as a synonym of narrative. The concept of the minimal story fits the structuralist search for the smallest units of a text. It has been developed to determine when one can speak of a narrative. If a character says, "Yes, I can come tomorrow," does that mean we have a story? No, Gerald Prince says, since a story consists of at least three ingredients: an initial situation, an action or event, and an outcome.[4] Connections must be temporal as well as causal. For instance, "John was happy, then he lost his girlfriend and as a result he became unhappy." Rimmon-Kenan criticizes Prince's definition and submits that a temporal connection is sufficient to speak of a minimal story.[5] For us meaningful relations suffice, and they might even be metaphorical, metonymical, or thematic, *as long as the reader considers them significant*. "Yes, I can come tomorrow," does not amount to a narrative, because it does not connect events in any meaningful way. "He could not come then because he was ill," does constitute a narrative since it does make a meaningful connection between events. In this case the link is simply causal, but different links can also create a minimal story. "It was raining hard, in the streets as well as in his heart," is a minimal story, too, as it makes a significant metaphorical (or symbolical) link, and it does not imply causality or temporal sequence.

2. TELLING AND SHOWING

In order to avoid complicating the following discussion, we will temporarily assume that we can distinguish more or less easily between events and reality on the one hand and their narrative representation on the other. A narrative never provides a perfect copy of the reality constituting its subject. A person who narrates what has happened to him will always summarize, expand, embellish, and leave out certain aspects of his experience. Since a narrative text is restricted to language, it will never show reality directly. On the stage certain events can be shown, but this hardly applies to a novel. All this relates to the age-old distinction between what Plato called *mimesis* and *diegesis*.[6]

Mimesis Mimesis evokes reality by staging it. This is evident in the theater, but narratives too have moments that tend toward mimetic representation, for instance literally quoted conversations. In this case the narrative almost literally shows what was said in the reality evoked by the text, and yet a complete overlap between narrative representation and the "real" conversation is out of the question. Short phrases like "he said" already indicate an intervention by the narrator. Furthermore, chances are high that the time necessary for the reader to process the conversation in the text will not exactly coincide with the duration of the original conversation. The latter even applies when reading a text meant for the stage, which after all approximates mimesis. There will probably be a major difference between the duration of the performance and the time necessary to read the text it was based on.

Diegesis Diegesis summarizes events and conversations. In such a summary the voice of the narrator will always come through. He colors narrated events, which are therefore no longer directly available. "The Map" recounts how the boy enters the store and asks about the enchanting map: "Monday afternoon, in the bookshop, I pointed to it. I did not have enough money, so that I had to wait until Saturday." This summary probably covers an unreported conversation in which the shopkeeper mentions the price of the map, and the boy concludes he will need his next weekly allowance in order to buy it. The narrator summarizes this situation instead of showing it.

The difference between diegesis and mimesis equals the difference, in the Anglo-American tradition before structuralism, between telling and showing, between summary and scene. In "The Art of Fiction" (1884) and other theoretical writings, Henry James established his preference for a narrator whom the reader can barely see or hear and who tries hard to show as much as he can.[7] In *The Craft of Fiction* (1921), Percy Lubbock favored showing to telling under the influence of James's novels.[8] A mimetic novel usually contains a lot of action and dialogue. In strongly diegetic texts, on the other hand, the narrator does come to the fore, so that he ostentatiously places himself between the related scenes and the reader. In postmodern narratives narrators can behave in such an extremely diegetic way that the reader starts to distrust them. So little is left of the original scene that you wonder whether the reported event actually took place.

Transition from mimesis to diegesis

Although mimesis and diegesis may look like a binary pair, they really constitute the two extremes of a continuum on which every narrative occupies a specific position. "Pegasian" appears more mimetic than "The Map," not least because Mutsaers shows conversation much more directly than Krol and because the time of narration in the Mutsaers narrative adheres more closely to the duration of a scene than it does in Krol. In "The Map," long periods such as the one in which the main character bikes around are summarized in a few sentences. In "Pegasian," the original conversation between the riding master and the female rider remains almost untouched. However, the difference between the two narratives is far from absolute. In narrative prose, there exists no such thing as pure mimesis or diegesis. Summaries always have their mimetic aspects, and mimetic representation always has moments of summary as well.

This combination of mimesis and diegesis has been typical of the novel from its very beginnings. On the one hand the novel is a diegetic genre, and in that sense it forms the opposite of drama, an avowedly mimetic genre that at least until the end of the eighteenth century dominated the literary system. Drama does not lend itself directly to narrative analysis, and therefore it is no coincidence that narrative theory has developed along with the novel. On the other hand novelists often defined their new art by pointing to the mimetic properties of their texts. Authors such as Daniel Defoe, Samuel Richardson, and Jonathan Swift wrote introductions to their novels in which they presented their "new" way of telling as a form of the "old" showing. They paradoxically defended the trustworthiness and prestige of the new diegetic narration by calling upon its mimetic opposite. Whatever found its way into their books was not supposed to be an imaginary summary by a narrator but rather a truthful representation of scenes that actually happened. The tension between summary and scene is inherent in every form of narrative, and it remains central to any discussion of contemporary prose – witness for instance the recurring polemic about the combination of fact and fiction in autobiography.

3. AUTHOR AND NARRATOR

It has become a commonplace that the author of a book must not be confused with its narrator. However, a total separation between these two agents proves inadequate. Autobiographical fiction, for instance, simply thrives on the close connection between its author, narrator, and main character.[9] Occasional discussions about supposedly improper statements in fiction also prove that the theoretical separation between author and narrator does not remain clear in practice. Sometimes authors are even sued for statements made by their characters or narrators. This goes to show that the connection between author and narrator often plays out on the level of ideology.

Wayne Booth has provided a theoretical analysis of this connection in his book *The Rhetoric of Fiction* (1961), one of the first classics of narratology. A narrative text, Booth says, is a form of communication, and therefore you always have a sender, a message, and a receiver. These three concepts do not simply translate into author, narrative, and reader. More communicative agents are involved. In his study, Booth does not deal with the empirical author in any great detail, but he inserts three more agents between author and narrative, which we will discuss one by one.

Implied author

The *implied author* does not actually appear in the text. He does not have an audible voice, and yet he forms part of the narrative. He constitutes the source for the aggregate of norms and opinions that makes up the ideology of the text. In other words, he is responsible for the world-view emanating from a narrative. This view can be established in a variety of ways, for instance on the basis of word choice, humor, and the manner in which characters are introduced. The implied author may have a different ideology than the characters or the narrator. Empirical authors may develop an implied author who is opposed to a specific world-view, but that does not prevent proponents of this ideology from speaking up in their novels. According to Booth, the distance between implied author and narrator offers an excellent criterion to test the latter's reliability. The closer the narrator's statements resemble the implied author's ideology, the more reliable he will turn out to be.

Problems with the implied author

This point about the proximity between the narrator and implied author does not hold. The implied author and the narrator's reliability are not offered in the text itself, but instead they are construed by the reader. There exist no objective procedures to derive the implied author from a narrative. The importance of the reader for the construction of the implied author shows through in the alternative names proposed for it by other critics. Seymour Chatman prefers *inferred author,*[10] Gérard Genette likes *auteur induit.*[11] The degree of the narrator's reliability is a subjective matter as well, which highly depends on the reader's preconceived ideas about reliability and trustworthiness.[12]

As a construction the implied author therefore depends on the reader and on the textual elements as they are interpreted by the reader. That turns the implied author into a paradoxical concept. On the one hand he is supposed to be at the root of the norms and values in a text, and in this way he would give the reader direction. Chatman defines the implied author as the "agency within the narrative fiction itself which guides any reading of it."[13] On the other hand the implied author depends on how the reader handles the text. Ansgar Nünning correctly suggests that the location of the implied author in the communicative structure of fiction is very unclear. In theory he occupies a position on the side of the sender since he connects to the author, but in practice he amounts to a construction by the receiver (the reader), who makes use of the message (the text) in order to arrive at this construction.[14] The exact position of the implied author remains vague. Nünning criticizes Chatman because the latter first says that the reader constructs the implied author and then lets this construction coincide with the text: "The text is itself the implied author."[15] Eventually Chatman combines reader and text in a definition of the implied author as "the patterns in the text which the reader negotiates."[16]

Such a blurring of the borderlines between sender, message, and receiver is wasted on structuralist narratology, which attempts to separate these elements as strictly as possible. No wonder Genette opposes the concept of the implied author. He maintains the strict separation between the empirical author, who remains outside the text (and therefore also outside narratology), and the narrator, who belongs to the text (and to narratology). Genette considers an intermediate figure such as the implied author entirely superfluous.[17] Opposites meet in connection with this issue. Anti-structuralist theorists, who do not regard language as a formal network but rather as subjective expression, hold the same opinion as Genette. Peter Juhl, who studies literature on the basis of intention and expression, contends that a literary work can only say and mean something when readers and critics connect it with an empirical author who guarantees the seriousness and authenticity of the text. The real author must not be hidden behind an imaginary construction, since that would mean statements in a text lose their value: "The propositions which a work expresses or implies are expressed or implied, not by a fictional 'implied author,' but by the real, historical person."[18]

The concept of the implied author thus appears highly problematic. Narratology can function perfectly without using the term. Furthermore, a theory that does use it might degenerate into anthropomorphism (since the term humanizes an element allegedly pertaining to the text) and biographism – (since readers and critics often enhance the implied author with elements from the author's real life).[19] Biographism is inherent in an approach like Juhl's that eventually reduces the implied author to the real author. We only accept the implied author as an intermediate position; that is, as a construction resulting mainly from the interaction between text and reader. The reader can consider the implied author as a reflection of the real author, but both these authors in fact amount to constructions by the reader and so, obviously, does the reflection.

Other narrative agents

Next to the implied author, who remains invisible in the text, Booth places the *dramatized author*, who does become visible. This is the traditional authorial narrator, whom we will also encounter in the theory developed by Franz Stanzel. Such a narrator does not function as a character in the fictional world, since he hovers over the narrative, but he does become visible through his first-person narration. The dramatized author only appears as a narrator, not as a character. Edgar Allan Poe's story "The Masque of the Red Death" provides an excellent example. This story deals with the mass slaughter within a fortified monastery by the red death. Not a single person survived, and so the narrator was not present as a witness either. Yet sometimes he becomes visible as the agent in charge of narration: "It was a voluptuous scene, that masquerade. But let me first tell of the rooms in which it was held."[20]

Booth also conceives of the *dramatized narrator*, who does appear in the story as a character. He takes part in the scenes he describes, either as an observer or as an agent. The *undramatized narrator*, finally, tells the story without being seen. He constantly shows the action through the eyes of the characters so that he remains out of sight. He never uses the first person, which distinguishes him from the dramatized author. "Pegasian" could be thought to sport an undramatized narrator who would then show us everything through the two main characters. "The Map" has a dramatized narrator who appears as an agent in the story he tells.

Summing up, three agents may appear between author and text: the implied author, the dramatized author, and the narrator – dramatized or undramatized. This division implies both a hierarchy and a shift. The first agent sits closest to the author, while the last occupies the position closest to the text. In chapter 2, structuralist narratologists will prove very explicit about their preference for such neatly separated levels.

Visibility and presence

Even the most humble undramatized narrator still comes up with a certain amount of summary. Narrative never comes down to purely mimetic representation. A narrator is not absent when he is hardly noticeable. Visibility and presence are two different dimensions, and one of the biggest merits of structuralists such as Genette and Mieke Bal is the fact that they have pointed this out. Those who confuse invisibility and absence conflate two characteristics and end up with the erroneous view proposed by Chatman in his classic study, *Story and Discourse* (1978). He speaks of "nonnarrated stories" and proposes a quotation from a conversation or diary as an example of "nonnarrated representation." According to Chatman, the narrator is absent whenever he represents dialogues as a kind of stenographer or diary fragments as a kind of collector.[21] In our view there is definitely still a narrator in these cases, although he is not directly visible. We agree with Rimmon-Kenan who contends that there is always a narrating agent, even in the representation of dialogues or written fragments. The agent who presents these elements to the reader may be invisible, but he cannot be absent.[22] Chatman's confusion of the two also shows through in the continuum he posits, which moves from absent narrators over covert narrators to overt narrators. The latter two concern visibility; the former deals with presence. By placing them on one line, Chatman denies the difference between the two dimensions.

4. NARRATOR AND READER

If a story forms part of a communicative situation in which a sender transmits a message to a receiver, then the latter must also be given his due in narrative theory. The sender does not turn out to be one easily identifiable agent, and we will see that the receiver of a story does not simply add up to a monolithic entity in the guise of *the* reader either.

According to Wayne Booth, every text envisions a specific reader with a particular ideology and attitude. This reader forms the counterpart to the implied author, functioning as his second self. Just as the narrator's reliability depends on the close ties between narrator and implied author, the reliability and the quality of reading depend on the similarity between the implied author's ideology and the ideology of the reader: "The most successful reading is one in which the created selves, author and reader, can find complete agreement."[23] Booth does not use the term *implied reader* for this reader, but he borrows the concept of the *mock reader* coined by Walker Gibson in 1950.[24] In reception theory, however, the implied reader does appear, although it must be said that Wolfgang Iser's definition of this concept hardly corresponds to Booth's mock reader. For Iser, the implied reader is the sum total of indications and signals in the text that direct the act of reading. Important indications can be found in passages resulting in a problem or mystery, the so-called gaps. Iser submits that in the course of its history literary prose has come to include more and more of these gaps.[25]

Mock reader and implied reader

Just like the implied author, the mock reader is an abstraction that cannot be heard or seen in the text. All the problems mentioned in connection with the implied author also apply here.[26] Just like his counterpart, the mock reader occupies an intermediate position. He is neither the concrete individual reading the text nor the agent explicitly addressed by the dramatized author or narrator. For this particular agent, narratology usually reserves the term *narratee*, a concept coined by Gerald Prince.[27]

Narratee

Just like the narrator, the narratee can be either dramatized or undramatized. In an epistolary novel, the addressee of a letter often acts as a character in the narrative, but that is not really necessary. The undramatized narratee may stand either close to the mock reader or far removed from it. In the collection containing "Pegasian," Charlotte Mutsaers also writes a "letter to [her] brother Pinocchio." This letter, which starts with "Dear Pinocchio," has an obvious narratee, but he never appears in the story and in that sense remains absent from it.[28] A good understanding of the narratee therefore also requires a clear distinction between visibility and presence.

Every text has a narratee, even though she or he remains invisible. Neither "Pegasian" nor "The Map" exhibit an explicitly acting narratee, but the two stories are obviously addressed to someone. Just as there is always an agent of narration, there is also always a narratee. Here we deviate again from Chatman, who posits a *nonnarratee* as the counterpart to his nonnarrator.[29] We do agree with Chatman's suggestion that narrator and narratee do not have to mirror each other when it comes to their visibility. A narrator who acts as a character does not have to address a similar narratee. The narrator-character in "The Map" does not address another character. Conversely, a narrator who does not act as a character may very well address specific characters, perhaps in order to scold or applaud them. In that case the narratee belongs to the universe of narrated events, whereas the narrator remains outside of it.

Two conclusions can be drawn. First of all, each side of the communicative spectrum in narrative has its own specific agents. Secondly, these agents do not necessarily mirror each other. The implied author addresses the mock reader; the dramatized author and the dramatized or undramatized narrator address the narratee, who can exist on various levels. He can belong to the narrative universe or hover above it like the dramatized author. He can stand close to the mock reader as well as very far from it.

The communicative situation of narrative can be schematized as follows:[30]

Sender: author → implied author → dramatized author → (un)dramatized narrator
↓
Narrative message
↓
Receiver: (un)dramatized narratee → mock reader → real reader

Classical structuralist narratology restricts this interaction between sender, message, and receiver to the agencies within the text: narrator, narrative, and narratee. This partly harks back to the Russian formalists, who opted for a strict separation between regular and literary communication.

Literature and daily communication

Calling upon speech act theory, Mary Louise Pratt argues that this separation comes down to "the poetic language fallacy," and she proposes to integrate the narrative communication of a literary text into the study of regular, day-to-day "natural narrative."[31] This proposal nicely conforms to speech act theory, which starts from the idea that every form of communication must be seen as an act, more specifically as a contextual interaction between speaker and hearer. Only in a concrete situation do words get their meaning and can some statements exert coercive power. According to Pratt, the reader always considers the interaction between narrator, narrative, and narratee as a reflection of the "natural" communicative interaction between speaker, message, and hearer.[32] The reader places literary narration into a larger context that provides conditions for successful communication such as comprehensibility, honesty, and the belief in what is being said. To the degree that a literary text meets these requirements, it assumes an authority that allows its statements to be considered meaningful.[33]

Such an insistence on context has the advantage of showing which requirements must be met before a literary text can be recognized, understood, and analyzed. Structuralist narratology does not concern itself with these requirements, since it takes recognition and understanding for granted. It does not ask where they come from and how they become possible. Yet this shortsightedness enables the narratologist to analyze the building blocks and mechanisms of literary narration from up close without worrying about the larger, non-literary context.

Adapted from Wallace Martin, *Recent Theories of Narrative* (Ithaca NY: Cornell University Press, 1986 [1994]), 154.

5. CONSCIOUSNESS AND SPEECH

One of the crucial problems of narrative analysis concerns the ways in which the characters' statements and thoughts appear in the text. In principle, the difference between sentences that have actually been uttered and unspoken thoughts does not really matter. In both cases we are talking about ideas and emotions belonging to characters, which an actual conversation may of course render more clearly than an unspoken reflection. An actually speaking character may have ordered his thoughts better than someone who is thinking or dreaming, but this does not always have to be the case. Conversations can be very tentative and chaotic, while a sequence of thoughts can be quite clear. We will indicate the reproduction of both thoughts and conversations with the term *representation of consciousness*, and we will address this matter at length since it constitutes one of the major challenges to narrative theory.

Representation of consciousness

The central problem of consciousness representation comes down to the relationship between the representing agent and the one who is being represented. If a narrator represents a character's thoughts, one may ask to what extent this representation will be pure and authentic. The reader may think that he or she gets the character's actual ideas, while in fact he or she may only get formulations and opinions belonging to the narrator, who paraphrases the ideas in question. We have mentioned this briefly in the introduction in connection with "Pegasian," and at that point we distinguished three forms of representation: direct speech, indirect speech, and free indirect speech. We will now develop this division with the help of an authoritative study about consciousness representation in literary narrative, *Transparent Minds* (1978) by Dorrit Cohn.

Cohn distinguishes two kinds of consciousness representation, which imply two different relationships between narrator and character. First of all, the narrator who represents consciousness can *coincide* with the character whose thoughts he represents, in which case the narrator most often uses the first person. He can possibly represent his ideas and feelings in the second person – for instance when he tells himself, "You're too slow; you're getting old" – but in fact this "you" comes down to a split-off from the I-figure. Secondly, the narrator who represents consciousness can *differ* from the character whose thoughts he represents, in which case he uses the third person. The second person could be used here when the narrator addresses the character. "Pegasian" is narrated in the third person, and for this Cohn coins the phrase "third-person context." "The Map" constitutes a first-person narrative, which Cohn refers to as a "first-person context."

Third-person consciousness representation

According to Cohn, third-person representation has no less than three types, which roughly correspond to indirect, direct, and free indirect speech. Cohn calls the first type *psycho-narration*. Here an omniscient narrator presents a character's consciousness without literally quoting as in "He sincerely believed she would make him happy." In psycho-narration the characters' unconscious may be represented since the narrator has unrestricted access to their interior selves. In fact, this method provides the only way to render the emotions and thoughts of which the character is not aware. It is also the most traditional method of consciousness representation. "Traditional" here does not mean that this method would be old-fashioned nor that it would have been completely mapped. In psycho-narration the border between reporting narrator and represented character often becomes difficult to draw. Which words must be attributed to the narrator, and which to the character? Doesn't the narrator alter the original words? Is he perhaps being ironic?

Psycho-narration

Dissonance and consonance

The various relationships between narrator and character can be placed on a sliding scale between dissonance and consonance. A narrator can be at odds with the thoughts and statements of the character. To illustrate such dissonance, Cohn discusses a passage from *Death in Venice* by Thomas Mann. The main character, Gustav von Aschenbach, thinks it is too late to flee from the fateful city, but the narrator doubts this: "Too late, he thought at this moment. Too late! But was it too late? This step he had failed to take, it might quite possibly have led to goodness, levity, gaiety, to salutary sobriety. But the fact doubtless was, that the aging man did not want the sobering, that the intoxication was too dear to him. Who can decipher the nature and pattern of artistic creativity?"[34] This quotation shows that a so-called omniscient narrator may also entertain doubts and develop uncertainties and that dissonance does not necessarily mean that the narrator distorts a character's thoughts. In this passage you can clearly see what the main character thinks and how the narrator reacts. A conflict between narrator and character does not automatically mean that the narrator censors or alters the character's consciousness. Neither does it have to mean that the narrator entirely distances himself from the character. The melodramatic exclamation,

"Who can decipher the nature and pattern of artistic creativity?," could be seen as an echo of Aschenbach's typical pathos, in which case the narrator adopts an aspect of the character after all – but of course this adoption may be meant ironically.

Consonance does not seem to leave the narrator a voice or contribution of his own. He renders the character's thoughts and reflections without any trace of criticism or rejection. The narrator's consciousness almost seems to coincide with the character's, making it impossible for the reader to separate the two clearly. Something of the sort happens in "Pegasian," in which the narrator does not distance himself from the thoughts arising in the minds of his characters. Neither does he side with one of them. It is difficult to figure out whether he prefers the riding master or the female rider. As the narrator does not intervene, or hardly anyway, consonant psycho-narration comes close to literal consciousness representation.

Literal consciousness representation by means of quotations constitutes the second type in a third-person context. Cohn calls it *quoted monologue*, a term she prefers to more traditional ones such as interior monologue and stream of consciousness. In any case, this variant comes down to the direct quotation of a character's thoughts in the first person and in the present tense. In his capacity as the quoting agent, the narrator can largely efface himself. He can even cover up the tracks pointing to his presence, including little phrases such as "he said" or "he thought."

Quoted monologue

In *Ulysses* one often notes that an omniscient narrator relinquishes his position to a character, so that psycho-narration turns into quoted monologue. For instance: "He stood at Fleet street crossing. Luncheon interval. A sixpenny at Rowe's? Must look up that ad in the national library. An eightpenny in the Burton. Better. On my way."[35] The first sentence clearly features the narrator. He could continue the psycho-narration as follows: "Bloom thought it was time for a lunch break. He asked himself whether he would have a six-pence lunch at Rowe's." Instead the narrator goes for direct quotation of the stream of thoughts in Bloom's mind.

As long as a monologue is set in the first person and the present tense, it is easy to decide whether the sentences originate from the consciousness of the character or from that of the narrator. Person and tense obviously indicate quotation and therefore quoted monologue. But when person and tense are absent, things become more complicated. "Pegasian" features the following passage: "And it wouldn't hurt to consult a few books on cavalry. Horse riding without background information doesn't make sense for anyone." These opinions belong to the riding master, but since they appear out of context, it is impossible to decide whether they amount to a quotation. Maybe the narrator is present here in the form of free indirect speech, which could characterize the sentence prior to this passage: "Little girls who have never personally experienced this heavenly feeling did well not to shoot off their mouths." The past tense ("did") might suggest that this is not a quotation, but a free indirect representation of consciousness. Perhaps this method of representation continues into the next few sentences.

Narrated monologue

Free indirect speech brings us to the third type of third-person representation, *narrated monologue*. As has already been mentioned, free indirect speech is suspended between direct and indirect speech. Here is a simple example:

Direct speech:	He asked her, "Can you leave tomorrow?"
Indirect speech:	He asked her whether she could leave the next day.
Free indirect speech:	Could she leave tomorrow?

Free indirect speech drops the introductory main clause ("He asked her whether") so that the reported sentence becomes the main clause. It also holds on to the word order of the quotation (in this case the inversion in the original question), and it does not adapt indications of place and time ("tomorrow" is not replaced by "the next day"). Exclamations and interjections which disappear in normal indirect speech are kept. A quotation like "No, no, I have done it today," becomes "No, no, he had done it today" in free indirect speech. These are all characteristics of direct speech, but other than that, free indirect speech does apply the typical changes of indirect speech. It changes the tense and switches the personal pronoun.

Confusion and ambiguity

The combination of direct and indirect speech often does not allow a reader to decide who is saying what. Indeed, the words pronounced or thought by the character are mixed with those spoken by the narrator. A classic case is *Madame Bovary* by Gustave Flaubert. Quite a few readers considered this novel shocking because they attributed the character's ideas to the narrator, whom they would then identify with Flaubert. To them, instead of Madame Bovary trying to negotiate her infidelities in free indirect speech, it was Flaubert himself who presented morally reprehensible action as a form of bliss.

The confusion between character and narrator appears clearly in the following passage in *Madame Bovary*: "Her soul, wearied by pride, was at last finding rest in Christian humility; and, savouring the pleasure of weakness, Emma contemplated within herself the destruction of her will, leaving thus wide an entrance for the irruption of His grace. So in place of happiness there did exist a higher felicity, a further love above all other loves, without intermission or ending, a love that would blossom eternally!"[36] The narrator speaks in the first sentence; in the second, Emma Bovary comes in through free indirect speech. Readers who do not notice the shift could imagine that it is the narrator who ecstatically glorifies eternal love.

The fact that free indirect speech has caused scandals in the course of literary history points to the ideological implications of a certain narrative strategy. Narrated monologue combines the character's ideology with that of the narrator's, and because of this ambiguity the reader has a hard time figuring out the ideology promoted by the text. What does the implied author look like in *Madame Bovary* or "Pegasian"? Does Flaubert's narrator really consider Emma's adultery an escape to happiness? And does the narrator in "Pegasian" agree with the final lines of the story that advocate taking off regardless of the means? Narratologist and reader will have to decide for themselves where to draw the boundaries between implied author, narrator, and character. A traditional reader will want to draw them as clearly as possible even if the text rules out an unequivocal choice.

The potential confusion increases when it is no longer possible to tell the person of the narrator from that of the character – in other words, when the narrator is talking about himself. In third-person representation, the use of the first person clearly signals a quotation from the character. In a first-person narrative this is not the case anymore. Here a sentence in the first person can bc a representation of the consciousness either of the narrating I or of the experiencing I (the I as character), and very often it becomes difficult to make the distinction. Where does the experiencing I start and where does the narrating I end? Usually a space of time separates the two figures, and a typical autobiography, where the older and wiser I tackles his younger and more naive self, can serve as a good example. Sentences such as "At the time I did not know things would take a different course" prove that there is a clear distinction between the narrating I of the present and the experiencing I of the past. But often it is not that simple.

While at the beginning of "The Map" one can easily distinguish between the eager boy and the disappointed narrator, it becomes much more difficult to do so near the end. The story deals precisely with the way in which initial enthusiasm changes into indifference. This confusion between I-narrator and I-character is even bigger in Gerrit Krol's novels. They feature many short fragments separated by a double space. It is often impossible to assign a time reference to these fragments, so that one is unable to decide whether the speaker is the I in the present or the I from the past.

First-person consciousness representation

Self-narration

Cohn's three types in the third-person context reappear in the first-person context. The first-person equivalent of psycho-narration is *self-narration*. Here the I-narrator summarizes his memories. He does not quote himself as a younger man, but instead he talks, in a way similar to indirect speech, about the ideas and feelings he had. Self-narration too can be consonant or dissonant. The latter is the case in the following passage from *Feed for Psychologists (Voer voor psychologen)*, an autobiographical novel by Harry Mulisch in which the narrating I (the older and wiser Harry) belittles the experiencing I (his younger counterpart): "Again my magic had immediately assumed a black and shady shape. At that time I also started to write, in the most appalling conditions one can think of, artistically speaking. Appalling because my orientation was entirely spiritual . . . and the artistic endeavor is in fact the most unspiritual of all."[37] These are clearly the words of the narrating I. His comments do not intend to create the impression they accurately represent what young Harry exactly thought about art and the spirit. There is hardly any indirect speech here in the literal meaning of the term. Instead of a truthful recording, the reader gets a crude summary. If psycho-narration and self-narration are indeed related to indirect speech, then the latter must be considered in the largest possible sense as the summary account of what a character has said or thought.

In consonant self-narration the critical voice of the narrating I remains absent so that it seems as if the narrating I's formulations are completely determined by what the experiencing I thought or felt at the time. The novel *Destination for Ashes (Asbestemming)* by the Dutch author A. F.Th. van der Heijden provides a clear example. The narrator, who also happens to be called Van der Heijden, describes how during his father's funeral he for the first time in his life develops the feeling of fatherhood: "Under a high arch of music, deep down there, I clutched my son against me. I do not say this after the fact, the understanding came about at that very moment: that's where my fatherhood was born. Hardly ever was I so intimate with a human being as then."[38]

Self-quoted monologue

For Cohn, the quoted monologue of the third-person context becomes *self-quoted monologue* in a first-person context. In this first-person version of the quoted monologue the narrating I quotes itself as character. Here's an example from the novel *Sunken Red* by the Dutch author Jeroen Brouwers: "All I thought was: since she's dead anyway, I'll tchoop her doll with the eyes."[39] In the absence of quotation marks, if the introductory main clause ("all I thought was") were dropped, the reader would only have the use of the present tense to decide whether it is the quoted younger I who is talking or the reporting older I. But if the present tense is used for a general truth, then there is a problem. The I-figure from *Sunken Red* describes a memory of torture he witnessed as a child in a Japanese internment camp, and the following sentence appears after a colon: " – the sun is the cruelest instrument of torture the Japs have at their disposal, the sun is the symbol of the Japanese nation."[40] Do these words belong to the boy or to the older narrator who is writing the story?

Self-narrated monologue

This kind of ambiguity grows in Cohn's third type of first-person consciousness representation, the *self-narrated monologue*. Here the use of free indirect speech causes the present tense of the quotation to become past tense. As a result, narrative passages dominated by the narrating I (Cohn's self-narration) surreptitiously shift to indirectly quoted monologues in which the character is talking (self-quotation). In "The Map," the young I-figure discovers a map of Dorkwerd village. His thoughts are rendered as follows: "I could be surprised by the degree of detail and especially by the name I read: Dorkwerd. The village I knew so well and which I had never seen on a map!" The first sentence contains words by the narrator and is an example of self-narration; the second sentence can be seen as an example of free indirect speech reproducing the thoughts of the character, and it can therefore also be seen as an example of Cohn's self-narrated monologue.

Readers of a novel or story seldom consciously stop to make a distinction between the many ways of representing the consciousness of characters. However, this does not mean that the distinction would be irrelevant. On the contrary, a certain variety in consciousness representation makes for many of the characteristics a reader can attribute to a text. Quoting thoughts, for instance, may become monotonous, especially if short phrases such as "he thought" or "she believed" are repeated over and over again. On the other hand, quotations may reinforce the reader's impression of truthful narration. Alternation in consciousness representation may also determine the rhythm of the text. Thus a long interior monologue may be followed by a brief summary of thoughts. By choosing a specific method of consciousness representation, the narrator can manipulate the audience. If he criticizes a character's emotions, he helps the reader toward a specific interpretation that would perhaps be developed less quickly with the help of quotation. In conclusion, consciousness representation is of paramount importance for the understanding and interpretation of narrative. Readers who decide to ignore this fact may end up making the same mistake as those who were shocked by *Madame Bovary*.

6. PERCEPTION AND SPEECH

In the introduction we already briefly mentioned perception in "The Map." We asked whether the little boy who is looking at the map is the same as the narrating agent. We suggested that the I-who-remembers is most probably the speaker, while the I-who-is-being-remembered is the one who looks at the map. A similar problem exists when the narrator differs from the character, that is to say, to use Cohn's words, when we are dealing with a third-person context. If a character remembers something, does that character automatically become the narrator of this memory? Or does one have to say that there is an omniscient narrator who represents the memories of a character in the form of Cohn's consonant psycho-narration? In that case the character is the perceiving agent, while the narrator remains restricted to voicing his perceptions.

The novel, *A Weekend in Ostend (Een weekend in Oostende)*, by the Dutch author Willem Brakman illustrates this problem. Blok, the main character, goes to the toilet and remembers the family visits from his youth. "Once in the toilet he drew the little bolt. . . . Those visits were strange affairs, no streamers, no swimming pool, no tea . . . but gaps one helped each other through by exchanging already endlessly repeated stories. . . . Thus the word 'ear' was an unavoidable ticket to the story of Blok's father and his hospitalization."[41] Who says here that the visits were strange affairs? A structuralist working in the tradition of Mieke Bal and Shlomith Rimmon-Kenan would, as we will see later in great detail, make a distinction between the narrator and Blok. Blok imagines the events, but he does not narrate them as can be derived from a formulation such as "Blok's father."

Point-of-view: Friedman

This distinction between the perceiving and the narrating agent is relatively new. The older so-called *point-of-view* tradition combined perspective with narration and thus mixed the figure who perceives with the one who narrates.[42] We wish to dwell for a moment on a classic representative of traditional point-of-view theory, Norman Friedman. He popularized the terms that are still often used outside the discipline of narratology, such as omniscient narrator and I-witness. The latter is symptomatic in that it proves to what extent traditional theory conflated perception (eye) with speech (I). The I-witness makes up one of the seven positions on Friedman's point-of-view scale, which extends from maximal diegesis to maximal mimesis.[43]

Seven points-of-view

At the pole of diegetic summary Friedman places *editorial omniscience*; that is, the omniscient authorial narrator who stands above the fictional world and summarizes everything in his own words. He is clearly visible and addresses the reader in the first person so as to show what he thinks about the people and things he describes. If the narrator makes his presence slightly less felt, he moves to the second position on the scale, which Friedman calls *neutral omniscience*. Here too the reader gets a clear idea of the narrator's appraisal of the characters and events, but this narrator no longer speaks in the first person and does not directly address the audience anymore. The sentence "She was a nice and well-educated woman" is an example of neutral omniscience. If this sentence is changed to "I can safely say that she was a nice and well-educated woman," then we have editorial omniscience.

Moving in the direction of the mimetic pole, Friedman conceives of two different I-narrators who no longer stand above the fictional world but instead belong to it, appearing as characters. The *I-witness* tells the story in his own words but lacks the omniscience of the authorial narrator. A well-known example of this is Dr Watson, Sherlock Holmes's faithful assistant and witness to his adventures. The *I-protagonist*, on the other hand, is the typical narrator of autobiographical novels. He talks about himself. The narrator of "The Map" occupies this position.

In addition, Friedman comes up with two different "character-narrators." He describes the first one with the formulation *multiple selective omniscience*. This means that the story is being told from the perspective of at least two characters, so that the reader is offered non-identical versions of the same event. These characters do not speak in the first person but rather through an inconspicuous omniscient narrator. The novel *The Rumours (De Geruchten)* by Hugo Claus nicely illustrates this position in that the events surrounding the protagonist René Catrijsse are considered by constantly changing characters.[44] The second character-narrator occupies the position Friedman calls *selective omniscience*, which means that only a single character provides the perspective on the narrated events. In the above quoted passage from *A Weekend in Ostend*, Blok provides this perspective. "Pegasian" presents a borderline case, because it shows both the view of the riding master and that of his pupil but still devotes most of its attention to the latter.

According to Friedman, selective omniscience has no real narrator. The reader looks almost directly into the minds of the characters.[45] This aspect separates selective from neutral and editorial omniscience. The latter two clearly exhibit the intervention of an evaluative narrator. However, we disagree with Friedman when he submits that it would be possible to look directly into the mind of a character without the help of a narrating agent. We would prefer to describe this method of representation as consonant psycho-narration. Just as Cohn, we believe that a narrative always implies a narrating agent. The narrator may not be visible, but he is nevertheless present.

The seventh and final position on Friedman's scale is supposed to approach pure mimesis. In this *dramatic mode*, events would mostly be shown, almost without any summary or transformation. The point-of-view becomes that of a camera, which (or so Friedman likes to have it) registers without interfering in the action. On account of its numerous dialogues, a novel in this mode starts to resemble a play. The dramatic mode is almost always limited to parts of the text, but with its more than six hundred pages of conversation and almost nothing else, *JR* by William Gaddis comes close to realizing the ideal that was described by Friedman long before this novel came out. A camera can only register the outsides of people and things; thus interior processing remains unseen. According to Friedman, the dramatic mode does almost completely away with mediation,[46] which was the basic aspect of all the other positions.

The first two of these mediate by means of omniscience; the two I-narrators mediate because they tell the story; and the character-narrators mediate since they perceive and present people and events. For us even the dramatic mode still contains a mediating agent whose minimal visibility helps to create the impression of objective, mimetic representation.

Narrative situation: Stanzel

Franz Stanzel's theory[47] is somewhat reminiscent of Friedman's approach since he too sometimes gets into trouble as a result of combining perception and narration. Stanzel, however, maintains that every narrative implies a mediating agent, so that a completely mimetic representation of events is impossible. His concept of mediation (*Mittelbarkeit*), which includes forms of perception as well as narration, results in three basic narrative situations (*Erzählsituationen*), which evoke Friedman's editorial omniscience, his two I-narrators, and his two character-narrators. Stanzel distinguishes between the authorial narrative situation in which the narrator hovers above the story; the first-person narrative situation in which the I-figure takes the floor; and the figural narrative situation in which the narrator seems to disappear in order to make room for centers of consciousness situated in the characters.

Stanzel describes these three situations with the help of three scales, each representing a gradual development between two poles. The first scale is the person scale, which evolves from identity to non-identity. A narrator may or may not be identical to a character. If narrator and character coincide, then we have an I-narrative, and if they don't, a he- or she-narrative. This distinction overlaps with Cohn's separation between first-person and third-person context. Stanzel's second scale concerns perspective, which goes from entirely internal all the way to completely external. In the former you see the events through the eyes of a character in the story and in the latter through the eyes of an agent who stands above the fictional world, for example, an authorial narrator. The final scale is that of mode, Stanzel's term for the degree to which the narrator comes to the fore. This scale slides from the pole of the teller-character, where the narrator is clearly present, to its opposite, where his visibility comes close to zero. The latter is occupied by what Stanzel calls the reflector, a character whose mind perceives the events and thus gives the reader the impression that he or she has direct access to the character's mind.

Although these three scales with their opposite poles are clearly reminiscent of the first six positions on Friedman's scale, Stanzel comes up with a different and, more importantly, more detailed system. He combines his three scales into a circle:

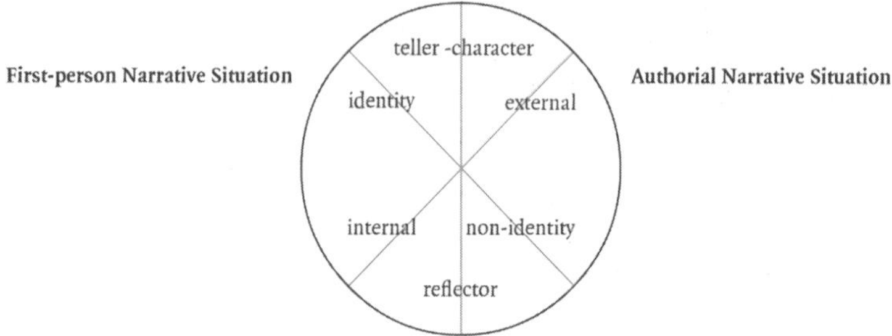

Each of the three basic narrative situations occupies one-third of the circle. The segment of the authorial situation runs from the teller-character pole on the mode scale to the pole of non-identity on the person scale. In the middle of this segment sits the pole of external perspective, which constitutes the primary characteristic of the authorial situation since an authorial narrator first and foremost stands outside the world he tells about. Secondary characteristics include the fact that the narrator is not identical with the character who is the subject of the narrative and the fact that the narrator is clearly present (as opposed to disappearing in favor of a character).

The first-person narrative situation is mainly characterized by identity since the narrator and the character who is the subject of the narrative coincide. It also features the clear presence of a narrator, and internal perspective, since one sees everything through the eyes of a figure who appears in the story. Finally, the figural narrative situation has as its basic characteristic the presence of a reflector rather than of a teller-character. The narrator seems to have disappeared, so that everything becomes available through the reflector. This automatically means that the perspective is internal and that the narrative is told in the third person, which on the person scale implies non-identity.

Gradations according to Stanzel

Stanzel's circular representation has the advantage that the relationships between the various methods of narration appear very clearly. The various methods do not exist separately, but instead they grade into each

Adapted from F. K. Stanzel, *A Theory of Narrative* (Cambridge: University Press, 1984), 56.

other. There are three clear cases of gradation. First of all, authorial narration can develop into figural narration when it crosses the junction between the identity scale and the circle; that is, when the narrator who does not coincide with any of his characters yields the floor to these characters to such an extent that his voice becomes indistinguishable from their perceptions and ideas. This situation applies in the case of free indirect speech, which as we have seen before occupies the borderline between authorial representation and character-oriented representation. Secondly, an emphatically present authorial narrator can use the first person so regularly that he approaches the border with first-person narration. No wonder it is the teller-character pole that constitutes this borderline in Stanzel's system. When this first-person narrator surrenders every form of authorial pretense, he restricts himself to his own internal perspective and crosses over to first-person narration. In its extreme version, this surrender results in self-quoted monologue in which case the reader sees only what goes on in the mind of the I-figure. Thirdly, the border between first-person narration and figural narration can be transgressed when fragments of quoted monologue appear framed by descriptions of the character who speaks the monologue. We have already encountered an example of this from *Ulysses* in which the character of Bloom switches from being a reflector in a third-person description to a speaker in the first person.

In order to map all these transitions, Stanzel has extended his circle. In the middle of each scale he has drawn a perpendicular line so that on the circle it marks the spot where one side of this scale (for example, that of the teller-character) crosses over into the other (for example, that of the reflector). Stanzel combines the three scales and their respective perpendicular lines in two concentric circles:[48] *(See next page)*

Stanzel holds that this circle covers all possible narrative situations. All narrative texts would fit into this system. When a narrative deviates from one situation, it approaches another. The circle would also clarify a particular historical development. The reflector would hardly show up until modernism in the early part of the twentieth century. Traditional novels would all be located in the domains of authorial and first-person narration.

Although Stanzel's double circle is an impressive systematization, we will not follow his proposal in this handbook. As we will explain

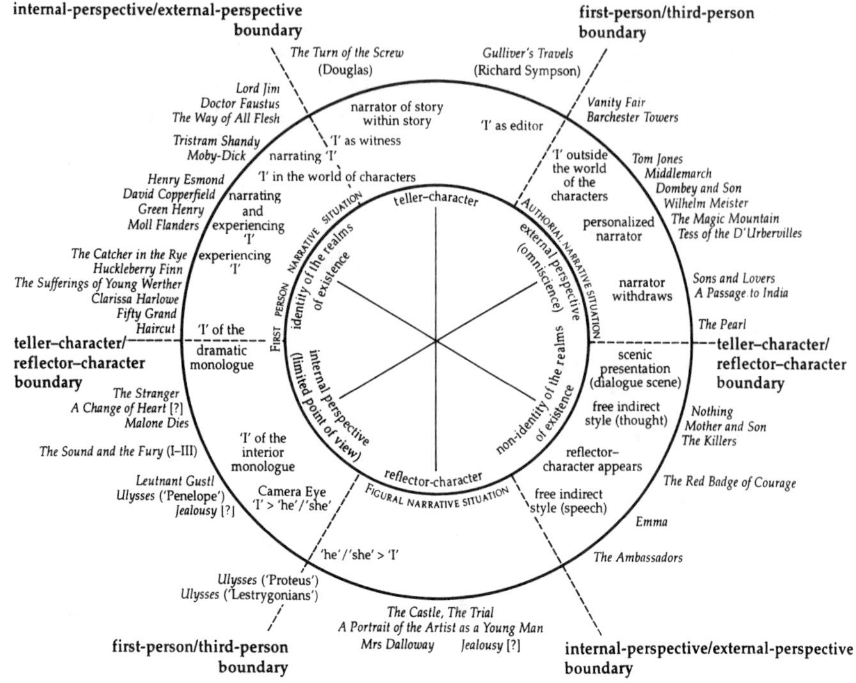

when discussing structuralism, we believe it is absolutely necessary to distinguish between the agents of speech and perception. They belong to different levels. The agent of perception is part of the story as it is told, while the agent of speech is responsible for the telling. In spatial terms this distinction would result in different layers that Stanzel's circle cannot accommodate. His circle is a flat plane that does not distinguish between perceiving and talking but instead considers both as forms of mediation.

This circle is one-dimensional in other respects as well. It only deals with narrative situations and does not say anything about a great many essential aspects of narrative and narratology. What about the manipulation of time? Or what about the difference between summary and scene? How do events connect into a plot? All these questions are taken up in

From Susana Onega and Jose Angel Garcia Landa, *Narratology: An Introduction* (New York: Longman, 1996), 162. Used with permission.

great detail by structuralist narratology, but they fall outside the scope of Stanzel's circle.

Cohn on Stanzel's mode and perspective

In an important discussion of Stanzel's system, Dorrit Cohn suggests that the difference between the scales of mode and perspective is untenable.[49] According to her, an internal perspective inevitably means that you are looking into or from the mind of a character, and it therefore implies the reflector mode. An external perspective means equally inevitably that events are represented by an agent who stands outside and above the characters and who therefore occupies a place on the teller-character side of the mode scale. The perspective scale is redundant since it coincides with that of mode. That leaves us with two scales, the one related to person, which distinguishes between I and he, and the one for mode, which distinguishes between narrator and reflector. Cohn holds that a teller-character shows through as soon as you see the difference between the speaking agent and the character who is the subject of his speech – or, to put it in her terms, when there is dissonance. To her the reflector illustrates consonance since in that case the narrator becomes so absorbed in the thoughts and feelings of the character that the two figures seem to coincide. To sum up, Cohn simplifies Stanzel and accommodates his view on mode into her theoretical frame of consonance and dissonance. Her circle looks as follows:

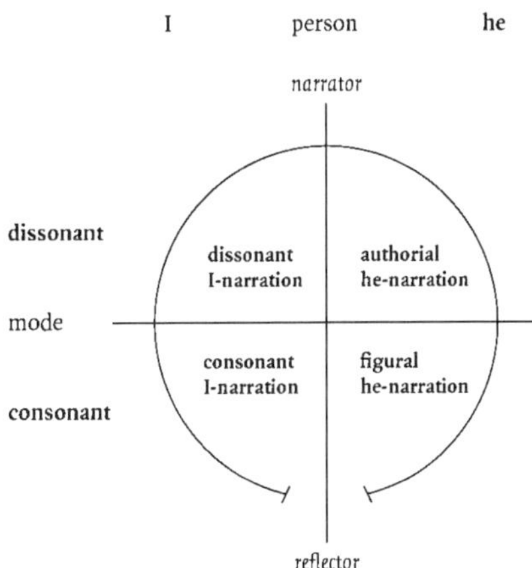

Adapted from Dorrit Cohn, "The Encirclement of Narrative: On Franz Stanzel's *Theorie des Erzählens*," *Poetics Today* 2, no. 2 (1981): 157–82.

Cohn further believes that there can be no gradual or inconspicuous transition between figural narration in the third person and consonant first-person narration. According to her, the example from *Ulysses* does not quite show that one method of narration develops into the other, but rather how strongly the two differ. Here is the passage again: "He stood at Fleet street crossing. Luncheon interval. A sixpenny at Rowe's? Must look up that ad in the national library. An eightpenny in the Burton. Better. On my way." The reader will notice that the third-person narrator of the first sentence is suddenly replaced by an I-narrator. The distinction between I and he is therefore not cancelled at all. Instead of a vague osmosis, the passage shows abrupt change, while Stanzel maintains that one form imperceptibly changes into the other. Cohn therefore leaves a gap on the circle between consonant first-person narration and figural third-person narration.

Stanzel's reaction to Cohn

Although Stanzel has a lot of praise for Cohn's criticism, he rejects this gap.[50] Stanzel would read the Joyce example differently. For him, its second and third sentences ("Luncheon interval. A sixpenny at Rowe's?") do not allow the reader to decide whether they belong to the first-person narrator or the third-person narrator. In general, there are only two indications from which to conclude who is talking: the explicit use of I or he, and the tense of the verb (past in the case of the third person, present in the case of the first). Sentences without an indication of the person and without a verb therefore float between I and he, so that one cannot speak of a rift or an abrupt transition. Here is another example: "His heart quopped softly. To the right. Museum. Goddesses. He swerved to the right."[51] The passage begins and ends with a third-person narrator, while the other Joyce passage started in the third person and ended in the first. Between beginning and end, both passages feature similar brief sentences without a verb or any indication of the person. If you interpret these snippets on the basis of the passage's last sentence, you would probably read "Lunchbreak" in the first passage as an example of first-person narration, while you would probably consider "To the right. Museum" in the second as an example of third-person narration. There are no clear borders or sudden rifts here, Stanzel would say, and he holds on to the continuation of the circumference at the bottom of the circle.

Cohn and Stanzel agree that gradation is definitely possible at the top of the circle, where the authorial narrator changes into the first-person narrator. A visible authorial narrator speaks and does so in the first person. The remnants of his authorial status shine through in the dissonant I-narrator who, just like an authorial narrator, belongs to a world which is different from that of the characters.

The six topics we have dealt with in this chapter all result in a binary relation, which often comes down to an opposition: story and plot; showing and telling; author and narrator; narrator and reader; consciousness and representation; and perception and speech. In structuralism, which we will address in the next chapter, these six individual topics are combined into an encompassing and hierarchical system. This can be seen as substantial progress since it transposes the various aspects of narrative analysis into a unified whole. In the structuralist system some binary oppositions are qualified and developed, so that they sometimes turn into three-part relations. Thus the connection between story and plot will be extended to the three basic levels of structuralist narratology: story, narrative, and narration. This too is an improvement since we have often had to establish that dual oppositions do not answer to the complexity of a concrete narrative text. As we will see, the structuralist approach tries to accommodate for this complexity.

Chapter 2

Structuralism

Contemporary narratology finds its roots in the work of the French structuralists. Issue number 8 of the journal *Communications* usually figures as the official starting point of the discipline. This issue, which came out in 1966, contained nine articles with proposals for concepts and methods to study narrative texts. Some of these articles have acquired classic stature. This certainly holds for the plot analysis proposed by Roland Barthes, which we will discuss shortly, but other contributions by A. J. Greimas, Claude Bremond, Umberto Eco, Gérard Genette, and Tzvetan Todorov have remained important as well.[1] In his *Grammar of the Decameron* published three years later, Todorov introduced the term "narratology": "We wish to develop a theory of narration here. . . . As a result, this book does not so much belong to literary studies as to a discipline that does not yet exist, let us say narratology, the science of narrative."[2] The French structuralists recognize the Russian formalists as precursors of this scientific discipline. Especially Vladimir Propp's analysis of fairy tales can be seen as an embryonic example of structuralist narratology.[3]

Division into levels

The structuralist distinction between the text as it appears and its underlying patterns also stems from the formalists. As we will see, these Russian literary theorists made a distinction between the abstract chronology of events and their concrete sequence in a narrative text where they often do not follow in chronological order. Structuralism is characterized by the gap between surface and deep levels. In the collection *What Is Structuralism?*, Todorov explains that structuralism does not deal with the literary text as it presents itself to the reader but rather with an abstract deep structure.[4] The science of narratology, rather than investigating the surface, should study that which is fundamental to narrative.

This approach has led to the division of the narrative text into three levels. Genette describes the surface level with the term *narration* – the same in the French original and in our English translation – which comes down to the formulation of the story.[5] Narration refers to the concrete and directly visible way in which a story is told. Word choice, sentence length, and narrating agent are all elements that belong to this level. Genette situates the second level slightly under the surface and calls it *récit* in French, which we will translate as *narrative* in English. Narrative is concerned with the story as it plays out in the text. Whereas linguistic formulation was central to narration, the organization of narrative elements is central to narrative. Narrative does not concern the act of narration but rather the way in which the events and characters of the story are offered to the reader. For instance, a novel starts with the death of the male protagonist and then looks back to his first marriage from the vantage point of his son, after which it looks forward to the end of that marriage from the perspective of his second wife. So the level of narrative has to do with organizational principles such as (a)chronology and perspective.

Genette's final and deepest level is *histoire*, which we translate as *story*, not least because its most concrete form coincides with Forster's concept of story – the chronological sequence of events – as we have presented it in the first chapter of this handbook. This level is not readily available to the reader. Instead it amounts to an abstract construct. On this level, narrative elements are reduced to a chronological series. The story of the example above would first have the man's first marriage, then the end of that marriage, and finally the man's death. Here the protagonist does not appear as a concrete character but as a role in an abstract system. The setting is reduced on this level to abstract characteristics such as high or low and light or dark.

Problems with the division

There has been endless discussion about the advantages and disadvantages of such an approach. We limit ourselves to a few remarks that will be useful for the rest of this book. First of all, structuralist narratology only deals with the concrete text via an abstract detour, notably the construction of a so-called deep structure that ideally remains so abstract that it only consists of symbolic and formal elements. The narratologist's ideal was the concept of distinctive feature in phonology. Such a feature does not have a meaning of its own, but it causes differences of meaning. The contrast between voiced and voiceless is a distinctive feature. For instance, phoneme /b/ is voiced and /p/ is voiceless. In itself the difference does not mean anything, but it does result in the difference between such words as "bath" and "path." Narratology never reaches such an abstract and exclusively formal level. All the elements structuralists isolate in the story as formal components of deep structure invariably carry meaning that destroys their dreams of an absolute formality.

Secondly, deep structure in principle has to be as universal as possible, but in practice it differs from structuralist to structuralist. The deep structure proposed by Barthes is different from Todorov's, but it also differs from those of Bremond and Greimas. In devising a deep structure one can apparently settle for different levels of abstraction. In its least abstract form, the story is the chronological sequence of events, but try to go any further and difficulties abound. Greimas's semiotic square is far more abstract than Barthes's narrative grammar. Greimas reduces a narrative text – and sometimes even an entire *oeuvre* – to four terms he combines in a square, which in its schematic form looks as follows:

Greimas calls the relation between term 1 and 2 one of contraries, for instance life versus death. Between term 1 and non-term 1 (or term 2 and non-term 2) there is a relation of contradiction. For instance, the combination of life and non-life is contradictory. The connection between term 1 and non-term 2 (or between term 2 and non-term 1) is described by Greimas as one of implication. Life implies non-death, and death implies non-life.[6] One could reduce narrative texts to a number of squares and explain textual development as a combination of these squares and their terms. Here is a stock example: A girl is in love with a poor man but has to marry a rich one whom she hates. This situation implies at least two squares, one (A) in which term 1 is prohibition and term 2 order, and another (B) in which term 1 is love and term 2 hate. The initial situation combines prohibition (A term 1) with love (B term 1), and order (A term 2) with hate (B term 2). If, as a result of various adventures, the girl is allowed to marry the man she loves after all, the story develops into a combination of non-prohibition (A

Adapted from A.-J. Greimas, *Sémantique Structural: Recherche de Méthode* (Paris: Larousse, 1966), 180.

non-term 1) with love (B term 1), and of non-order (A non-term 2) with hate (B term 2). All stages between beginning and end can be described as a combination of certain terms in certain squares. This approach resembles the reduction of a movie to a set of slides. If one applies such a reduction to an entire *oeuvre* – which then appears as a single square – a number of essential aspects will inevitably be lost.[7]

Barthes counters Greimas's abstract and static square with a dynamic sequence of functions that connect more closely to the order and development of events in the actual text. When later in the book we try to systematize events and actions in our discussion of story, we rely on Barthes's system because it is more concrete and dynamic than Greimas's. However, we conclude that discussion with the remark that our choice does not reflect *the* structuralist treatment of events in the narrative text. There are as many opinions on this subject as there are structuralists.

This variety of deep structures points to a third problem related to this issue: how does one arrive at a particular deep structure? Here too the structuralists fail to come up with an answer. There are no clear discovery procedures.[8] Instead of being based on actual texts, deep structures are simply posited.[9] There is a considerable risk that texts will be manipulated until they fit the model. In other words, the model sometimes takes precedence over the concrete text, and the theory becomes more concerned with itself than with the literary works it supposedly investigates.

Narratology and geology

It seems as if structuralist narratology, with its division of narrative texts into three layers, adopts a geological model. Critics of structuralism have termed this spatial treatment of the text "spatialization." They have two basic reproaches with regard to this procedure. To begin with, spatialization underestimates the importance of time. A narrative text unfolds in time not only when it comes to its events but also when it comes to the act of reading, which always takes up a certain amount of time. Structuralist narratology represents a narrative text by way of schemata and drawings that are sometimes reminiscent of geometry. Textual elements are literally and figuratively mapped. The resulting map provides a static and general view that does not do justice to the dynamics of the concrete, and sometimes quite chaotic, process of reading. Secondly, the structuralists tend to focus on the lines of separation between the three layers, so that gradual transitions are often overlooked.

In their search for the differences and gaps between the levels, they fail to appreciate gradations and similarities.[10]

Advantages of the model

These points of criticism do not detract from the fact that structuralist narratology is the first large-scale attempt to combine all aspects of narrative analysis in a convenient system. The model resulting from the combination of the three levels allows a reader to link all the central aspects of a narrative text. One can see, for instance, how characterization connects with the setting or the method of narration and the perspective from which events are perceived. This leads to congruities that not only offer better insight into the formal organization of the text but also enable the reader to join content and form. Encompassing structuration is and remains structuralism's major merit since it clarifies both textual content and form. That is why this particular brand of narratology continues to provide an indispensable legacy even to those readers whose main interest lies in later approaches.

We will elucidate the three levels of the narrative text with reference to three important structuralist narratologists: Gérard Genette, Shlomith Rimmon-Kenan, and Mieke Bal.[11] Unfortunately, these critics do not use the same terms for the levels. In order to avoid confusion, we combine all the terms in a figure, whose left column contains the concepts we will favor in this handbook. From our choice one will notice that we no longer use the term *plot*, which we provisionally worked with in the first chapter when discussing E. M. Forster. While the emphasis of the term *plot* seems to be on what we call narrative, its meaning spills over into our *narration*.

	Genette	**Rimmon-Kenan**	**Bal**
story	*histoire*	story	fabula
narrative	*récit*	text	story
narration	*narration*	narration	text

1. STORY

Just like any deep structure, the story is an abstract construct that the reader has to derive from the concrete text. The figure below shows that the story consists of three aspects that will be discussed separately but that in fact always intermingle. In the course of the discussion, the terms in the figure will gradually become clear.

Actions/Events	– functions	☐ cardinal
		☐ catalyzer
	– indexes	☐ pure
		☐ informative
	– combinations	☐ arbitrary = pure + informative
		☐ implication = catalyzer + cardinal
		☐ mutual implication = cardinal + cardinal
		↘ sequence
		↘ embedding, . . .
Actants	– subject/object	
	– sender/receiver	
	– helper/opponent	
Setting	– bipolar scales and boundaries	
	– as an index connected to actant and action	

1.1. *Events*

The story is an abstract level. In the first place it refers to the chronological sequence of events that are often no longer shown chronologically in the narrative. The Russian formalists used the term *fabula* for this chronological sequence (story) and *sjuzhet* for the specific way in which it was presented in the text.[12] Thus, the *sjuzhet* covers both narrative and narration in our terminology.

Several proposals have been made to order events on this abstract level. The Russian formalists consider the motif as the story's most basic component. So-called bound motifs are indispensable for the *fabula*, while unbound motifs are far from essential. A murder, for instance, is a bound motif, while the road an assassin travels to shoot his victim may well be considered as an unbound motif since it is not crucial. His clothing and his age are unbound as well. Unbound motifs may be important on the level of the *sjuzhet*, but they are not on the level of the *fabula*. Digressions about the killer's clothing, age, and psychology are important for suspense, but they are unimportant for the development of the action. Formalists also distinguish between static and dynamic motifs. The latter change the progress of events, while the former do not. Bound motifs are usually dynamic and unbound motifs most often static, but this is not a rule. In principle, the description of a character's mental makeup constitutes an unbound motif, but this makeup may result in certain actions that give a decisive twist to the course of events. A murder is usually a bound motif, but if it does not bring about any change, it turns out to be static after all.[13]

Functions

Roland Barthes has refined these distinctions in his "Introduction to the Structural Analysis of Narrative."[14] He distinguishes functions and indexes. Functions are elements whose interrelatedness is responsible for the horizontal progress of events; that is, their linear development. The relationship between these elements can take many forms of which temporality, causality, and opposition are the most common. "X buys a gun" is a function that leads to "X uses the gun to kill Y." The function, "X is in love with Y," is opposed to "Y hates X," and the tension between these two functions brings about a development in the story. Functions belong to what Jakobson calls a syntagm, a horizontal sequence of contiguous elements. Elements are contiguous if their relationship comes down to a direct connection between terms such as part and whole, cause and effect, producer and product, pole and opposite. The link between buying the gun and using it is one between intention and execution. The killer buys the gun in order to use it. Jakobson calls these contiguous relations metonymical.[15]

Indexes

Indexes, on the other hand, do not bring about the horizontal progress of events. They refer to a different plane, which means they function vertically. The many telephones on James Bond's desk in the sixties amount to an index of his importance. As a character he belongs to a different plane from the telephones, but he does get extra weight thanks to these instruments. The connection between the two planes could be called symbolic since the telephones symbolize Bond's importance. Here Jakobson would speak of paradigmatic or vertical relationships and of metaphors instead of metonymies. Instead of contiguity between elements on the same plane, the Bond example features similarity between elements on different planes. The set of telephones reflects Bond's busy life. In musical terms one could compare functions to melody and indexes to harmony or counterpoint. Melody derives from the horizontal progress of the score, while counterpoint arises from vertical accumulation.

Cardinal functions

Barthes distinguishes between two kinds of functions. A cardinal function implies a risk, which means it harbors a choice or a possibility. A question provides a minimal example of this type of function since asking a question leaves open the possibility of ignoring it. When the telephone rings, it may or may not be answered. More generally, almost all crucial events of the story belong to this category. An assassination attempt is a cardinal function and includes the possibility of failure. Narrative suspense largely rests on the risk central to this type of function.

Catalyzer The second type of function described by Barthes is the catalyzer, which does not involve a risk but instead merely assures the continuation of what the cardinal function has started. When the telephone rings and Bond is in the room, he can walk to the phone, let it ring for a few moments, and then pick it up. All the movements between the moment the phone rings and the moment he picks it up are catalyzers, but the ringing and the answering remain cardinal to the whole sequence.

Pure index For the indexes Barthes offers a two-fold division as well. A pure index is an element the reader must interpret. Bond's clothing, his taste, and his preference for certain drinks are all interpreted by the reader as symbols of Bond's sophistication and virility. *Informative index* Next there is the informative index, which is mainly important for spatio-temporal description and which does not require symbolic interpretation or the solution of a mystery. "It was seven forty-five and it was raining," makes up an informative index. Obviously, this type may turn out to be a pure index when for instance the time indication enables the reader to accept or reject the suspect's alibi.

Combinations A structure implies elements in a specific relationship to each other. In the present case the elements are the functions and the indexes, and the relations between them generally fall into three types. The combination of pure and informative indexes is arbitrary. In a self-portrait, for instance, direct information about age and place of birth will appear side by side with suggestive indexes the reader must interpret as indications of character. The relation between cardinal functions and catalyzers is that of implication. The catalyzer completes the cardinal function and is therefore implied by it. Lastly, two or more cardinal functions have a relation of mutual implication, since one cannot do without the other. A murder cannot do without a murder weapon and vice versa: the gun is not a murder weapon without the actual murder.

For Barthes the combination of cardinal functions leads to sequences. They are independent units whose opening action has no precursor and whose conclusion has no effect. "Seduction" is a sequence. It starts with certain tactical moves and then results in success or failure, after which it is over. Sequences can in their turn be combined, for instance through embedding. Sequence A (seduction) can contain a sequence B (for instance a story about the heroic deeds of the seducer) that may or may not lead to the successful completion of A. The insertion of B literally causes suspense because it temporarily suspends the continuation of A.

Here is how Barthes systematizes story events: he starts from minimal components such as functions and indexes, proceeds to create minimal relationships between these components (arbitrariness, implication, mutual implication), and so arrives at larger units in the story such as sequences and their combinations.

James Bond

It goes without saying that such a system works best with narrative texts in which many things happen. No wonder then that Barthes refers to James Bond. Bond stories contain clear sequences like "the murder," "the hero is summoned," "the hero starts an investigation," and "the hero solves the murder." In order to illustrate Barthes's theory, we will analyze the story "From a View to a Kill"[16] in which the sequence chronology is very clear. The *sjuzhet* hardly deviates from the *fabula* because the presentation of events in the text closely approximates the story chronology. Only when Bond is keeping a watch on a suspicious location in the woods does a short flashback briefly disturb the chronology. According to the Russian formalists, such a minimal difference between the abstract story and the concrete presentation of events is typical of non-literary texts or of texts that hardly merit the literary label.

The Bond story starts with a murder sequence. An agent of the British secret service is driving his motorbike on a road through the woods. His mission is to deliver secret documents, but he gets shot by a man who has disguised himself so that he can approach the agent without being suspected. The killer then covers the traces of the murder as best as he can. This sequence can be divided into three cardinal functions: the pursuit, the shot, and the cover-up. There are many indexes. An attentive reader knows from the first few lines that the killer on the motorbike is not a positive character. He has eyes "cold as flint," "a square grin," and "big tombstone teeth." His face has "set into blunt, hard, perhaps Slav lines."[17] A Bond reader will interpret these descriptions as characteristics of a criminal, probably from Russia. The mention of the time and place of the murder – seven in the morning in May, somewhere near Paris – constitutes an informative index.

By identifying functions and indexes, one can get a better understanding of each sequence. The second sequence, for example, could go under the heading, "the hero is summoned." A beautiful girl snatches Bond away from a sidewalk cafe and tells him about the murder. In this sequence there are more indexes than cardinal functions because information is more important than action. In the third sequence, Bond is briefed at the headquarters of Station F. This briefing rounds off the first sequence, since Bond (and the reader) gets to hear what came of the cover-up. The remaining suspense of the first sequence is now totally gone. The briefing is followed by the first investigation at SHAPE (Supreme Headquarters Allied Powers Europe) where staff are less than cooperative. Bond nevertheless manages to formulate a hypothesis, which amounts to the cardinal function of this fourth sequence – "the hero's first investigation." Bond tests his hypothesis in "the hero's second investigation," sequence number five, in which he observes the secret hideout in the woods of the killer and his two accomplices. Obviously the hero's hypothesis proves to be correct. In the sixth sequence, Bond devises a plan to apprehend the criminals, which he carries out in the seventh and final sequence. This sequence perfectly mirrors the first. Bond has taken the place of the agent on the motorbike and now he is being shot at just like the agent in the beginning. He tricks the killer and clears the secret hideout, after which he explores his interest in the beautiful girl.

Advantages Such a systematization of events offers a number of advantages. First of all, it provides an overview of the various links between the sequences. The seventh sequence mirrors the first; the third one concludes the first; and the fifth one confirms the hypothesis of the fourth. The ways in which the author of this story builds up suspense thus become clear. This method also enhances the reader's understanding of numerous details that become more meaningful when seen as a pure or informative index. Elements that might have seemed irrelevant in a superficial reading now acquire the importance they deserve owing to this more searching analysis. For instance, it cannot be a coincidence that the murder is committed on a road through the woods where the criminals are hiding. As we will see in our discussion of the setting, criminals are constantly associated with nature, whereas the hero appears affiliated with culture, the city, and sophistication in general.

Disadvantages Barthes's systematization becomes more difficult and less relevant for stories with few events. In "Pegasian" for instance, sequences are difficult to distinguish. One could see the horse-riding lesson as the first sequence, and the text's lesson ("As long as you take off") as the second. The cardinal function for the first sequence could be condensed as "dressage." In this view, indexes would be made up of all symbols of drill and submission such as the "real pair of riding breeches" and the "background information" that would teach the pupil respect and politeness. The fact that one of the crucial indexes has to do with a pair of pants could then be seen as the symbolic combination of "dressage" and "dress" (in the meaning of clothing in general). This may, indeed, appear somewhat far-fetched, but obviously any systematization by the reader will have something arbitrary. There is no cogent method one can simply apply in order to arrive at the deep structure of events. The reader has an important role. The Bond story could be divided into three as well as thirty sequences. Rather than fixed elements that can be abstracted from the text, structures are constructs that are always partly dependent on the reader.

Other views

The choice for Barthes's system has something arbitrary as well since many other options are available. For instance, rudimentary systematizations of story events can be found in Propp,[18] who has developed thirty-one functions in his analysis of Russian fairy tales, and in Eco,[19] who has distinguished nine crucial moves in a typical Bond novel. The relatively linear or even deterministic sequence of these functions or moves only appears on the level of deep structure. In a concrete fairy tale or Bond novel, that system will transform in various ways.

Claude Bremond

Claude Bremond's systematization is less linear. He starts from so-called pivotal functions, which always leave open the possibility of success or failure. Barthes's sequence becomes a succession of three pivotal functions in Bremond. First there is possibility, which is followed by realization, and finally there is completion.[20] For instance, a woman can devise the plan to kill her husband in order to inherit his wealth. The murder sequence starts with the possibility of carrying out the plan or not. If it is carried out, then the murder attempt may be successful or fail. If the murder succeeds, then the woman may or may not inherit the money. Just as Propp and Eco, Bremond envisages various transformations taking place between the relatively simple three-function structure and the often complicated developments in a concrete narrative text.

We have opted for Barthes's system because it is far less hampered by such a complex series of transformations and because it does not start from frameworks as rigid as those offered by his colleagues. Barthes's indexes, functions and sequences are open concepts that the reader has to fill out with elements from the text. They do not impose a specific order or interpretation, and in that respect they are still quite directly geared to a concrete narrative text.

1.2. *Actants*

Events cannot be conceived independently from the agents who are involved in them. We describe these agents with the term "figures," which we will shortly specify as *actants* following Greimas. The term does not refer to the actual manifestation of a character in the text but rather to the specific role a character plays as an abstract agent in a network of roles on the level of the story. Here too every structuralist has developed his or her own networks and systematizations. Bremond, for instance, conceives of two fundamental roles, a passive one and an active one. Active figures steer and direct events, even though they often do not consciously develop a strategy. A prime example of such a figure is again James Bond. Passive figures such as the agent who is killed at the beginning of "From a View to a Kill" undergo events. On top of this, there are three criteria for going into the details of figure characterization: influence, modification, and conservation. Influence typifies figures – such as a seducer or an informant – who exert direct influence on the course of events. Modification marks figures who improve or aggravate the situation, while conservation distinguishes those who try to avert a change.[21] This explanation of Bremond's criteria consistently presents the figure as an active agent, but obviously there are also passive figures who are influenced, modified, or stopped in their effort toward change. The same character can be at once both active and passive, depending on the viewpoint. The female rider in "Pegasian" actively wants to improve her situation, but she is "passively" helped by the riding master, who at first sight seems to hinder her.

A. J. Greimas Greimas's actantial model is better known than Bremond's systematization of roles.[22] In its simplest and most useful version, this model consists of six roles or actants. These terms are synonymous with "figures." There is a subject, who carries out the action and who strives for a specific object. This quest is inspired and provoked by a *destinateur*, whom we will call "sender" following Cok van der Voort.[23] Greimas calls the agent who benefits from the quest the *destinataire*, which Van der Voort translates as the "receiver." The agent who assists in the quest is the helper, while the agent who thwarts it is the opponent. This results in the following system:

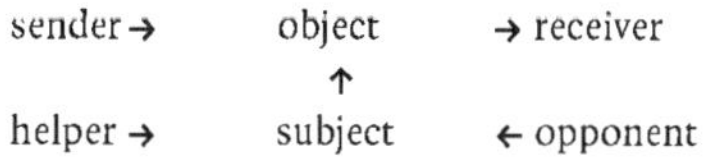

sender →	object	→ receiver
	↑	
helper →	subject	← opponent

These are all abstract roles that should not be confused with actual characters. One character may play all the roles. In the case of someone who wants to quit smoking, one could say the subject is the smoker and his object quitting. The sender is also the smoker – he himself wants to stop, he himself thinks it is necessary – and the receiver is the smoker as well – he will benefit from giving up. The smoker's willpower is the helper and his old addiction amounts to the opponent. This example shows that roles do not have to be played by real characters. Also an emotion, a motivation or an idea can function as an *actant*, for instance as the sender.

Just as one character can play all the roles, one role can be played by many characters. Bond can get help from people such as the beautiful girl or the man from intelligence, but his helpers can also be state-of-the-art weapons or even more abstract things such as his courage and resourcefulness.

Advantages

This story structure has the advantage of being simple and generally applicable. It can literally be applied to every narrative text. For instance, the Marxist philosophy of history can be represented with the terms offered by Greimas. Its subject is humanity and its object the classless society. History is the sender and humanity (or at least the proletariat) the receiver. The proletariat is the helper as well, whereas the capitalists play the role of the opponent. In the case of "Pegasian," the female rider is the subject, and the story's object is being able to fly. The horse – more specifically perhaps the winged horse Pegasus, the symbol of the muse linked to poetry – plays the role of the helper. Dressage and the riding master at first seem to act as opponents, but eventually they turn out to be helpers as well. The sender is the desire to overcome gravity, while the

Adapted from A.-J. Greimas, *Sémantique Structural: Recherche de Méthode* (Paris: Larousse, 1966), 180.

receiver is the girl and, on a larger plane, perhaps also the reader who understands the moral lesson.

Disadvantages

Simplicity and general applicability are at the same time the model's disadvantages. It seems just too easy to reduce all characters and motivations to six roles. If the role of the sender can comprise such diverse elements as a motive, an onset, a character who obliges or invites, and an order or a law, then one might ask whether it would perhaps be useful to specify the category of the sender somewhat further or even to divide it into a set of subcategories. The general applicability of the model also means that it lumps all kinds of narrative texts together and treats them indiscriminately, whether it is the Marxist philosophy of history, the story of the man who wants to give up smoking, or the story of the female rider who wants to learn how to fly.

Furthermore, Greimas does not offer an easy method to go from the actual narrative text to the actantial model. Different readers will come up with different actantial structures for the same story. In "Pegasian," the riding master could also become the subject, in which case the object would be the teaching of the necessary discipline. The sender would then be the riding master or, more generally, the demands of horsemanship. The female rider in this view is still the receiver, but she also acts as the opponent. The helper, finally, is the horse, which lets itself be trained. Complex texts with many events risk the development of totally diverging actantial models. Readers who appoint the murderer as the subject of a detective novel will obviously come up with a different model from those who choose the detective for this role.

Extensive narrative texts often complicate the application of the model. Does one need to devise one model for the entire text, or one for every chapter? Or maybe one for every sequence or an even smaller unit? If each of the seven sequences of "From a View to a Kill" is analyzed according to the actantial model, then it becomes clear that James Bond does not act as the subject in the first three sequences. He is absent from the murder sequence; in the second sequence ("the hero is summoned") he functions as the object; and in the third sequence ("the hero is briefed") he acts as the receiver since he acquires the information. It is only in the fourth sequence that he becomes an active heroic subject, thereby finally assuming the role one would expect of him. This abstract order shows how the main character is first announced and then patiently put together: he goes from absence to object, from object to receiver, and eventually from receiver to hero. Greimas enables the discovery of a structural principle that might otherwise remain unnoticed.

Action and events

In this way the systematization of actants, just like the systematization of the story's actions, ensures a better understanding of the macro- and microstructures of a narrative text. Actions and events differ from one another on the basis of actant involvement. An action derives from an actant, while an event happens to the actant. In naturalist novels events usually take precedence over actions. Human beings find it hard to resist the events that befall them. However, this contrast between actions and events does not amount to a fundamental distinction, since the actantial model allows for the interpretation of events as actions by abstract actants such as fate, death, old age or social class. In this way, both actions and events can be made to fit the actantial model.

This fact points to the interdependence between actions and actants. The reader will expect certain actions from a specific actant. By playing with these expectations, a narrative text can create suspense and take surprising turns. At the beginning of a detective novel, the reader might think that a given character is a helper, but his actions might slowly lead to the suspicion he could be an opponent. Conversely, the confirmation of expectations creates a certain predictability that some readers take as a guarantee of reliability. Certain deeds are expected of a hero. If he does not deliver, he will not be considered a real hero, and in that sense he is an unreliable character. One does not expect the same feats from an octogenarian as one expects from a hero like James Bond.

Actant and character

If we connect the actant to both its actions and its depth, then we are moving from abstract role to concrete character. Traditionally there exists an inversely proportional relationship between the amount of action and the degree in which a figure is psychologically developed into a many-sided character. The more action there is, the less profound the character. This may not always apply, but it certainly holds true for traditional genres such as the adventure novel and the detective novel.[24] Profundity is defined by the number of character traits and their variation. Forster has made the traditional distinction between, on the one hand, static, one-dimensional *flat* characters, and variable, many-sided *round* characters on the other.[25] This distinction is quite problematic. Leopold Bloom in *Ulysses* has many aspects, but he does not really develop. An allegorical character such as Everyman (from the eponymous medieval morality play) is notably flat, but he does develop.

Forster: flat and round characters

Rimmon-Kenan: *three dimensions*

Rimmon-Kenan proposes to determine the richness of a character with the help of three sliding scales, which together make a three-dimensional coordinate system.[26] The first scale indicates complexity and goes from a single characteristic on the one pole to an infinity of characteristics on the other. The second scale, which deals with development, runs from the pole of stagnation to that of infinite change. The third scale indicates the degree to which the text shows the character's inner life. At the left end of this scale Rimmon-Kenan situates characters of whom one only sees the outside, at the other end she places characters whose inner lives are described with great attention to detail. In a psychological novel, many characters will presumably occupy positions close to the right ends of the scales (numerous characteristics, significant development, and an insistence on inner life), while in an action-packed story, like the one about James Bond, most characters will appear closer to the left ends. In "The Map," the I-character is not very complex as few of his features are mentioned. On the other hand, there is considerable development since the young I who believes in the magic of mapping evolves into an older I who has practically no illusions left on this score. Of both I's, the reader sees mainly the interior.

Such a three-dimensional characterization of role makes the transition from an abstract deep level to the level of visible characters in the concrete narrative text. Chatman describes the role as the "syntagmatic reading" of a figure since the latter functions as an element in a horizontal chain of actions, a position in a network of connecting events. The paradigmatic reading considers the figure as a set of traits, a vertical stack of indexes referring to a personality and therefore to a concretely drawn character.[27] If one does not merely see the female rider in "Pegasian" as the role of a subject reaching for an object (notably "taking off"), then one arrives at the level of characterization and will describe her with adjectives such as playful, disrespectful, and relativizing.

1.3. Setting

There is more to the story than actions and actants. Events take place not only in conjunction with certain roles but also in a specific time and place. Such a spatio-temporal indication is usually described with the term *setting*. The Russian literary critic Mikhail Bakhtin prefers to speak of a *chronotope*, a textual combination of time (*chronos*) and place

Setting and chronotope

(*topos*).[28] According to him, the spatio-temporal setting constitutes the narrative and ideological center of the text because it gives form to figures and actions. Abstract themes like love and betrayal acquire a concrete form within and thanks to such a chronotope. Similarly, an abstract view of humankind and social reality can only be concretized if figures (humankind) and events (reality) are embedded in the chronotope.[29] Insofar as the text embodies a world-view, it contains an ideological dimension, which we will elaborate later in our chapter on recent developments in narratology.

At first sight, the spatio-temporal background against which the story develops appears relatively fixed. The Russian formalists categorize it as a static motif; Barthes would call it a pure or an informative index. Both terms are appropriate since the fictional universe does not cause the story to develop. However, story development is inconceivable without the setting, which makes it possible for actions to take place and actants to become involved in them. It is impossible to imagine roles and events without embedding them in time and space. Chatman's schematic representation of the story insists on the fundamental connections between actions, actants, and setting:[30]

Story according to Chatman

Story:	1. events	1.1. actions
		1.2. happenings
	2. existents	2.1. characters
		2.2. settings

Events are dynamic components of the story, while *existents* are relatively fixed points around which the story can unravel. Obviously, characters and setting can develop in the course of the story, but a certain stability remains – the subject remains the subject and the city remains the city, whatever changes they may undergo.

Setting and actions

Actions cannot be separated from the setting. An account of a chase requires the description of the scenery as it passes by at high speed. Moreover, the setting often amounts to an index for the action. In the story discussed earlier, it is no coincidence that James Bond unmasks the killer in the same environment where that very killer used a disguise to shoot an agent. Although the road through the woods is not a highway, as an index it refers to culture, while the woods themselves are part

Adapted from Seymour Chatman, *Story and Discourse: Narrative Structure in Fiction and Film* (Ithaca NY: Cornell University Press, 1978), 26.

of nature. Once Bond has shot the killer on this road and removed his accomplices from the woods, nature has resumed its innocence and attraction. The final scene takes place in the woods. Bond talks to the beautiful girl, and his words show that nature has dropped its connotations of terror for those of eroticism: "Bond took the girl by the arm. He said: 'Come over here. I want to show you a bird's nest.' 'Is that an order?' 'Yes.' "[31]

Setting and actants

This example proves that the setting can also function as an index for the actants. Good westerners live in the civilized city space, whereas bad Russians live in the natural habitat of the forest. The clash between them plays out in a space between these two environments, and also in an in-between time, the period between night and day (seven o'clock in the morning).

Many stories have a typical setting, a commonplace that provides the cliché-ridden environment for stock themes or *topoi*. Bakhtin has shown that every genre and every type of discourse develops its own spatio-temporal patterns, or chronotopes.[32] His examples include the picaresque novel, which centers around "a road that winds through one's native territory," and the idyll, which is determined by "the immanent unity of folkloric time,"[33] but one could also think of the Gothic novel with its combination of the haunted house and events taking place at night. The story's credibility rests to a large extent on the interaction between actions/events, actants, and setting.

Setting in Mutsaers

In "Pegasian," the setting is not very clear, but some indications are nevertheless available. The story concerns a lesson during which many horses trot around in a "carousel." The association with a merry-go-round provides an index of the story's central theme, dressage and discipline. The horses do not run around in nature, and their circuits in the riding school make them as unfree as the wooden horses on a merry-go-round. This image therefore conjures up three different spaces: nature, the riding school, and a fairground.

Setting in Krol

Space and time are important in "The Map" as well. The boy discovers the near-divine map on a Sunday, and he sees it through a forbidden gap. The map's attraction can largely be attributed to the fact that the peek was unexpected and actually prohibited. Later on, it allows a look at the entire environment of his youth, at all the roads and pathways he biked as a boy. In this respect, the map provides a visible and spatial representation of his youth. But as soon as that representation is complete, the fun is over.

The description of setting requires a constant questioning of the terms and criteria for its characterization. Just as in the case of events and roles, there is no clear method to distill the setting from a text. Structuralism likes to work with binary oppositions that can form the basis of a sliding scale. Following Mieke Bal, one could investigate space relying on pairs such as inside versus outside, high versus low, and far versus close.[34] It is no coincidence that the interminable tortures in the work of de Sade almost always take place in the closed, dark space of an underground dungeon. These spatial characteristics may feature as indexes of hell.

Bipolar scales

The structuralist will use similar oppositions to characterize time: short versus long, continuation versus interruption, day versus night, light versus dark. In his story, "The Leak in Eternity" ("Het lek in de eeuwigheid"), the Dutch author Willem Frederik Hermans indulges in the opposition between a long darkness and a brief period of electric light that switches off automatically. Just as the light comes on briefly in an eternity of darkness, human life appears briefly in an eternity of death.[35]

Borderlines

The central aspects of this space and time characterization are the drawing of a borderline and its potential transgression. Actions and actants who transgress these borders often play a central role in the story. A burglar or spy is unthinkable without the violation of the border between private and public, open and closed. Murderers and rapists do not respect these borders either. In the bourgeois novel, the hero often repairs borders, while in the adventure novel he is likely to overturn the bourgeois system. Transgression, for that matter, may be a step on the way to recovery. In the medieval story, "Karel ende Elegast," the title character Karel goes out stealing in order to discover who stands inside and who stands outside the feudal space. Of course the stealing takes place at night and includes a journey through a dark wood. Night and the wood form part and parcel of the chaos that normally threatens order but which in this case brings about its restoration.

2. NARRATIVE

Narrative constitutes the second level of structuralist narratology. This level no longer concerns the abstract logic of sequences but rather the concrete way in which events are presented to the reader. As can be seen in the following figure, the analysis of narrative consists of three main parts: time, characterization, and focalization.

Time	– Duration	☐ ellipsis	
		☐ acceleration/ summary	
		☐ scene	
		☐ deceleration	
		☐ pause	
	– Order	☐ direction = anachrony (versus achrony)	
			* analepsis
			* prolepsis
		☐ distance	* internal
			* external
			* mixed
		☐ reach	* punctual
			* durative
	– Frequency	☐ singulative	* simple
			* plural
		☐ iterative	* external vs. singulative
			* internal vs. singulative
		☐ repetitive	
Characterization			
	– Direct		
	– Indirect: metonymy		
	– Analogy: metaphor		
Focalization			
	– Types	☐ external/ internal	
		☐ fixed/ variable (2)/ multiple (> 2)	
	– Properties	☐ space: panoramic/ simultaneous/ limited	
		☐ time: panchronic/ retrospective/ synchronic	
		☐ cognition: omniscient / limited	
		☐ emotion: objective / subjective	
		☐ ideology	* explicit / implicit
			* unequivocal / polyphonic

2.1. *Time*

Structuralism analyzes *time* by studying the relation between the time of the story and the time of narrative. For instance, a central event in the story may well remain untold in the narrative; or an event that takes very long in the story might be mentioned briefly and casually in the narrative. In order to systematize the various aspects of time, Genette uses three criteria: duration, order, and frequency.[36]

Duration

Duration is measured by comparing the time necessary to read the account of an event to the time an event takes on the level of the story.

The first of these two dimensions builds on the act of reading in order to determine how long an action or event lasts on the level of narrative. Since these actions and events take place in the narrative as it is being told, this dimension is usually called the *time of narration*, even though what really matters here is the time of reading. In the figure below, this time on the level of narrative appears as TN. The second dimension is usually called *narrated time* and refers to the duration of events on the level of the story, which is why it appears as ST (story time) below. Since Günther Müller already introduced the distinction between the time of narration and narrated time in 1948, it existed long before the advent of structuralist narratology.[37] Bal distinguishes five possible relations between TN and ST, which we represent on a sliding scale as follows:[38]

ellipsis	acceleration	scene	deceleration	pause
$ST = n$	$ST > TN$	$ST = TN$	$ST < TN$	$ST = 0$
$TN = 0$				$TN = n$
$ST >\infty TN$				$ST \infty< TN$

At the ellipsis pole, an event that does happen in the story is absent from the narrative. As a result, story duration becomes infinitely longer than duration in the narrative. Events that remain untold can be very important. A crime novel, for instance, will effect more suspense when the execution of a planned murder or assault does not appear in the narrative. In a psychological novel, things that remain unsaid can be essential because they may point to repressed or dismissed traumas. *Ellipsis*

Acceleration is another term for summary. An event that takes a long time can be summarized in one sentence, so that the time of narration is shorter than story time. In "The Map," the narrator says, "and the roads I had not had yet, that is where I went." The bicycle rides, which must have taken quite some time, are summarized very briefly, which makes the narrative move faster than the story. *Acceleration*

Scene indicates an almost perfect overlap of the duration of an event with that of its representation or reading. A dialogue that appears word for word in a novel will take almost as long in the text as in the story. The equation sign, however, is of course a fiction since the time of narration *Scene*

Adapted from Mieke Bal, *Narratology: Introduction to the Theory of Narrative*, 2nd ed. (Toronto: University of Toronto Press, 1997), 102.

and narrated time are never entirely identical. For instance, it is almost impossible to make pauses in the story conversation last equally long in the text. A brief line such as, "The conversation came to a stop," is an example of acceleration rather than a scene.

Deceleration Deceleration occurs when the time necessary to read the description of an event turns out to be longer than the event itself. A text can halt, for instance, at the moment a killer points his gun at his victim. This would take merely a second in the story, but it can be described in dozens of pages. Deceleration, therefore, is very useful to create or decrease suspense. Thus an almost scenic description of a fight may be followed by a deceleration in which the narrator enters at length into a brief event such as the arrival of the police. The Dutch author Gerard Reve likes to use this strategy: in his novels, extended virtuoso descriptions decelerate the action, which often does not amount to much. Since these descriptions, which circle the unspeakable secret appearing in every Reve novel, are there to justify the passivity of the protagonists, one could say that form adheres to content. At the beginning of *The Book of Violet and Death (Het Boek Van Violet En Dood)*, the narrator even makes Reve's habit explicit: "No, nothing much happens: I meet someone; I meet that someone again once or twice, and then he tragically disappears."[39] The rest of the narrative comes down to one giant deceleration that continuously postpones the little action there is.

Pause Pause represents an extreme form of deceleration. Nothing happens anymore, the story comes to a standstill. A clear example of this occurs in *Max Havelaar* by Multatuli. Stern, the narrator, discusses the precarious balance between the continuation and the standstill of the narrative. By way of example he brings up "the heroine who is leaping from some balcony four floors up." Instead of describing that action, he brings it to a halt: "Only then, with a bold contempt for all the laws of gravity, shall I leave her floating between heaven and earth until I have relieved my feelings in a detailed picture of the beauties of the countryside."[40] Seventy pages later the narrator returns to the moment where he introduced the pause: "I would give a good deal, reader, to know exactly how long I could keep a heroine floating in the air while I described a castle, before your patience was exhausted and you put my book down, without waiting for the poor creature to reach the ground."[41]

The combination of ellipsis, acceleration, scene, deceleration, and pause determines the rhythm of the narrative and contributes to suspense or monotony. Narrative texts with continuous acceleration or deceleration create a much more dynamic impression than texts that always opt for the same type of duration. Sketches such as "Pegasian" mostly go in for acceleration, and indeed, the riding lesson is described only briefly. "The Map" summarizes an entire period in a few sentences, and it deals with a substantial part of the narrator's youth in a few paragraphs. This summarizing method of representation is relinquished only briefly in order to describe how the boy sees the map in the shop window. This brief change has an effect similar to that of zooming in with a camera; it enables the reader to concentrate on a specific detail or fleeting event.

Time of narration

When trying to establish duration, the definition of the time of narration presents a major problem. How does one measure the time the narrative devotes to an event? Is that the time required to describe the event or to read about it? Usually, reading time functions as the norm, but this speed obviously differs from reader to reader. Structuralists then take recourse to a purely quantitative element: the number of pages. Forty pages to describe one minute means deceleration, while one page to describe a year comes down to acceleration. This means that time is reduced to space, more specifically "the amount of space in the text each event requires."[42] By the reduction of temporal development to a certain number of pages, time is stripped of its dynamics. This connects with the already mentioned spatialization characteristic of the structuralist approach.

Narrated Time

Another problem with duration is the definition of narrated time. Some narrative texts, such as the *nouveau roman* and postmodern encyclopedic novels, make it very difficult to reconstruct the story or even the events. In his encyclopedic novel, *Vegetables (Groente)*, the Dutch author Atte Jongstra presents a collage of texts taken from manuals, cookbooks, and reference works, and he even includes pictures. This novel no longer has a story made up of chronological and causal connections. How, then, to establish the duration of events? If this does not work, it also becomes impossible to search for the relation between the time of these events and that of their description, which means the structuralist definition of duration does not apply here.

Order

A similar problem arises with regard to *order*. Order is determined on the basis of the relation between the linear chronology in the story and the order of events in the narrative. If it is impossible to reconstruct story events and to order them into a clear chronology, order in a narrative text cannot be assessed by using the structuralist method. If it is possible to order events nicely on the story level, for instance in a sequence from one to five, then one can see how the narrative complicates that order, for instance into the sequence four, two, five, one, three.

Genette specifies order with reference to three categories: direction, distance, and reach. Specification always depends on a clear primary narrative. This primary narrative or *récit premier*[43] functions as a norm or, in spatial terms, as a measure for the location of events in time. The primary narrative is not the same as the story, because it is visible in the text and does not necessarily contain all the events of the latter. Still, the primary narrative poses the same problem as the story. If a novel does not allow the reader to establish its primary narrative, one can forget about order altogether. A text brimming with associations, such as Joyce's *Finnegans Wake*, cannot be approached with this method.

Direction Two directions are possible with regard to the primary narrative: forwards and backwards. If the primary narrative, for instance, shows the last three weeks in the life of the protagonist, all memories of his youth and all anticipations of life after death would fall outside this narrative. Such a memory would be an example of *analepsis*, and such an anticipation an example of *prolepsis*. English here uses *flashback* and *flashforward*,[44] while in German, Eberhard Lämmert popularized the pair *Rückwendung* and *Vorausdeutung*.[45]

If the analepsis or prolepsis concern the element in the foreground of the primary narrative, Genette calls them homodiegetic. For instance, if a dying man remembers a moment from his own life, this would constitute a homodiegetic analepsis. If, however, he remembers something about a person who does not appear or has only a minor role in the primary narrative, then the analepsis is heterodiegetic. The dying man may remember a boyhood friend who has disappeared, which may lead to a story about that friend and some related details concerning him, none of which the dying man has experienced himself.

Defining direction can often be tricky. Suppose the dying man remembers something from his adolescence, but then looks ahead from that period to his twenties. The prolepsis with respect to his adolescence is an analepsis with respect to the primary narrative. "The Map" features a mild version of this: "because I had had all roads, nothing was added anymore, and one day I would remove the map from the wall." This one day represents a prolepsis with respect to the period in which the boy was biking around but an analepsis with respect to the moment at which the narrator remembers his youth.

The situation becomes more complex when the various memories are not clearly dated. Many autobiographical novels contain a whirl of memories and anticipations that connect associatively and are very hard to locate. In such a case, the reader does not know whether memory A goes backwards or forwards with respect to memory B. Genette uses the term *achrony* for passages that cannot be dated. Prolepsis and analepsis, on the other hand, only exist if they can be clearly located in time. They are examples of *anachrony*, a departure from the chronology in the primary narrative.

Order is not just a matter of direction, but also of distance, which concerns the temporal gap between primary narrative on the one hand and prolepsis or analepsis on the other. The dying man may remember an event that took place two days ago, which therefore falls within the primary narrative; or he may remember something that happened fifty years ago, which clearly remains outside the primary narrative. If the remembered or anticipated period falls within the primary narrative, Genette speaks of an internal analepsis or prolepsis. External is when this period falls outside the primary narrative. And finally there is mixed analepsis or prolepsis, which covers a memory starting before the primary narrative but ending within it, or an anticipation beginning within the primary narrative and ending outside it. *Distance*

Apart from direction and distance, order is also characterized by reach. This term refers to the stretch of time covered by the analepsis or prolepsis. If the memory concerns one particular event, then the analepsis is punctual. If it comprises an entire period, the flashback is durative or complete. The analepsis in "The Map" is durative since it describes the complete extent of time from the discovery of the map until its removal. *Reach*

Although the number of terms enumerated here suggests a rather abstract system, investigating order in a narrative text is of great importance. The more an author indulges in flashbacks and flash-forwards, the more complex the narrative becomes. This also leads to all sorts of new relationships between the various periods. If, on the same page, the text refers to three or four periods from the life of the protagonist, chances are that one will start to see connections between these periods.

As a result, themes may emerge more clearly or suspense may increase. In *Sunken Red* by Jeroen Brouwers, the main character's thoughts go back and forth between very divergent moments: the Japanese internment camp, the boarding school, the sexual relationship with Liza, the garden party, the birth of his daughter, and the death of his mother. All these stages connect through the joint image of his mother's disgrace. The turmoil in the novel's time structure formally reflects the unrest and roaming typical of the I-character.

Frequency

Frequency refers to the relation between the number of times an event occurs in the story and the number of times it occurs in the narrative. Obviously, there are three possibilities here: less often, more often, and just as often. When the event occurs just as often in the story as it does in the narrative, Genette uses the term *singulative*. Something that happens once and is described once, is a simple singulative, while a reoccurrence in the story that is described just as often in the text is a plural singulative. The discovery of the map in Gerrit Krol's story provides an example of a simple singulative. If the boy had visited the store more than once, and if each of these visits had appeared separately in the text, then that would have been a plural singulative.

Singulative

Very often such an exact coincidence does not seem appropriate. If you describe something that happens regularly every time it happens, the text may become monotonous or endless. For story events that happen repeatedly but are only presented once in the text, Genette uses the term *iteration*. The first sentence of Marcel Proust's *Remembrance of Things Past* offers a good example of this second type of frequency: "For a long time I used to go to bed early."[46] The formulation, "for a long time," probably covers thousands of days on which the protagonist went to bed early. Iteratives are prevalent in the description of habits. Some examples from "From a View to a Kill": "Bond always had the same thing – an Americano – Bitter Campari – Cinzano"; "When Bond was in Paris, he invariably stuck to the same addresses"; "After dinner he generally went to the Place Pigalle."[47] In "The Map," the clause, "I occasionally traveled somewhere by train," is an iterative since the journey is only mentioned once but will have taken place many times.

Iteration

Iteratives can be combined with singulatives. A party described singulatively can contain an iterative such as "He repeatedly harassed his neighbor, until she could not take it any longer and left the table." Genette calls this an internal iterative since it remains within the temporal limits of the singulatively described party. If it were to fall outside these limits, Genette would call it external. For instance, the description of the party could contain a sentence such as the following: "That is what he would do for the rest of his life: harass people who did not ask for it."

Repetition

Genette calls the third type of frequency *repetition* by which he means the repeated description in the text of an event that takes place only once on the level of the story. Thus the main character in *Sunken Red* continues to ruminate on the scene in which his mother is beaten by a Japanese soldier. Repetitions of this kind often embody various standpoints, that is to say, the same event is considered by various characters. With postmodern novels it can be hard to decide whether the various standpoints relate to a single event or various events, or whether they are sheer invention. *A Fabulous View (Een fabelachtig uitzicht)* by the Dutch author Gijs IJlander includes several versions of a walk during which a dead animal, possibly a squirrel, is found. The characters entertain widely diverging views of what happened, which may lead the reader to doubt their truthfulness. The narrator, a stuffed squirrel, does not decide the matter, and perhaps the characters' views are even his fabrication.[48] For such a complex and undecidable case, structuralism, which functions only on the basis of clear event reconstruction, cannot offer a solution.

2.2. *Characterization*

Next to time, *characterization* makes up the second dimension of narrative. While story deals with abstract roles, narrative involves their concretization. The central question in this respect concerns the way in which a character is represented in narrative. This question not only calls for a list of characteristics but also for ways in which these characteristics can be woven into the text. According to Rimmon-Kenan,[49] we can discern three methods.

Direct characterization

Firstly, a character can be described *directly*.[50] This type of characterization occurs in many traditional novels that introduce a character with an enumeration of character traits. These traits may relate to psychological states as well as to outward appearance. Direct characterization always takes the form of specifying and evaluative statements such as the following: "Mister Hoorn was a warm and honest individual, though his casual conversation and jokes could not be called brilliant. But stupid, no, that he was not."[51]

A central question in this connection relates to the origin of such statements. Does the character itself pronounce them? Or do they come from an omniscient narrator, or another character? The answers to these questions have a profound influence on the reliability of the characterization. Direct characterizations belong to the most straightforward strategies to inform the reader, but they can easily be (ab)used to send the reader in the wrong direction. At the beginning of the story, "A Rose for Emily," by William Faulkner, the characterization of "noble" Emily is emphatically positive, but the reader soon realizes that those positive statements are mistaken and misleading.[52]

Indirect characterization

The second type is *indirect* characterization.[53] This type is based on metonymy; that is, it works with elements that are contiguous with the character. Actions, for instance, often follow naturally from a character's identity. Discourse too says a lot, literally and figuratively. The words and style used by a character betray his social position, his ideology, and his psychology. The character's physical appearance and his environment can be telling too. Ben, the main character of *Postcards from America* (*Ansichten uit Amerika*) by Willem Brakman, moves house a number of times, but his environment continues to resemble a labyrinth. His house is "very intricately designed," the streets form an obscure network and "become hard to follow." "The labyrinth of small streets"[54] comes up in all sorts of contexts related to Ben and therefore says something about the claustrophobic and paranoid world-view of this character.

Characterization through analogy

Thirdly, characters can be described with the help of *analogy*, which leads to metaphor instead of metonymy.[55] In "Pegasian," the main character's identity is partly established through implicit comparison with the horse. Just like the horse, the female rider wants to break free from the ground and take off. The latter refers to the text's message. The fact that metaphors often refer to a specific ethic or ideology also appears in Theodor Adorno's study of the images Kafka uses to describe his characters. Kafka often compares his characters to animals and objects, and this metaphorical typification shows how unhuman humankind has become.[56]

For Rimmon-Kenan, the name is an example of characterization through analogy.[57] To the extent that the name points to an aspect of the character or to a contiguous element pertaining to it, we believe it still belongs to metonymic characterization. Thus, the names Goodman and Small describe metonymically, whereas Castle or Roach do so metaphorically. In the former case, elements are put forward that belong to the semantic domain of humankind, while in the latter case, other domains come into play. In the novel *Bint (Bint)* by the Dutch author F. Bordewijk, the pupils of a class called "Hell" have suggestive names such as "Saint's Life" and "Precentor." Such metaphorical or symbolical names may of course refer to the opposite of what they suggest. A character called Castle may well be weak, in which case his name is ironic, to say the least.

Similar to the name, the alter ego or second self presents a borderline case between metonymical and metaphorical characterization. While the connection between the protagonist and a witness may be called contiguous, the blending of Jekyll and Hyde brings about a metaphorical osmosis of two different personalities. Metonymical characterization does not lead to osmosis, but its metaphorical counterpart does. The borderline between the two is not always clear. Two supposedly distinct characters may resemble each other in so many ways that one could still speak of identification or blending. This is true, for instance, of the alter egos in *The Discovery of Heaven* by Harry Mulisch.

Problems with characterization

The structuralist treatment of characterization almost reaches the level of semantic, content-related analysis. Since structuralism has wanted to develop a largely formal approach, it does not come as a surprise that characterization does not belong to the more detailed or innovative domains of structuralist narratology. The concrete description of a character differs from text to text, and therefore it does not really appeal to a structuralist, who is out to expose general principles and procedures.

The difficulty in reducing characterization to general and structuralist statements is further borne out by the impossibility to define what a hero actually amounts to. Bal has drawn up a list of characteristics, including "the hero occurs often in the story," "the hero can occur alone or hold monologues," "certain actions are those of the hero alone," and the hero "maintains relations with the largest number of characters."[58] A relevant question is not only how many of these characteristics have to apply before one can speak of a hero but also whether the hero concept is at all relevant for non-traditional texts such as the *nouveau roman* or for classical genres such as the epistolary novel and the novel of manners. In the *nouveau roman*, the hero seems to disappear in favor of an impersonal quasi objectivity; in the epistolary novel, all correspondents being more or less equal, there is no center; and in the novel of manners, intense interaction between groups and classes makes a criterion such as "certain actions are those of the hero alone" irrelevant. More generally, one might ask whether a narrative text always needs a hero.

The fact that structuralist narratology holds on to concepts such as hero and villain suggests that it still deals with characterization in a very anthropomorphic way.[59] Coming from a theory that explicitly dissociates itself from subjectivist and humanist approaches to literature, this may be surprising. Indeed, structuralists do not like empathic readings, which analyze the emotions displayed in the text. And yet they too risk treating constructs of words as people. In postmodern novels characters lose many of their human traits: they blend into one another, they say they are inventions of a narrator or of the text, they disappear as suddenly as they appear. Structuralism hardly knows what to do with such non-anthropomorphic characters, which proves the extent of its remaining anthropomorphism.

The treatment of literary character as a set of traits may lead to static enumeration. Barthes famously considers a character as a set of minimal semantic elements or semes.[60] In this approach, character development is reduced to a change in the set, and dynamics come down to a sequence of two or more different stages of the set. Obviously, it is not at the level of character analysis that structuralist narratology has made its most significant contribution.[61]

2.3. *Focalization*

Focalization, on the other hand, does belong to the crucial insights narrative theory owes to structuralism. The term refers to the relation between that which is focalized – the characters, actions, and objects offered to the reader – and the focalizer, the agent who perceives and who therefore determines what is presented to the reader. So, we are talking here about the relation between the object and the subject of perception. We avoid the verb "to see" on purpose, because all senses are involved. Perception, for that matter, can imply cognitive functions such as thought and judgment. "The Map" features the following clause: "I had to recognize that I occasionally traveled somewhere by train. . . ." The I-character is the center of perception – in this case an act of recognition that is not visual and not even sensual but that rather pertains to thought. The riding master's perception expressed in the following sentence from "Pegasian" seems related to emotion and attitude: "Now the riding master doesn't feel like explaining anything anymore."

Focalizer and focalized object

The terms we will use in the following discussion, "focalizer" and "focalized object," are problematic. They suggest there are centers of perception in a narrative text that approximate human beings and that apparently think and feel as we all do. One might ask in the first place whether a text actually contains such distinct centers and, secondly, whether it is useful to study them so anthropomorphically. Genette has avoided this problem by speaking consistently of focalization, without subject or object. Bal, on the other hand, who has refined the theory of the French narratologist, believes it is necessary to distinguish between a perceiving agent and a perceived object.[62] Genette did not like her revision at all,[63] but the distinction between focalizer and focalized object has in the meantime been accepted probably because it can help clarify the rather vague and monolithic concept of focalization.[64]

One of those clarifications has to do with (un)reliable perception, which can be described thanks to this distinction between a perceiving subject and its object. The relation between these two is crucial for the reader to gauge the information provided by the text. If a character is constantly seen through the eyes of a single focalizer, one may wonder whether this view is reliable. Is it really true that a woman is a flirt if you only see her through the eyes of her partner? Conversely, one character might be perceived by so many focalizers that the reader has too much information to be able to arrive at a coherent and reliable image.

Types of focalization

Internal and external

We will discuss focalization using the three criteria that we will also refer to in our section on narration: types, characteristics, and textual indications allowing for the determination of these types and characteristics. Two questions must be answered in order to determine focalization *types*. The first concerns the position of the focalizer with regard to the fictional universe. If the focalizer belongs to it, he is internal; if he remains outside of it, he is external.[65] Edgar Allan Poe's story, "Metzengerstein," provides a clear illustration of this distinction. A fire breaks out in the stables of the Berlifitzing family, which has been on bad terms with the Metzengersteins for ages. The reader sees the young baron Von Metzengerstein's reaction through the eyes of an agent who is not in the room with the baron: "But during the tumult occasioned by this occurrence, the young nobleman himself sat apparently buried in meditation, in a vast and desolate upper apartment of the family palace of Metzengerstein." One could imagine this as a scene caught by a camera on the shoulder of the narrator, who does not appear in the story. Next, however, "his eyes were turned unwittingly to the figure of an enormous, and unnaturally colored horse." From then onwards, the reader sees the scene through the eyes of the young baron: "The horse itself, in the fore-ground of the design, stood motionless and statue-like."[66] This switch between external and internal focalization can be compared to the occasional image change during the live transmission of a Formula One race. Most of the time the camera is placed above or on the side of the circuit, but sometimes the viewer finds himself inside the race because the images come from a small camera installed on one of the cars. Of course this focalization is not perfectly internal, since the viewer does not really see through the eyes of the driver.

Narrative texts with numerous levels complicate the relation between internal and external focalization. Let us return to *A Weekend in Ostend* by Willem Brakman. The main narrative deals with Blok. When he is perceived by the narrator, who never appears as a character in the story, focalization is external. For instance, "In the evening, all spruced up, he pedaled on the borrowed bike to the birthday party." Focalization becomes internal when Blok hears the waltz entitled "Gold und Silber" ("Gold and Silver"), "which moved him to tears, because it made him think of everything at once."[67] Things get more complicated when Blok starts to tell a story about his Uncle Anton. In the beginning of this story, the account is filtered through Blok's perception, as for instance in "On a beautiful summer night it was so hot and tepid that even the dead in the graveyard rapped on the lids and called out: 'Please . . . just for a moment.' "[68] This is external focalization with respect to the story about Uncle Anton since the reader's perception entirely depends on Blok, who does not appear as a character in the story he tells. With respect to the main narrative about Blok, however, this quotation amounts to internal focalization since the reader sees everything through Blok, the protagonist of the main narrative. But when Uncle Anton's perceptions start to infiltrate Blok's story about him, focalization in this secondary story also becomes internal. For instance, "Uncle Anton came walking by with his calloused little hands; he was amazed to hear how her fair sex was emitting all this seductive language."[69]

External and internal, therefore, must not be seen as absolute concepts, especially when the text features several embedded stories. Internal focalization on the level of the main narrative can become external on the level of a secondary narrative. Even when there is no embedding, the focalizer can be hard to determine. At the beginning of the novella "Sugarplums" ("Suikerpruimen") by Huub Beurskens, the character Stein appears to be the (internal) focalizer, but certain passages suggest (external) focalization by the narrator. At one point Stein and Patty John are sitting on a restaurant terrace: "In between the private yachts and the small fishing boats, the dark water reflected the many little colored lamps."[70] Who sees this? Stein or the narrator? Impossible to decide.

The alternation between internal and external focalization is always present in narrative texts. It is also ideally suited to manipulate the reader, who often does not see that information has been filtered through the perception of a character or the narrator. As a result, the reader might treat subjective information provided by a character as objective information coming from a detached narrator. This possibility is inherent in what, following Dorrit Cohn, we have called consonant psychonarration, where the narrator adheres so closely to the character's perceptions that it becomes difficult to distinguish between the two.

Nevertheless, the distinction is not to be neglected. Even if character and narrator coincide in a first-person text, there still exists a difference between internal and external focalization.[71] If the narrating I considers something the experiencing I did, then there is external focalization if the scene is perceived by the narrating I, and internal focalization if it is perceived by the experiencing I. Here is an example from "Sugarplums": "I was annoyed at it, probably because of a kind of professional jealousy, I now think."[72] Since the experiencing I felt the annoyance, it is internally focalized; since the narrating I gives his reasoning for the annoyance, it is externally focalized.

Focalization and person

The examples show that the choice of internal and external focalization does not depend on person. First-person narration can be focalized externally, while third-person narration can be focalized internally. "I was very arrogant at the time," is an example of external focalization, while "he considered her extremely arrogant" is focalized internally.

The type of narration, therefore, must not be confused with the type of focalization.

Internal and external focalizers can either remain on the surface, or they can penetrate the things they are perceiving. In a crime novel, very often only the killer's external characteristics appear, so that the reader has to search for his motivations. This adds to the suspense, and it enhances the reader's eagerness to solve the mystery. When focalization penetrates a character, it results in the observation of emotions, cognitive functions, and psychological detail. These can either be perceived by a detached narrator (in which case focalization is external) or by a character (in which case it is internal). The potential combinations and alternations between the various types of focalization also enable an author to create and sustain suspense. If the first chapter of a novel contains the description of a character's thoughts and they include plans for a murder, he or she will appear as the most likely suspect for the murder committed in the second chapter. But in order to keep the reader guessing, the text may stick to the seemingly innocent exterior of the character in the following chapters, so that it becomes impossible to decide immediately whether he or she is really guilty.

Stability As we mentioned before, types of focalization are determined on the basis of two criteria. The first concerns the focalizer's position: external or internal. The second criterion has to do with stability. If the events of the story are perceived by a single agent, then Genette calls this *fixed* focalization. If the events are perceived by two characters who constantly alternate, Genette speaks of *variable* focalization. Of course there can be more than two centers of perception, and in that case Genette speaks of *multiple* focalization. These three types could also be seen as positions on a sliding scale, starting with single or fixed focalization and ending with multiple or alternating focalization.[73]

"Pegasian" features variable focalization. Sometimes the reader is guided by the female rider's perceptions ("What are those flaps for, in fact?"), sometimes by the riding master ("And it wouldn't hurt to consult a few books on cavalry"). "The Map" also has variable focalization, since the reader is now made to look through the eyes of the boy ("The village I knew so well and which I had never seen on a map!"), now through those of the narrating I ("I haven't kept it either"). In the two stories, the alternation of the perception center reflects a thematic confrontation between the unorthodox and naive view on the one hand and the disciplined and adult view on the other. View here combines ideology and frame of mind.

Showing the same event through a number of focalizers adds variety, but it often also complicates the narrative. In "Sugarplums," Patty John betrays her husband, Stein, with Ruben. Their first sexual encounter is initially presented through Ruben, and then through Patty John. Here is Ruben: "Before I went out with her into that urine-reeking Pigeon Alley, and she pushed me against the wall and stuck her tongue between my lips, in the humid August night, I had quickly relieved myself of some extra pressure."[74] And here is Patty John's perspective: "It was a humid August night when, in a narrow alley that reeked of vomit, urine, pigeon shit and, she imagined, horse chestnut blossoms, she let herself be opened, lifted, and rammed."[75] In Ruben's perception, Patty John is the more active person since she pushes him against the wall; in Patty John's experience, Ruben is more active than she is since she lets *him* open, lift, and ram her. The fact that they both feel taken advantage of reflects one of the problems in their relationship. Their initial passion rapidly deteriorates into passivity. They both feel misled since their partner has failed to deliver on his or her promises. These content-related aspects are underscored by the choice of variable focalization, which shows how differently the lovers interpret their first sexual encounter.

Properties of focalization

The different types of focalization (internal versus external and single versus multiple) can be specified with reference to a number of properties that Rimmon-Kenan prefers to call *facets*.[76] The first two properties concern the focalizer's spatio-temporal perception. In terms of space, the focalizer can impose a panoramic, simultaneous, or limited view on the reader. In the case of a panoramic view, the focalizer controls the entire space of the narrative. The beginning of Malcolm Lowry's *Under the Volcano* adopts such a panoramic view: "Two mountain chains traverse the republic roughly from north to south, forming between them a number of valleys and plateaus. Overlooking one of these valleys, which is dominated by two volcanoes, lies, six thousand feet above sea level, the town of Quauhnahuac."[77]

Space

There is simultaneous focalization when the reader perceives what happens in different locations at the same time. Harry Mulisch, for instance, repeatedly illustrates his principle of "octavity" (the same and yet different) by showing divergent events taking place at the same moment. He suggests that these events resemble each other like a musical note and its octave. The simultaneity of events in different locations is traditionally represented by formulations such as, "In the meantime . . ." or "While this was going on . . ."

A less traditional way of showing simultaneity is the use of columns or of text strips on top of one another, which results in a simultaneous presentation of different narratives. In *Minuet*, Louis-Paul Boon places a collage of newspaper clippings at the top of the page. Below comes the "normal" narrative text. The first sentence of the newspaper section is as follows: "A farm laborer found a naked girl tied to a tree in a snow-covered field." The cold suggested in this sentence provides a link with the first sentence of the regular text: "My work in the refrigerating chambers was rather monotonous: checking temperatures which had to remain at freezing point day and night."[78]

With respect to space, next to panoramic and simultaneous focalization, there is also limited perception. This is the typical situation of a character since his or her perceptions are most often coupled with the limited space in which he or she moves. Rimmon-Kenan holds that the panoramic and simultaneous views are only possible for external focalizers, but we disagree.[79] A character can perfectly imagine what happens elsewhere. Imagination forms part of the focalizer's perception. Such panoramic views are therefore possible, not only owing to an actual position (from an airplane for instance), but also owing to the character's imagination.

Time Just like spatial perception, temporal perception can be divided into three types. A panchronic focalizer surveys all time periods. He can look back and look forward. The beginning of Poe's story, "Metzengerstein," illustrates this: "Horror and fatality have been stalking abroad in all ages. . . . The families of Berlifitzing and Metzengerstein had been at variance for centuries. . . . The origin of this enmity seems to be found in the words of an ancient prophecy."[80] This prediction amounts to a flashforward. If the narrative only looks back, focalization is retrospective as is the case in the typical autobiography where the narrating I considers the experiencing I. Finally, perception can take place simultaneously with the events, in which case there is synchronic focalization.

Obviously, the various temporal and spatial focalizations can alternate. In *Sunken Red*, the narrating I remembers his childhood in the Japanese internment camp. In the following passage, the first sentence is retrospective, while the second one is prospective within the retrospection: "*Then* it left me untouched. I was not to be touched by it until much later." Then there is a passage with synchronic focalization: "I see the Jap beating a woman with a rattan cane."[81]

Apart from time and space, psychological properties play an important role in the further description of focalization. With "psychology," we mean the cognitive, emotional, and ideological aspects of perception.[82] On the level of cognition, there are focalizers who know everything and there are those whose knowledge is limited. In this context, omniscience is no longer directly related to the act of narration. Traditional omniscient narration is thus redefined as a form of narration in which an omniscient agent is the focalizer. Normally speaking, this will be an external focalizer: the center of perception is occupied by a narrating agent outside the fictional universe. Characters can also pretend to be omniscient and to look in other people's heads, but such passages will seem more speculative and less reliable than those informed by an external focalizer. In *The King of Waltzes (De Walsenkoning)* by the Dutch author Louis Ferron, the main character, also called Louis Ferron, makes it seem as if he can look into his mother's mind. He addresses her in his imagination at the occasion of her marriage: "You could already see the golden mountains he promised you."[83]

Cognitive properties

Focalization manipulates the reader. By switching from an omniscient focalizer to a limited one, the reader can be kept in suspense. The beginning of the medieval narrative *Karel ende Elegast* is focalized through an omniscient agent from whom the reader learns that an angel tells the king to leave his castle and start stealing. When Karel meets a black knight in the woods, the omniscient focalizer relinquishes his position to the king. Since the reader is now limited to what Karel feels and perceives, he knows just as little as Karel about the identity of the black knight. The character's fear and tension are transmitted to the reader. If an omniscient focalizer informed the reader that the black knight was the other central character Elegast, the story would have been less exciting.

Emotional properties

On the emotional level, focalization can be detached or empathic. The relation between focalizer and focalized object is crucial in this respect. If only the outside of the focalized object is perceived, focalization is detached. If, on the contrary, there is constant speculation about the thoughts and feelings of the focalized object, then perception is empathic. The above passage from *The King of Waltzes* provides an example of empathic focalization.

Ideological properties

The ideology inherent in every form of perception can either be given explicitly or be implied in narrative. The way in which the external focalizer in "From a View to a Kill" perceives the non-Western criminals is telling. Their eyes are cold, their faces angular, and their language incomprehensible. The conservative "capitalist" ideology emanating from the Bond stories is reinforced by their internal focalizer, James Bond, who observes and judges the Russians in exactly the same way as the external focalizer.[84] In "Pegasian," the ideology is expressly stated at the end when the narrator or the female rider suggests that lightness is important, "as long as you take off." However, this preference was already implicit in the first passages focalized through the female rider.

It is not always possible to establish a text's ideology in an unambiguous way. The longer and the more complex a narrative, the more ambiguous the ideology usually becomes. In this respect much depends on the number of focalizers and their position. If the narrative works with one external focalizer, chances are high that the ideology will be relatively unequivocal. If, however, dozens of characters function as focalizers, the result is polyphonic ideology, and the reader will have a hard time reconstructing the dominant view. But even in the case of a single external focalizer, textual ideology may be hard to delineate. Thus Gerard Reve's novels often have a fixed external focalizer, and yet his omnipresent irony makes it impossible to decide just how literally one should take his statements about blue-collar workers, women, and migrants.

The structuralists did not deal at length with the ideological analysis of focalization. That is hardly surprising since this enquiry leads away from a discussion of form into a discussion of content. Attention to ideology is the most important recent shift in the study of focalization. In our third chapter, we will present new approaches that emphasize the ideological aspects of perception in narrative.

Textual indications

When establishing the types and properties of focalization, the reader has many textual indications at his disposal. Descriptions of focalized objects or people may help him to decide, for instance, between an internal or an external focalizer. Suppose the wife of Judge Jack Jones enters her husband's study. If the text reads, "Judge Jones looked moody," one can attribute this perception to an external focalizer, since the woman probably would not think of her husband as "Judge Jack Jones." If, however, the text reads, "Jack seemed moody again," it is probably the woman who is responsible for this perception. Terms of endearment provide an extreme example of elements pointing to perception by a character rather than by an external focalizer.

Style too can provide indications of the focalizer. Childhood memories with many complicated and technical observations are probably externally focalized because a child would not achieve such intricacy. When Harry Mulisch discusses his childhood in *Feed for Psychologists*, he often uses a style that is not childish at all and that suggests perceptions have been filtered by the adult he has become. As a nine-year-old, Harry sees a puzzle, and there follows a very intellectual description of its top-right corner.[85] One would be inclined to conclude that a child could never see the puzzle that way, but naturally the text might also suggest that nine-year-old Harry was a genius. This ambiguity shows that textual indications can help but do not necessarily lead to an unequivocal conclusion. Here too the reader plays an important role. Too bad for the structuralist project, but texts seldom impose their structures.

Textual indications of focalization also include linguistic features such as register and the type of language. If a story is told in a neutral version of standard language, and suddenly dialect and swear words appear, this can mean that the events are no longer perceived by a neutral (external) narrator but by an (internal) character.

A great number of words can suggest a distance between the perceiving and the narrating agent, and as such they indicate that there is no internal focalization. In first-person texts, time indications often have this function. In "Now I know what I did not even suspect then," "then" and "now" imply external focalization. Words of modality are also often used to distinguish external from internal focalization. In "It's possible I thought at the time that everything would go just swell," the modal phrase "it's possible" shows that these are the thoughts of the narrating I about the experiencing I, which implies external focalization.

The list of textual indications can be endlessly extended, but this is not unproblematic. In principle, structuralist narratology wants to separate focalizer from narrator as strictly as possible. This becomes difficult if the particularities of narration are considered as indications of focalization. If word choice, for instance, is related to world-view, the boundary between narration and focalization may become fuzzy.[86] We have repeatedly encountered this problem, which is inherent in the structuralist attempt at categorization.

3. NARRATION

Narration forms the third and least abstract level of structuralist narratology. It is concerned with formulation – the entire set of ways in which a story is actually told. While the story is not visible in the text, narration involves the concrete sentences and words offered to the reader. While narrative was mostly concerned with the perception of events, narration mostly deals with the way in which these are worded. Attention goes to the narrating voice, to speech instead of perception, to narration instead of focalization. This implies two central areas of investigation: first, narrating (including the narrating agents) and second, the way in which these agents present a character's consciousness. These two concerns can be summarized as follows:

Narrating – Narrator types
- □ level: extradiegetic/ intradiegetic
- □ involvement: heterodiegetic/ homodiegetic
  ↓
  - *autodiegetic
  - *allodiegetic

– Properties
- □ temporal : subsequent/ prior/ simultaneous/ interpolated
- □ visibility : covert/ overt
- □ reliability : high/ low
- □ status : authority
  - * diegetic
  - * mimetic

Representation of consciousness
- – Diegesis/ mimesis
- – Indirect speech/ free indirect speech/ direct speech
- – Diegetic summary/ summary, less purely diegetic/ indirect content paraphrase/ indirect discourse, mimetic to some degree/ free indirect discourse/ direct discourse/ free direct discourse

3.1. Narrating

Similar to focalization, narration also expresses a relationship between an active subject and a passive object. In this case this relationship is the one between the narrator and that which is narrated. Again similar to focalization, this relationship brings about different kinds of narration that can be further described with the help of several properties.

Although Genette avoids the term *narrator* and mostly replaces it with less personal concepts such as *narrating instance*,[87] one cannot deny that here again structuralism catches a textual aspect in all too human terms. Most narratologists use the term *narrator*, and we will do so too since the use of less anthropomorphic terms such as *narrating instance* does not prevent this instance from being characterized by means of such anthropomorphic criteria as "reliability" and "detachment." This has led to a great deal of criticism,[88] but the distinction of various narrator types remains relevant for narrative analysis.

Narrator types

The narrator type depends on the relationship between the narrator and that which he narrates. The first criterion here concerns the relationship between the level of the narrator and the level on which the events he narrates take place. If the narrator hovers over the narrated world, he is extradiegetic. An intradiegetic narrator, by contrast, belongs to the narrated world and is therefore narrated by an agency above him. If a character is presented by a narrator with no other narrating agent above him, this narrator is extradiegetic. If the character in question starts to tell a story, he becomes an intradiegetic narrator. The difference between the two is a hierarchical one. The extradiegetic narrator occupies the highest place in the hierarchy, while the intradiegetic narrator sits one step below. In order to make the distinction, one simply has to answer the following question: "Is this narrating agent narrated by another narrating agent, or not?"

Extradiegetic and intradiegetic

Although an extradiegetic narrator occupies the highest level, this does not automatically mean that he is the most important narrating agent in the text. Turgenev's novella *Asya* begins as follows: "I was then about twenty-five (N. N. began) – as you can see, these matters belong to years long passed."[89] The extradiegetic narrator is the one who says "N. N. began." In the rest of the text, he does not appear again, and the reader always hears the intradiegetic narrator, the man who is described with the letters "N. N." The hierarchically lower narrator is much more important than his higher colleague.

Narratee

The extradiegetic or intradiegetic narrator mostly addresses an extradiegetic or intradiegetic audience, which in chapter 1 we called the narratee. The extradiegetic narrator mostly speaks to an extradiegetic narratee. These so-called addresses to the reader do not involve the empirical reader at all but rather an agent who does not appear in the story and yet functions as the narratee. In "The Cask of Amontillado" by Poe, the extradiegetic narrator addresses such an audience: "The thousand injuries of Fortunato I had borne as I best could; but when he ventured upon insult, I vowed revenge. You, who so well know the nature of my soul, will not suppose, however, that I gave utterance to a threat."[90] Intradiegetic narrators mostly address other intradiegetic agents; that is, other characters.

But, as we have already suggested in the first chapter, cross bonds are possible. An intradiegetic narrator can speak to a higher agent who occupies a position outside his narrative world. A character can, for instance, complain about his narrator. In *Chapel Road* by Louis Paul Boon, a male character relates how a female character has complained about "boontje," the narrator of their story: "She talked about the chapel road book, from which she's been removed, she says." She also thinks "that we're neglecting too many of our heroes," and concludes, "You're a useless writer if ever there was one."[91] Conversely, an agent outside the fictional world can speak to an internal agent. For instance, an extradiegetic narrator can address his protagonists. In *Slaughterhouse-Five*, the narrator has the same name as the author, Vonnegut. This Vonnegut repeatedly surfaces in the story of his protagonist, Billy Pilgrim, and he often talks with his creation.[92] Structuralism considers both cases as narrative transgressions for which Genette has coined the term *narrative metalepsis*.[93] Although the structuralist recognizes the existence of such transgressions, he is keen on establishing and maintaining the boundaries.

Metalepsis

Problems with the narrator type distinction

The distinction between extra- and intradiegetic narrators causes a number of problems of which we will discuss only two. First, one could ask whether any character who starts speaking automatically becomes an intradiegetic narrator. When a character says, "Yes, I sure do," it appears irrelevant to analyze this statement as intradiegetic narration. It is of course an intradiegetic statement, that is, a statement by an agent within the fictional world, but it does not really amount to a story. This brings us back to a problem we considered at the beginning of this handbook: How can one define a story? And what is the most basic form of a story? Which minimal requirements must a stretch of text meet in order to qualify as a story? There is no generally accepted definition of a minimal story yet, and it will probably never materialize. In the first chapter, we defined a story as a sequence of events that the reader connects in a way he considers meaningful. Needless to say, that which is meaningful for one reader does not have to be so for another. Fortunately, the problem of the minimal story is not crucial to the distinction between extradiegetic and intradiegetic passages. Indeed, it does not affect the distinction between the two levels; the question is simply whether an intradiegetic passage should be considered a story.

Mise en abyme

Secondly, and more importantly, a problem arises when various levels and stories are embedded in a frame narrative. When the embedded story mirrors or summarizes the story on the higher level, this leads to the so-called *mise en abyme*. To begin with, this causes a terminological problem. Imagine the abovementioned intradiegetic narrator N. N. talks about a character O. O., who in N. N.'s story starts telling his own story, say about P. P., who in his turn tells a story about someone else, and so on. How to describe all these narrators? The narrator who starts talking in intradiegetic narration (in our example O. O.) can be called an intra-intradiegetic narrator. Rimmon-Kenan calls him hypodiegetic, Genette metadiegetic.[94] The latter term is especially confusing since it suggests that a narrator who stands lower on the hierarchical ladder (and therefore sits "deeper" in the narrative) in fact stands "above" the ladder (and must therefore be placed higher). To avoid confusion, we prefer to distinguish between a narrator on the first level (extradiegetic), a narrator on the second level (intradiegetic), a narrator on the third level (intra-intradiegetic), and so on.

Hierarchy between narrative levels

With respect to embedded stories, it is not just the terms that are confusing. Sometimes it is also hard to maintain the hierarchy. Certain texts with embedded stories reverse the whole hierarchy on their deepest level and make it seem as if the supposedly highest level is actually narrated from what was thought of as the lowest. In our example, the character P. P. would then be the agent who said or wrote, "N. N. began." If the stories by N. N., O. O., and P. P. mirror each other in this way, the result is a paradoxical form of *mise en abyme*, which Lucien Dällenbach describes as "the aporetic duplication (a sequence that is supposed to enclose the work that encloses it)."[95] The paradox or aporia resides in the fact that the deepest level would contain the highest. Such embeddings undermine the structuralist effort to place all levels in a clear vertical hierarchy.

Again, *A Weekend in Ostend* provides an example. The first or highest story is the one about Blok. It is told by an extradiegetic narrator who never appears in it. The second or lower story is told by Blok and concerns his uncle Anton. Here Blok is a second-level or intradiegetic narrator. He relates how Uncle Anton met a prostitute, and they were going to get married. Then Uncle Anton starts to tell a story as an intra-intradiegetic or third-level narrator. His story deals with a riveter. At the end of this embedding, the text returns to the highest level at which we find Blok's conversation partner Uncle Julius. He summarizes – for a colonel who has just arrived – the story told by Blok. He says, "And he told me in his turn how his Uncle Anton turned into a poet when he stood in front of a floozie, but that he had to let that talent decline because of the circumstances, since he lived in a dark street with, if I understood well, a dairyman, a few greengrocers and a garage manager."[96] This sentence upsets the text's hierarchy of levels in two ways. First of all, it is Blok and not Uncle Anton who lives in the dark street, which means Uncle Julius conflates the second- and third-level narrators. Secondly, the formulation, "if I understood well," creates a paradox, since Blok has never told Julius anything about the dark street. Julius apparently knows things only the reader can know. In other words, an agent inside the story knows things that have been told to agents outside it. This confusion of internal and external has to do with narratees since the external narratee falls in with the internal narratee. Structuralist categorization fails in the face of texts such as this one by Brakman.

Blok

Narrator involvement

Homodiegetic and heterodiegetic

Apart from the difference between intra- and extradiegetic, there is a second distinction on the basis of which one can establish narrator types. This distinction no longer concerns the hierarchy of levels, but rather the narrator's involvement in what is narrated. Either the narrator has experienced that which he is narrating, in which case he is homodiegetic, or he has not, in which case he is heterodiegetic. If his experience is personal, the degree of his involvement may vary. Perhaps he has only seen things from afar, or perhaps he played the central role in the proceedings. On this sliding scale from marginal to central involvement, one can place the traditional distinction between witness and main character. If the homodiegetic narrator is the protagonist of the story he tells (such as Pip in *Great Expectations* by Charles Dickens), Genette calls him autodiegetic.[97] The prototype here is the autobiographical narrator. Genette has no separate term for the narrator who deals with things he has only witnessed. We accept Van der Voort's proposal for this situation and use the term "allodiegetic."[98]

Six types

When combined, level and involvement result in six types. First of all, there is the extradiegetic and heterodiegetic narrator, probably the most classical one: he hovers above the story – meaning he is not narrated by another agent – and deals with things he did not experience. This narrator can be inconspicuous if he narrates exclusively in the third person, or he can occasionally appear in the first person. Poe's "Masque of the Red Death," which we have previously referred to, provides an example of the latter. The I-narrator is not narrated by another agent, and he has not experienced the terrible events he relates. "Pegasian" too presents an example of an extradiegetic heterodiegetic narrator, this time without the use of the first person.

Secondly, there is the extradiegetic and autodiegetic narrator. He stands above the events he narrates, but he *has* experienced them. More precisely, he was their central character. An example of this type is the I-narrator in "The Map." The narrating I stands at the top of the hierarchy and tells a story in which he played the central role as a child. If he were to give us his father or mother as the main character, he would become a witness, and such an extradiegetic narrator would be allodiegetic. A famous example of this is Dr Watson. He has no narrator above him (so he is extradiegetic) but he is a mere witness of the things he relates (which makes him allodiegetic).

For the intradiegetic narrator, the same three possibilities apply. A character can relate things he has not experienced, in which case he becomes an intradiegetic and heterodiegetic narrator. He can also give us events he has witnessed, in which case he becomes allodiegetic, or events where he played the central role, in which case he becomes autodiegetic.

Advantages of the hierarchy

There are many advantages to this systematization of narrators, which we prefer to Stanzel's circle. To begin with, Genette avoids the confusion of Stanzel's system. Whereas Stanzel conflated speaking and perceiving agents by combining reflectors and narrators into one scheme, Genette's six types are all speaking agents. Genette specifies Stanzel's reflector as a combination of a particular narrator with a particular focalizer. An example of a reflector in terms of Genette would be an extradiegetic narrator who shows everything through the perception of a character and remains in the background while doing so. This means that for Genette there can be no scale beginning with "reflector" and ending with "teller-character," because that would mean one starts with focalizer and ends with narrator, two agents that for Genette belong to different levels of the text. They cannot be shown on a sliding scale.

Stanzel's person scale resembles Genette's degrees of involvement. The "identity" Stanzel spots in I-narration corresponds to the homodiegetic narrator, while non-identity corresponds to the heterodiegetic narrator. Stanzel's scale of perspective is not a question of narration for Genette but of focalization. Stanzel's internal and external perspective amount to Genette's internal and external focalization respectively.[99] This comparison proves to what extent Stanzel's circle confines to the same plane elements that for structuralists belong to different planes or levels. As a tool for narrative analysis, Genette's system is more transparent.

Problems with the hierarchy

And yet this transparency, as we already have had to establish more than once, derives from a theoretical construct that is not always borne out by actual narrative texts. Concrete texts are often more complicated than theories and do not always easily submit to classification. *A Weekend in Ostend* already showed that the distinction between intradiegetic and extradiegetic narrators is occasionally far from clear. The same novel also proves that the distinction between hetero- and homodiegetic narrators is sometimes impossible to maintain. Uncle Anton tells a story about a riveter. It resembles a traditional heterodiegetic story since Anton relates things he himself has not experienced. But as the riveter is dying, he hears the voice of his wife, who asks, "Are the lights out, Anton? . . . and the gas turned off? . . . closed the upper window?" And then the text reads, "The riveter wanted to nod obediently," which suggests he is also called Anton.[100] Maybe the riveter is Uncle Anton, in which case he would be a homodiegetic narrator. This is impossible to decide, so it is up to the reader to settle the matter. A traditional reader is likely to say Anton is a heterodiegetic narrator who happens to have the same name as his hero. Such a reader would argue that a narrator can never describe his own death. A reader versed in postmodernism might either consider Anton a homodiegetic narrator or leave the question open altogether.

Properties of narration

One can further specify the various narrator types on the basis of three *properties*. First of all there is the temporal relation between the moment of narration and the moment at which the narrated events take

Temporal properties

place. Here Genette discerns four options.[101] The most traditional one is that of subsequent narration (narration after the events), of which "The Map" provides an example. Although the past tense of the verb is most common here, subsequent narration can also occur in the present tense. A sentence such as, "I am fifteen and I think everything still has to happen," is a seamless fit for a subsequent narration by a fifty-year-old. Often in this connection, the use of the present tense has a special meaning. In "Self-Portrait with Turban" ("Zelfportret met tulband"), Harry Mulisch uses the present tense for nine crucial events from his past.[102] He calls each one of them a "today" because it makes itself felt until the moment of narration. This continuity has its symbolical expression in the use of the present tense for events in the past.

The second temporal option is one that involves prediction, which Genette calls prior narration. For instance, a character can narrate how someone else will end up. Prediction can be expressed with the help of the present or the future tense or a combination of both as in, "You will see. In seven weeks you will be a wreck. You don't have a job anymore then, or a wife. You drink all day and you think things can't get worse."

Simultaneous narration, the third temporal type, requires the use of the present tense because only that enables the perfect coincidence of action and narration. As examples, Genette mentions both the *nouveau roman* and directly quoted monologue. In both cases the narrator wishes to create the impression he tells you everything the moment it happens. Obviously this is only a trick – if the narration were really to coincide with the action, the narrator would be talking and experiencing at the same time. "Pegasian" amounts to simultaneous narration.

Finally there is interpolated narration. For instance, in a novel action can be alternated with a letter that provides a comment on it. In such a case, there is always more than one narrative level. An epistolary novel has the story told in the letters (of the letter-writing characters), and (at the other level) the story told about these characters between those letters. An example of such interspersed narration can be found in chapter 18 of *Max Havelaar* in which Havelaar's letters "To the Bantam Resident" constantly interrupt the action.

Narrator visibility

Next to time, visibility is the narrator's second property, which can be represented on a sliding scale from a nearly invisible narrator to one that is extremely visible. Rimmon-Kenan speaks of a covert and overt narrator.[103] The difference resides mainly in their narrative procedures: a covert narrator quotes a lot, does not present himself in the first person, and tries to avoid evaluative descriptions as much as possible. An overt narrator resorts to paraphrase instead of quotation; he will definitely talk about himself and therefore use the first person; and he will often showcase his own opinions. "Pegasian" has a covert narrator, "The Map" an overt one.

At this point we feel we should repeat our earlier remark that visibility must not be confused with presence. An invisible narrator remains present, and a visible narrator does not have to play a role in the story he tells. In other words, he does not have to be homodiegetic. He can perfectly well talk about things he has not witnessed, as for instance in Poe's "Masque of the Red Death."

Narrator reliability

The narrator's third property concerns reliability, which can also be represented on a sliding scale from a completely reliable narrator on one end to an entirely unreliable one on the other. As we have already said in the first chapter, a method does not exist to establish reliability in any objective way. Of course, a text can contain many signs of (un)reliability. If a narrator maintains he has said something when he has not in fact done so, that can be seen as a sign of unreliability. This impression will be enhanced by contradictory statements on the part of the narrator and by confessions that he is confused and fails to see connections. If a narrator says at the beginning of his story that he is better at imagining things than at giving a precise account, that does not make him more reliable either.

But even such almost binding signals the reader might interpret in unexpected ways. The above examples of supposed unreliability may be felt to contain a suggestion that a correct and truthful account is necessarily mendacious. In this view, a traditionally coherent story is not as reliable as it may purport to be. Textual indications of reliability, such as internal coherence, are therefore not sufficient to decide the matter.

Narrator type does not provide a solution either. Perhaps extradiegetic and heterodiegetic narrators are more often reliable than their intradiegetic and homodiegetic counterparts if only because the former are more detached and can therefore be more objective. But this is not at all a general rule. Quite a few postmodern narrators are extradiegetic and heterodiegetic, but this does not prevent them from being totally unreliable. Other narrator properties such as invisibility or temporal distance do not guarantee reliability either. In the first chapter we showed that an intimate link between narrator and implied author does not suffice to test reliability, partly because the implied author is an entity constructed by the reader rather than one that can be mechanically derived from the text. All these arguments lead us to conclude that the decision concerning (un)reliability largely lies with the reader.[104]

The first two properties of the narrator – position in time and visibility – are relatively technical characteristics of the text. With reliability one enters the anthropomorphic domain and turns the narrator into a human agent. A structuralist does not want to venture too far in this direction, although, as we have seen, he often goes much further than he might want to. However, readers and critics who see the text as a message that is part of a communicative exchange between a sender and a receiver *can* develop such human features. One example of this is the so-called *status* of the narrator, a concept developed by Susan Lanser. Her paradigm is speech act theory, which means she sees a text as a way to create a reality through language. This creation depends to a large extent on the authority of the speaker, in this case the narrator.

Narrator status

The narrator's status has to do with "the authority, competence and credibility which the communicator is conventionally and personally allowed."[105] In practice, this comes down to the combination of "diegetic authority" (which the narrator possesses on the basis of his personality) and "mimetic authority" (which he develops through his style of narration). The former type of authority comprises social identity, which for Lanser includes elements such as "profession, gender, nationality, marital situation, sexual preference, education, race, and socioeconomic class."[106] The most common social identity, according to Lanser, is that of a white heterosexual middle-class man, but this leads us to the ideological aspects we will discuss in the third chapter of this handbook. Mimetic authority consists of three elements that must be conveyed by style: honesty, reliability, and competence. A narrator can lie and talk about things he does not really know, or he can be honest and well informed. The problem with this list is, first of all, that it can be endlessly extended[107] and secondly that the characteristics in question are often very difficult to extract from the text. How does one determine the social identity of an extradiegetic and heterodiegetic narrator who never comes to the fore?

Perhaps these characteristics rather have to do with the unspoken prejudices of the reader (who might for instance expect the narrator to be white and male) than with concrete textual features of the narrator. Strictly speaking, this discussion takes place outside the structuralist treatment of the narrator, but one could also say that it exposes the structuralist's blindness. Indeed, his treatment is not devoid of ideological prejudice either, and furthermore it displays similar shortcomings: the structuralist description of the narrating agent is sometimes anthropomorphic, it can be endlessly extended, and it does not always follow logically from the wording of the story.

Textual indications

Nevertheless, for a description of the narrating agent the reader can definitely let himself be guided by various *textual indications*. However inconspicuous the narrator may be, there will always be traces of his presence. Each description is his and betrays his ways of formulation. If one analyzes setting on the level of story and spatio-temporal focalization on the level of narrative, it is possible to check how exactly the narrator describes and formulates this setting and focalization. The narrator of a James Bond story shines through in the many evaluative descriptions of the woods or the city or the secret service headquarters. The same holds for his descriptions of characters and events.

Furthermore, narrators can be discerned on the basis of elements that are not immediately visible on the level of story and that of narrative. Things that have not happened, and that therefore do not belong to the story, can surface in narration because for instance the narrator might assign a certain importance to something that could have happened but eventually did not. Things which characters are unaware of in narrative can also assume importance in narration, and yet again they betray the presence of the narrating agent. They also show that there is indeed a difference between the level of narration and the level of narrative.

In our discussion of the various narrative situations we have suggested more than once that there are hardly any textual elements leading directly to an unambiguous definition of the narrating agent. One has to combine and interpret an ever-growing number of indications. First person, for instance, does not automatically mean that the text features an intradiegetic narrator. Extradiegetic narrators too can come to the fore in the first person. The choice between first or third person is not even decisive for the distinction between homodiegetic and heterodiegetic narration. If the narrator talks about himself in the third person, he is still homodiegetic. In order to describe the narrative situation, one has to consider the entire text with all its embedded stories and combine the numerous relevant elements into a coherent whole.

Properties of narration can seldom be directly deduced from a textual indication either. The use of the present tense does not automatically

an original sentence like "Hell, I saved so many people in hi . . . hiding, so many people in hiding during that . . . that damned war." The first passage from "Sugarplums" could also serve as an example of indirect content paraphrase. "She still wanted to see what Ruben could really do" might correctly represent the content of something like "I wonder what Ruben can really do."

Of course, as readers we often cannot possibly know what the original sentence or thought was, so that we cannot tell what kind of summary we are dealing with either. The example of people in hiding could be a less purely diegetic summary if the character originally had a lot more to say about these people. It could also be a content paraphrase, but it might represent the original style quite faithfully as well if the original sentence went something like "I saved a lot of people in hiding during the war." When style *and* content are represented accurately in indirect discourse, McHale calls it *indirect discourse, mimetic to some degree*, which we will call semi-mimetic indirect discourse. "He said that, hell, he had saved so many people in hi . . . hiding, so many people in hiding during that . . . that damned war," might be an example. Thus, the simple sentence "He said that he had saved a lot of people in hiding during the war" may belong to three different types of consciousness representation: less purely diegetic summary, content paraphrase, or semi-mimetic indirect discourse.

Indirect discourse, mimetic to some degree

Once again, textual elements turn out to be non-coercive and can be read in different ways. Consciousness representation is therefore not just the work of a narrator representing the consciousness of a character but also – and often more importantly – the work of a reader trying to imagine the original version of a represented thought or utterance. In "The Map," we read, "What excited me was the thought that it now made sense *to have been everywhere*." If the reader imagines this to be the representation of a thought such as "it now made sense *to have been everywhere*," this could be a case of semi-mimetic indirect discourse. But maybe the young first-person narrator was thinking a lot more carelessly and incoherently at the time; so perhaps the style has not been represented accurately. In that case, we are dealing with a content paraphrase. It is also possible that the boy had a lot more going through his mind than the thought represented in that single sentence, which would make it a less purely diegetic summary.

These four initial kinds of consciousness representation are all

Free indirect discourse

variations of indirect discourse, which apparently can be interpreted in a very broad sense. The fifth type on McHale's scale is free indirect discourse. As we have seen, this variation occurs regularly in "Pegasian." An utterance by the riding master is represented as follows: "Little girls who have never personally experienced this heavenly sensation did well not to shoot off their mouths. And it wouldn't hurt to consult a few books on cavalry." This last sentence might in fact be a direct quotation.

Direct discourse

Free direct discourse

Direct quotation is the sixth step toward faithful representation; that is, toward more mimesis of the character and less summary by the narrator. According to Brian McHale, there is a seventh possibility, which represents thoughts or utterances even more accurately: *free direct discourse*, which differs from ordinary direct discourse in that digressions and supposedly irrelevant jumps in discourse and thought are also represented. The typical form is the quoted first-person monologue, which naturally leads us to Joyce's *Ulysses* again. Leopold Bloom is looking for a bar of soap in his pockets: "I am looking for that. Yes, that. Try all pockets. Handker. *Freeman*. Where did I? Ah, yes. Trousers. Purse. Potato. Where did I?"[112]

First problem with consciousness type representation

Although free direct discourse emphatically seeks to create the impression that it represents a character's consciousness virtually directly, it is of course "just" a convention. The "real" thoughts are as irretrievable to the reader as the "original" utterances we have just mentioned.[113] This constitutes an important problem inherent in consciousness representation. The term itself suggests that there are two levels and two phases: first there is consciousness and then its representation within a narrative. In typically structuralist terms, consciousness is considered the deep structure, while its representation is the superficial manifestation of that structure. But what we have said about the story as a so-called foundation also goes for consciousness: it is an abstract and hypothetical construct that often remains irretrievable. There is no way to ascertain what Bloom or Patty John were "really" thinking.

The constructivist alternative

This is why recent narratological approaches to consciousness representation abandon the mimetic conception in favor of a constructive or productive one. The first maintains the sense of an original, real reality (the words and thoughts of the character), represented as faithfully as possible after the fact. By contrast, the second approach sees this so-called real reality as an illusion produced by consciousness representation. Making use of a number of conventions, representation creates the impression of being an accurate reflection. This so-called reproduction is in fact a production. Monika Fludernik puts it as follows: "Reproduction is a process of evocation. . . . Mimeticism in representation is an *effect*, a fiction of authenticity."[114] From this perspective, the focus should be primarily on the strategies and conventions that give the reader the impression that this production is in fact the faithful reproduction of a so-called real reality.

Fludernik and typification

The crucial – and paradoxical – concept that Fludernik uses to refer to these strategies is *typification*.[115] In order to give the reader the sense that a representation is true to life, the narrator uses a number of typical, clichéd turns of phrase and stylistic means that are supposedly inherent in oral language (which supposedly has to be faithfully represented): swears, sighs, derailing syntax, banalities, repetitions, and so on. In the sentence "He said that, hell, he had saved so many people in hi . . . hiding, so many people in hiding during that . . . that damned war," the swearing and the hesitation create an impression of exact representation. There is a paradox here: on the one hand, these techniques create the illusion of verisimilitude, while on the other they are so conventional and stereotypical that they inevitably impoverish and distort the concrete reality (the thoughts and words of the character). The reader recognizes the clichés and accepts them as a warranty of authenticity, while in fact they are fakes. The reader only acknowledges the authenticity of a representation in the shape of a forgery.

That acknowledgment in the end depends on the frame in which the conventions of typification operate. One important example of such a frame is genre: a newspaper report requires a different typification than a postmodern encyclopedic novel. But frames can also be wider and refer to a whole set of social and cultural conventions activated through typification. When a narrator, in a story about a restaurant, quotes a waiter's reply, the frame of the setting evokes certain expectations in the reader that determine whether the reply will be recognized as believable or not.[116] We will look more closely at the use of frames in narrative theory in the third chapter of this handbook.

Representation of consciousness and persuasiveness

In addition to typification, the narrator has other means at his or her disposal to make the reader believe that a representation is accurate and true to life. The comparison of different versions of an account is probably the most common example. At the beginning of "Sugarplums," the narrator seemingly quotes Patty John, who reproaches Stein for his predictability: "Never anything truly surprising or even nasty, for all I care; you're so mortally dependable." The sentence is in quotation marks, making it seem reliable, but the exactness of its reproduction is cast into doubt in the very next sentence: "She probably didn't say it that way, but to Stein it could be put in those words and it still could."[117] The quoting agent is therefore not the extradiegetic narrator but the character Stein. At the end of the novella, the quotation crops up again, this time in a fragment focalized by Patty John. It turns out Stein's reproduction was very accurate: "Never anything truly surprising or even nasty, for all I care, Stein; you're so mortally dependable."[118] The identity of the quoting agent in this case is not entirely clear. It is probably the extradiegetic narrator or maybe Patty John recalling her own words verbatim. In any case, the strategy is obvious: the repetition of the quotation is meant to convince the reader that the consciousness representation is very precise and accurate.

It is no coincidence that this example involves direct rather than indirect discourse. Since utterances are usually ordered quite carefully, quoting them may be perceived as more truthful and convincing than the putatively exact reproduction of often disorderly streams of thought. Perhaps readers tend to think of a quoted utterance as an authentic representation; whereas they do not believe that a narrator could ever be capable of representing the chaotic swirl of thought in language. More generally, forms of representation at the diegetic end of the spectrum seem more dubious than those at the mimetic end because diegetic representations are only rough paraphrases. The intervention of the narrator is so strong that readers are not inclined to accept these representations as exact reproductions of a character's consciousness.

Second problem with consciousness representation

This brings us to another problem of consciousness representation: the relationship between narrator and character. In the case of the diegetic forms – the first four on McHale's sliding scale – it is impossible to determine to what extent the words of the summarizing narrator are a faithful copy of the words and thoughts of the character. After all, we do not have access to the so-called original.[119] The one thing that is certain, however, is the identity of the narrating agent: the narrator is talking here, not the character. From free indirect discourse onwards – McHale's final three forms – the problem is reversed. We get a better view of "the original." In theory, then, we should be better able to see what the character "really" thought or said. But in the case of free indirect and free direct discourse, the narrating agent becomes a major problem. Who speaks the words we hear in these two forms of consciousness representation?

Dual voice and polyphony

Most traditional answers to this question assume that two agents are speaking at the same time: the narrator and the character. A dual voice, in other words.[120] Bakhtin expands this notion to a polyphony of voices, which he does not so much consider the product of anthropomorphic centers such as characters and narrators but rather a combination of various discourses. This creates a hybrid language that rules out any unambiguous identification of a single speaker or discourse.[121] Ann Banfield takes this theory one step further and argues that there is no speaking center in free indirect discourse. Sentences with this kind of discourse are "unspeakable": they are not uttered by any speaker but are indicated and constructed on the basis of a number of syntactic signals such as inversion ("Would he still love her tomorrow?") and a shift in subject (the "he" in the example was originally an "I").[122] Free indirect discourse thus becomes a mechanism of language, a grammatical process that Banfield studies from an abstract, Chomskyan perspective; it is no longer dependent on concrete and clearly identifiable centers.

Fludernik's typification is paradoxical in this connection as well. On the one hand, typical turns of phrase make the representation impersonal – in that sense "unspeakable" – while at the same time they typify the speaking characters and/or reporting narrator. Swearing and hesitation are both typical of a swearing stutterer (the character, let's say, not the narrator) *and* of the linguistic frame to which the representation belongs. Insofar as they typify the stutterer, they suggest that the narrator is letting the character do the talking; to the extent that they are stereotypical mechanisms of representation, however, they imply that the narrator is mostly letting linguistic conventions take over. In this way language, personality, and impersonality come together in typification.[123] The question of who is speaking makes way for an investigation into the typical turns of phrase that language enforces, enabling and at the same time distorting subjective expression. According to Fludernik, this means that the eternal problem of free indirect discourse (who is speaking?) is not of vital importance to narratology.

Structuralist solution to the second problem

To a structuralist narratology, however, these kinds of solutions are not acceptable. Hybrid forms of language, utterances without speakers, and impersonal expressions of personality go against the structuralist predilection for distinct forms and unambiguously definable centers. Still, that preference is not very realistic, at least in this context. As we mentioned before in our discussion of Dorrit Cohn, free indirect discourse does not always allow us to separate the words of a narrator from those of a character. It is especially difficult in the case of a first-person narrator, where free indirect discourse often makes it impossible to distinguish between the narrating I and the experiencing I. In free direct discourse, which naturally makes use of first-person narration, the problem becomes particularly challenging. Because the narrator in this case appears to make way entirely for the character, some narratologists claim that the character should be considered the narrator. In other words, a character is talking about himself or herself and is therefore a homodiegetic narrator. Others suggest that there is an invisible heterodiegetic (often also extradiegetic) narrator trying to represent a character's consciousness as accurately as possible by using free direct discourse. The positions of different theorists on this matter are not always very clear. They tend to overlap, and an individual narratologist sometimes displays contradictory opinions. In order to illustrate this, we will take a closer look at the prototypical form of free direct discourse: quoted monologue.

The case of the quoted monologue

When quoted monologue takes up an entire book, we might say there is an extradiegetic and homodiegetic narrator at work, narrating from the highest level and talking about himself. Because the narrator wants to represent his inner world as directly as possible, the focalization is internal. There is hardly any observation through the narrating I, who is after all nearly invisible: our observations completely follow the experiences of the I as character. In a diagram from *Narrative Discourse Revisited*, Genette appears to characterize quoted monologue as follows: extradiegetic and homodiegetic plus internal focalization.[124]

According to Genette

When quoted monologue is embedded in a larger narrative, however, things change according to Genette. As an example, he cites Molly Bloom's famous monologue, which makes up the last chapter of *Ulysses*. Molly Bloom is not at the highest level: she is being narrated by an extradiegetic and heterodiegetic narrator who in the rest of the novel also narrates Leopold Bloom and Stephen Dedalus. Focalization is still internal, but the extradiegetic narrator is now heterodiegetic as well: he or she no longer coincides with Molly Bloom, who is no longer a narrator but merely a focalizer.

So far everything seems logical. The difference between these two interpretations of the quoted monologue can be reduced to a difference in size: in the first instance, the monologue takes up the entire text; in the second case, it is only one part among many. In *Narrative Discourse*, however, Genette noted that the quoted monologue does not have an obvious narrator, "but that it should be emancipated right away . . . from all narrative patronage."[125] The quoted monologue, then, would be so mimetic that the reader is given a direct representation of the character's consciousness with the narrator disappearing into the background. This is where things get really confusing: first the quoted monologue is the work of a homodiegetic narrator, then of a heterodiegetic one, and now it turns out there might not be any narrator at all.

According to Cohn

Dorrit Cohn vented her exasperation at this lack of clarity in a letter to "Dear Gérard Genette."[126] To Cohn it does not matter whether a quoted monologue is part of a greater narrative or stands on its own. She is only interested in the kind of representation used in the monologue itself. Since the first person is used in those kinds of fragments, they are instances of what Cohn calls self-quoted monologue; that is, the narrator is talking about himself or herself and is therefore necessarily homodiegetic.

In his response to Cohn's letter, Genette maintains that the quoted monologue can be both heterodiegetic and homodiegetic.[127] The decision depends on the environment in which it appears: as part of a greater whole or as an independent narrative. Of course, this says nothing about the problem of the so-called effaced narrator, the abandoned "narrative patronage."

According to Chatman

Seymour Chatman discusses the effaced narrator in his analysis of the famous Molly monologue. While not explicitly building on Genette's theory, he generalizes the French structuralist's argument of the monologue-as-component. Any quoted monologue, Chatman claims, implies a narrator quoting the thoughts of a character. As the word suggests, a quoted monologue necessarily calls for a quoting agent, according to Chatman "a totally effaced narrator."[128] Following this line of reasoning, it does not matter whether or not we read Molly's monologue as an independent narrative. In either case there is a totally effaced narrator.

A synthesis?

Chatman's view can be connected with both Genette's and Cohn's. Chatman's invisible narrator is heterodiegetic when he uses a third-person text. That is the case for the narrator of *Ulysses*, who talks about Bloom, Dedalus, and Molly as "he" and "she." The invisible narrator is homodiegetic when he uses a first-person text. A quoted monologue with an "I" doing all the talking, without a visible frame narrative using "he" or "she," is thus a narrative with a homodiegetic first-person narrator. The reader barely notices the narrating I; we see the experiencing I almost directly, whose experience here consists of having memories.

This combination of Chatman's effaced narrator with Genette's heterodiegetic and homodiegetic narration and Cohn's first-person and third-person context suggests that we do not necessarily see the quoted thoughts of a character as a narration by that character. Genette claims that any memory belonging to a character immediately turns that character into an intradiegetic narrator.[129] We think of the memory as a story told by a heterodiegetic narrator when this narrator uses "he" or "she"; when the first person is used, the narrator is homodiegetic.

No doubt, this calls for an example. When Blok goes to the men's room in *A Weekend in Ostend* and remembers past parties, this is a character's heterodiegetically narrated memory. If Blok had been the narrator of the entire novel, it would have been written in the first person and the memory would have been narrated homodiegetically. The difference between the two does not show so much in the quoted thoughts (which always appear in the first person) but in the frame narrative. In *A Weekend in Ostend*, we read: "Finally, he thought he'd pay a visit to the men's room." The memory that follows is narrated by the heterodiegetic third-person narrator. If it had said, "Finally I thought I'd pay a visit to the men's room," the subsequent memory would have been narrated homodiegetically.

Conclusion: against

This brief account of a narratological polemic shows that the creation of unambiguous and generally accepted categories remains a utopian enterprise. Any classification proposed by structuralist narratology gives rise to borderline cases and problems that have yet to be – and probably never will be – solved. In many cases the structuralist is forced to acknowledge that concrete stories always upset theoretical demarcations. That does not mean, however, that these theoretical constructs should simply be cast aside. Even when a story transcends theory, theoretical notions still enable us to describe the workings of the narrative more satisfactorily, if only in purely negative terms, such as: "In *A Weekend in Ostend*, the narrator does not adhere to the difference between heterodiegetic and homodiegetic narrating agents nor to the hierarchical relationship between extradiegetic and intradiegetic." In those cases where structuralist narratology is limited to producing negative descriptions, other approaches that will be dealt with in the next chapter are more fruitful.

Conclusion: for

In a lot of cases, however, structuralist narratology *can* contribute to a detailed analysis of the form and content of a narrative text. The three diagrams we have used in discussing story, narrative, and narration may be used as guides to the narratological study of a novel or any other narrative. They not only afford a global perspective on the text as system but also a minute view of all kinds of details that might remain unnoticed without the benefit of these three diagrams.

Of course, the application of the system is only as good as the person using it. The diagrams have to be interpreted, leaving a lot of room for decisions on the part of the reader. Many times he or she will have to make choices that are not necessarily prescribed by the three diagrams or the narrative. One pragmatic decision that will always force itself upon the reader concerns the size of the analysis. If one wants to analyze every single part of a text in depth on all three levels, one will find that the analysis expands endlessly and becomes bloated beyond the dimensions of the story itself. Readers will have to decide for themselves where to stop the analysis, what units to use (for example, chapters or shorter scenes), how relevant certain details may be and so on. Even in the most rigorous kind of structuralist narratology, there is still room for the unsystematized and the subjective, which are inherent in any reading experience.

Chapter 3

Post-Classical Narratology

Like most theories, narratology came under fire long before the structuralist analysis of narrative texts had been worked out in detail. The French journal *Poétique*, for example, was still publishing supplements to Genette's chapters on focalization, when in the United States feminist narrative theory was already in full swing. This simultaneity is endemic to academic research, and as a consequence it is not always easy to determine exactly when the shelf life of a theory has expired.

Classical and post-classical

In the case of narratology, there is definitely a classical structuralist and a post-classical phase.[1] The post-classical approaches partly resist structuralism but at the same time rarely if ever make a complete break from it. As we will see, some concepts are adopted, while others are rejected or adapted. Our discussion of post-classical theories is thus not meant to create the impression that classical narratology is on the way out. It continues to exist, sometimes in adapted versions. University curricula usually even stick to the unadapted ones. This can partly be explained by the limited attention teachers can or want to devote to post-classical narratology and also by the usefulness of the structuralist model. Post-classical approaches are often still in an embryonic phase; their insights have not been worked into practical models yet. Most literature professors want to give their students a methodology for the interpretation of literary texts, and a lot of stories and novels lend themselves well to a structuralist analysis without incurring too many problems. More precisely, with the aid of structuralist narratology, students can be alerted to textual aspects that they might not have discovered all that easily otherwise. Moreover, whenever this didactic approach runs up against so-called experimental authors, this problem can be solved by the suggestion that these writers consciously play with narrative standards and expectations established by structuralist narratology.

Classical problems

Still, the structuralist method is marred by serious problems. We have already indicated some of these in our discussion of that methodology: the anthropomorphous approach to the text, the preference for clearly distinguishable levels that may be impossible to separate in practice, the hierarchical thinking that turns a text into an accumulation of layers, and so on. We suspect that the average teacher at least points out these difficulties, so that the narratological interpretations of the students are none the worse for them. The post-classical approaches, however, seek to do more than draw attention to these flaws: they want to find remedies for them.

Selection criteria

We will present some of these approaches, without trying to be exhaustive. Our selection is inspired by two considerations. First, the relevance of the approach for concrete interpretation. This might give the reader the impression that we have picked out those theories that harmonize with Mutsaers's and Krol's texts. To a certain extent, this is inevitable: a theory is usually selected in relation to a text and vice versa. More generally, however, we would like to avoid approaches that get caught up in abstraction. We will focus on those approaches that start from and end with concrete literary texts. The second consideration concerns the way in which the approach construes the relation between text and context. As will become clear, in our discussion of the context we will limit ourselves to three aspects of cardinal importance to the concrete interpretation of a literary text. First, we will discuss how ideology can be related to a text. Second, we will deal with the way in which the text evokes knowledge of what is probable and possible. Finally, we will present a number of new perspectives on the interaction between text and reader.

In all three cases we will try to avoid the abstract conceptions of classical narratology. Monika Fludernik, for example, will be shown to connect literary stories to everyday, non-literary experience, thereby escaping the classical definition of a narrative text as the manifestation of the sequence of events we have called the story. Abstraction seems to be inherent in the structuralists' three-layered model. Obviously, such a model can yield strong interpretations, as in the work of Genette, whose theoretical analysis ultimately offers an interesting reading of Proust. But the detour of abstraction distorts the actual text, which is read in function of an idealized model that ignores experience, ideology, and other so-called subjective and contextual elements as much as possible.

Unexplored approaches

Our emphasis on interpretation and the direct connection with the literary text explains why we do not pay attention to narratological approaches that choose to discuss the context but lose track of the text in the process. That is the case with, for example, empirical narratology, which concentrates on the psychological mechanisms of text processing and almost exclusively uses positivistic techniques.[2] Since most narratologists have not been trained for this kind of research, the empirical study of narrative processing has largely been developed by research psychologists. However, their interest in literary narrative is fairly limited. Representative contributions to the field, such as those by Richard Gerrig and by Gordon Bower and Daniel Morrow, seem to imply that literary narratives make up too complex a phenomenon to allow for the controllable testing conditions required by the positivistic approach.[3] In striving for the disambiguation typical of the hard sciences, literary narratology might lose its relevance as a tool for the development of interpretations that ideally keep the complexity of a text intact. In any case, empirical narratology turns the narrative and literary dimensions of the text into quantitative data. Something similar happens in sociological narratology, which is based on oral stories and which connects these stories to the social group in which they originate and circulate.[4]

Anthropological narratology starts from the observation that fairy tales, legends, and myths from different cultures and periods have many characteristics in common. Following the structuralist project, this approach locates the basis of this similarity in almost archetypal processes and structures such as initiation, quest, and rebirth.[5] René Girard, for example, reduces stories to the triangular structure of desire (A desires an object X because the admired B desires that object) and the scapegoat mechanism (A is blamed for all social disorder and expelled so as to restore order).[6] Psychoanalytical narratology explains stories starting from psychological processes such as displacement and condensation and from unconscious structures such as the Oedipus complex.[7] The basis of a story can be found in unconscious desires that only end up in the text after various filtering processes. Examples of these include metonymical displacement (which, for instance, lifts a part from its whole and thus pushes aside those aspects of the unconscious desire that are unacceptable for consciousness) and metaphorical condensation (which, for instance, merges different people into one character).

In our opinion, in all of these cases a literary text is subordinated to a non-literary conception of a story. The literary nature is repressed and the actual text is pushed aside in favor of an abstract pattern.

Cybernarratology

A marginal case, which we will only touch upon, is cybernarratology. This approach is mainly concerned with so-called "hypertexts"; that is, all kinds of digital texts that collect data in a network in which a (potentially infinite) number of nodes are connected to each other in a (potentially infinite) number of ways. Apart from language, graphics, sound, and video material can be part of the hypertext. Well-known examples are video and computer games, multimedia stories, interactive texts, and websites.

First characteristic: palimpsest

Two aspects of this type of text stand out. First, different layers of the text are often visible at the same time, for instance when a mouse click conjures up another text. This can be related to the postmodern notion of the text as a palimpsest. Palimpsests are pieces of parchment that bear traces of texts that have been effaced. When a new text is written on the parchment, the earlier texts are still evident. Even though this image has been canonized by the structuralist theoretician Genette, it is especially in postmodern literary theory that it has become a popular notion because this paradigm assumes that every text rewrites or overwrites other texts.[8] Small wonder that hypertext was welcomed as the palpable and concrete fulfillment of postmodern ideals such as networklike intertextuality and the endless production of meaning.

Especially in the beginning of the nineties, hypertext prophets such as George Landow and Jaron Lanier stirred up a nearly euphoric mood.[9] It almost seemed as if the new text type constituted the beginning of a total liberation not only from the constraints of paper text but also from social reality. In this connection, Lanier's notion of "virtual reality" is very important.[10] Hypertexts were claimed to present a different kind of reality in which things are realized that are merely possible in the real world – if they are not improbable or even outright impossible. These prophecies never came to much, and in some cases cybernarratology limits itself to the design of new terms and metaphors that give narratological discourse a fancy touch but that do not really contribute to the theory.[11]

According to Espen Aarseth, this type of cybernarratology all too often boils down to a terminological trade-off, in which cyberterminology is imported into literary theory, and terms from literary theory are exported to the study of cybertexts.[12] The difference between the textual and the hypertextual world is ignored, even though the dimensions of time and space, for instance, are clearly different in the two worlds – it is no coincidence that these are important aspects of postmodern narratology. Hypertexts showcase a visual and in certain applications even a tangible world representing time and space concretely, which is not the case in literary works. In fact, in the literary text, time and space are no more than metaphors, while traditional narratology pretends they are real – as if these texts actually staged a time, a space, and a world. Aarseth aims to correct these metaphors in literary theory, criticizing them from the perspective of hypertext studies.[13] This goes well beyond the familiar criticism of the structuralists' spatial three-layered model because Aarseth questions the world as it is construed by structuralist narratology at the level of the *fabula*. In order to resolve this problem, Aarseth develops a pragmatic model in which texts are no longer conceived of as worlds but as communication processes.

Second characteristic: the reader-player

This brings us to the second crucial characteristic of hypertexts: the importance of the reader, who often becomes a player. In most cases, this importance is theorized by means of the concepts of immersion and interactivity. Precisely because of his active involvement, the active reader/player loses himself in the computer game he is playing or in the digital text he is writing with the help of all kinds of computer techniques. According to Marie-Laure Ryan, this combination of immersion and interaction is not possible with literary texts. Literary texts that force the reader to participate actively – *textes scriptibles* or "writerly" texts to use Roland Barthes's terms – inevitably shatter the effects of realism experienced by the reader: they introduce distance and lead readers to consider literary procedures more closely, which disrupts the immersion.[14]

Ryan relates immersion to the phenomenological approach of reading as a complete conflation of subject (reader) and object (text). She connects interaction with the structuralist approach of the text as a game, a system of rules that induces action. As a combination of immersion and interaction, hypertext would be an object of investigation in which the two traditionally opposed approaches could meet. This would imply a reconciliation of the phenomenological conception of the text-as-world with the structuralist view of the text-as-game.[15] Ryan starts from this perspective on hypertext to enrich literary narratology. She is looking for narrative strategies that are geared toward immersion or tries to find strategies that aim to achieve precisely the opposite effect. She also sheds light on the paradoxical attempts to create the illusion of a hypertext in a text – a short-term illusion of the synthesis of reflection and immersion.

In this way, cybernarratology increases our understanding of the literary communication and reading process.[16]

Seen from this perspective, hypertexts demonstrate what literary texts do to a reader in an extreme and paradoxical way. In her now-classic study *Hamlet on the Holodeck*, Janet Murray reads the digital narrative text as an extreme version of the stories readers were confronted with before the digital "revolution." The immersion in a strange world as well as the possibility of interaction are much more manifest in digital text types than in non-digital ones. Murray relates this to a third characteristic of hypertexts: the ease with which the fictional world can be adapted.[17]

When they reoccur in our discussion of other new forms of narrative analysis, we will elaborate on the two aspects of cybernarratology we have touched upon here. The complex layering of the text as palimpsest and as virtual reality will be dealt with, among others, in the theory of possible worlds. And the importance of the reader for the realization of the text will be underscored by just about all recent narratological theories.

1. POSTMODERN NARRATOLOGY

First characteristic: no synthesis

There is no such thing as a clearly defined postmodern narratology. This is not surprising, considering the fact that the term "postmodern" is so vague and limitless that it can be used to denote an immense variety of things.[18] Yet at the same time this is precisely the first characteristic of postmodern narratology: it combines classical elements with new insights without striving for a kind of higher synthesis. Such a synthesis would constitute a "metanarrative," which has become an object of ridicule in postmodern thought.[19]

A good example of a narratological combination-without-synthesis can be found in Mark Currie's *Postmodern Narrative Theory*.[20] Currie bases his plea for an expansion of narratology to *socio-narratology*[21] on the typically poststructuralist idea that everything is a narrative and a text. Lacanian psychoanalysis has shown that identity is a construction of language; historiography of the Hayden White school shows that history exists only as a plot and a story; and the postcolonial approach of theorists like Homi Bhabha interprets the nation state as a narrative as well.[22]

According to Daniel Punday, the connection of the narrative text with social reality creates an interesting tension in postmodern narratology. On the one hand, it breaks the text open by leaving room for context, including the social relationships and the subjective idiosyncracies of reader and author. Punday argues that this makes the text more tangible: the story is embedded in the world of objects and subjects, things and bodies.[23] This embedding diminishes the autonomy and thus also the power of the narrative text. On the other hand, this connection between text and reality also extends this power since the contextual elements (such as reader and body) can only be grasped as narratives. If this produces a new totality, a new kind of coherence between the textual story and extratextual history, it may result in a "post-deconstructive" integration of text and context.[24]

These notions have at least two drastic consequences for literary narratology. First of all, the study of a literary text is no longer limited to its so-called intrinsically literary aspects. It also concerns – and rightly so, as we will outline in this chapter – elements that are excluded from classical narratology: ideology, biography, social position, and so on. Secondly, the notion of narrative has become so broad that anything can be a narrative text, and nearly any form of representation can have a narrative character. A film, the Gulf War, the news, and the capitalist economy, to list only a few – are all considered narrative constructions.

Second characteristic: no hierarchy

The disadvantage of this theory is that it has no fixed methodology and is therefore very dependent on the insights and qualities of the individual narratologist. This is even more the case than in classical narratology, and it brings us to the second characteristic of postmodern narratology. Narrative theory, too, resembles a story and this erases the boundaries between narrative text and narratology. This characteristic fits the typically postmodern combination of level (text) and metalevel (textual analysis), as well as its rejection of hierarchies. Andrew Gibson, for instance, argues in favor of a postmodern narrative theory that no longer adheres to hierarchically separate levels like story, narrative, and narration. A narrative text is not like a house with clearly demarcated floors but more like a horizontal and often cluttered conglomerate of the most diverse narrative elements. The attitude of the classical narratologist who puts himself or herself above the text and dissects it into different layers is rejected in favor of "narrative laterality."[25]

Obviously, the classical distinction between text and interpretation cannot hold and the supposedly objective position of the metalevel is an illusion. But the postmodern combination of levels threatens to turn narratology into a very fictional affair. Currie rightly notes that the literary analyses of poststructuralists such as Jacques Derrida and Paul de Man are often very personal fabulations that do not contain any clearly applicable method.[26] However, the search for ambiguities, for places where the text contradicts itself and where the dualisms it posits turn in upon themselves, might be considered a methodology of sorts.

Postmodern methodology

A postmodern narratologist might base his analysis of "Pegasian" on the story's ambiguous representation of consciousness: sometimes we do not know who is thinking or uttering what sentence. Whereas structuralists would try to arrive at a decision by investigating other textual elements, postmodernists would say that the undecidability of the question is crucial to any story and particularly to this one: it shows how unimportant the differences between the two protagonists are. Whether you follow the rigid method of the riding master or the casual approach of the rider, "Whatever. As long as you take off." The riding master is associated not just with the symbols of dressage such as the whip and the lesson but also with signifiers of freedom and elusiveness. He talks about "a very special kind of wind" and "this heavenly sensation." The contrast between riding master and rider is undermined because the master himself has something of the rider in him.

In "The Map" a similar approach might exploit the ambiguous relationship between "blind" and "all-seeing." On the level of the text, there is the antithesis between the shaded shop and the map it still reveals, despite the blinds. But what the boy learns to see in this way ("a whole table full of *new things*") soon loses its value: the map is starting to fill up and is no longer worth seeing ("and one day I would remove the map from the wall"). Hence the reference to "a blank map of the Netherlands": that which supposedly provides new insight is itself a form of blindness. A postmodernist would no doubt extrapolate this insight to the metalevel as well. First of all, to the level of narration itself: the older first-person narrator pretends to know and see more than his younger self, but in fact his narration is captive to the same illusion as the boy's bike trips. He thinks that he can map things, that he can see and survey his youth as it "really" was. Secondly, on the metalevel of interpretation: a postmodern or deconstructive reading is also a form of insight-through-blindness, blindness among other things to so many other facets of the story and to the inevitable blind spots in one's own point of departure.[27]

Third characteristic: monstrosity

These short analyses clarify the third characteristic of postmodern narratology: it primarily pays attention to everything that does *not* fit into a neat system, anything that undermines itself. Following Michel Foucault and Derrida, Gibson talks about the "monster," an aggregate of elements that resist classification in any structure.[28] That which is excluded by classical narratology becomes the center of attention. While classical narratology streamlines and tidies up narratives, the postmodern variety favors "savage narratives" that refuse to submit to the discipline of structuralist narrative theory.[29]

Monstrous time

What does the monster look like? What does not fit the classical paradigm but does find a place in the postmodern model? First of all, non-linear time. Postmodern narrative analyses show a preference for textual passages that are hard to date or that go against the separation of past, present, and future. They prefer the chaotic swirl of time to the domesticated time of structuralist diagrams. Consequently, they reject the notion of a generally accepted temporal framework – the *fabula* or story – but assume instead that any literary text is crisscrossed by dozens of different time frames and scales.

Ursula K. Heise describes this situation with the term "chronoschisms," referring specifically to "the incommensurability of different time scales."[30] However incommensurable they may be, in the postmodern experience of time they occur simultaneously. On the one hand, there is the fast and microscopic time, the nanosecond, the immediacy of so-called real time, which characterizes not only computer technology but also the economic distribution of goods. On the other hand, there is the slow and extended time of cosmology, which speculates about millions of years and the Big Bang. The two time dimensions cross each other in many different ways and make it impossible to establish a primary and normative time scale.[31] The mutually opposed times coalesce in an inextricable and contradictory present that Heise refers to as the "hyperpresent" and that Joseph Francese calls the "continuous present."[32] In the same vein, Punday describes postmodern time as a condensed and heterogeneous simultaneity without the modernist inclination to the integration of contradictions.[33]

Whereas structuralists attempt to systematize the various time scales in a literary text by connecting them with fixed points of reference such as the *fabula*, focalizers, or narrators, postmodern narratology focuses primarily on temporal elements of the text that make this kind of systematization impossible. This implies that postmodern narratologists do not believe in a primary, "real" time that can be reconstructed or in a stable subject giving sense and direction to that time.[34] Instead, they point out that stories can never be reconstructions of the past, because there was no "real" event first and a narrative repetition afterwards.[35] Narrators who reconstruct themselves through their memories do not end up with their "real" or "original" selves but with yet another construction, another story about themselves.

In "The Map," the past is only reconstructed as a pretense. Its fixedness is clearly suggested by temporal indications in the first four paragraphs, until the boy gets hold of the map. Each paragraph starts with an exact temporal setting: "On Sundays the Christian shops had their shades drawn"; "This bookstore's shades were drawn on Sundays. . . ."; "Monday afternoon, in the bookshop. . . ."; and "That Saturday . . . At one-thirty I brought it home with me. . . ." From then on, the temporal indications become more vague, revealing the illusion of mapping. The map makes everything hazy. The distance between then and now is obscured as well: the final paragraph constantly shuttles back and forth between the moment of the bike trips, an unspecified moment some time later ("one day"), and the present time ("I haven't kept it either"). There is no genuine reconstruction here.

Time of analysis

The paradoxical simultaneity of different time scales is not limited to the literary text. It is also part of the context, or more precisely, it only arises in the interaction with that context. The context not only refers to the social reality, which combines the most diverse time scales, but also to the actual reading experience. Narratologists who read and analyze a text read traces of other passages in every passage as well as traces of their own temporal concepts. The traditional narratological reconstruction of a single temporal evolution in a story or a novel is an extreme simplification, which is blind to its own background. It is established after numerous readings, and the earlier readings resonate in every new reading. This resonance disrupts linear evolution because the narratologist reads each passage with the previous and the following passages in mind.[36] Hence, heterogeneous simultaneity and the "hyper-present" also play a role at the level of analysis. It follows that the "real" temporal evolution of a narrative text can never be reconstructed and certainly not via a traditional straightforward development.

Monstrous causality

Monstrous space

The collapse of linear time also entails a far-reaching relativization of causality, which is after all closely linked with the linear succession of two moments, cause and effect. Spatial setting is relativized in the same way. A linear notion of time sees evolution as a line between two or more points, in other words, as movement in a clearly definable space. From that perspective, classical narratology represents the space of the text in anthropomorphous, almost Euclidian terms that require fixed centers and calibrations. Postmodern narratology, on the other hand, proceeds from a space that is in constant motion and has no established centers.[37] Space is motion, "the ongoing transformation of one space into another."[38] This chaos of different time scales has its spatial counterpart in the uncentered web, the labyrinth, or the rhizome.[39]

In the postmodern description of narrative space, the terms "multiplicity" and "metamorphosis" pop up time and again. Francese, for instance, characterizes postmodern space as a form of "multiperspectivism" and a "flux."[40] Punday relates "spatial multiplicity" to "alterity."[41] The latter term refers to the fact that space can never be defined in terms of its own characteristics and coordinates, because the definition depends on the reference to other spaces. Punday argues that the space of a particular narrative passage cannot be reduced to the description of the setting. Instead it should be seen as an entanglement because the setting refers to the setting of other narrative passages, to the reader's spatial conceptions, and to the narratives that are attached to that setting in social reality.[42]

Postmodern narratologists do not establish temporal or spatial axes in order to situate the events of a story. They consider the act of situating a misunderstanding because of its anthropomorphous and referentialist connection of the text with everyday human reality. The reader of "The Map" and "Pegasian" hardly ever gains a solid foothold in the spatial setting. The space that he or she reconstructs changes constantly and resists unambiguous and invariable representation. Those kinds of representations belong to classical structuralist narratology rather than to the narrative text itself.

Nevertheless, the "text itself" remains out of reach for postmodern narratologists as well. However much structured time-space may be a structuralist construct, the postmodern theoretician's dynamic and multiperspectivist time-space is no less of a construct. His starting points and preferences naturally color his analyses. There is a difference, however. Structuralists look for so-called objective analyses, for verifiable interpretations that are suggested by the text itself. That is why they downplay the narratologist's subjective preferences, prejudices, and views. Postmodern narratologists, on the other hand, make their own points of departure explicit, insofar as this is possible. We use the term *point of departure* because it indicates that this bias is often theorized by means of spatial imagery: it is about the narratologist's position, the place from which he analyzes the narrative.

Space of analysis

In this connection, Punday talks about the narratologist's situatedness. This is not a fixed point but an interaction. The analysis of a narrative text generates an interchange between literary clichés pertaining to the text (such as patterns of setting and narrative strategy) and interpretive habits. At the spatio-temporal level, this interaction links the textual setting to the extratextual space and time, which is referred to as "site."[43] A reader constantly oscillates between text and site, and that is why he can never grasp the spatio-temporal setting as it would exist in the narrative itself.[44] Inevitably, the act of analysis will always be colored by narratives that precede the analyzed text and that resonate in the form of literary clichés and interpretive habits.

Time and space, therefore, are not compelling characteristics of the literary text: they are constructs on the borderline between text and context. This context is often identified as postmodernity, and its characteristics are usually found in sociological and economic analyses.[45] The fragmented and multiperspectivist time-space of postmodernism is, for instance, related to the contemporary, late-capitalist means of production. David Harvey studies postmodern narrative time-space from the perspective of the accelerated mechanisms of production, distribution, and consumption,[46] thereby following in the footsteps of authors such as Fredric Jameson, Jean Baudrillard, and Jean-François Lyotard.[47] Such contextualizations of the postmodern text and textual analysis often point out that traditional spatio-temporal footholds are disappearing. This results from the increasing importance of non-real time-spaces such as the Internet and from the growing fetishization of objects that lose their clear position in the production process and that are consumed as self-contained entities.

Monstrous paraphrase

Let us return to the literary text. The monstrous characteristics covered so far all relate to what is traditionally called narrative content: time, space, causal logic. A second monstrous aspect is connected with narration and concerns non-paraphrasability. Classical narratology assumes that narrative elements can be paraphrased and translated into theoretical terminology without destroying what is crucial to the text. To postmodern narratology, any paraphrase necessarily amounts to a disruption. This ties in with our earlier observation: postmodern narratology sticks so closely to the story that it threatens to become a narrative itself.

Monstrous imagery

The distrust of paraphrase is linked to another central postmodern concern: the close attention to imagery; that is, metaphor and metonymy. Metaphors can never be put in other words; they resist any kind of paraphrase. Hence the considerable attention poststructuralists have devoted to metaphor.[48] A well-known example is Lacan's analysis of a metaphor taken from the story "Berenice" by Edgar Allan Poe. Egaeus, the protagonist, is convinced that Berenice's teeth are ideas.[49] This metaphorical connection between teeth and ideas can never be paraphrased or exhaustively described. Yet the metaphor is crucial to the story, which shows how the protagonist's obsession (fixed *idea*) leads him to dig up the apparently dead Berenice and extract her *teeth*. The dynamics and specificity of the story lie in its imagery, more precisely in the interaction between metaphor and metonymy. In psychoanalysis teeth are metonymically connected with the vagina (as body parts they are literally part of the same whole) and ideas are metonymically linked with fears and delusions. The metaphorical connection between teeth and ideas thus refers, via a metonymic shift, to the vagina and fear; that is, to castration anxiety, which in its turn is a metaphorical combination of body and mind.[50]

The central metaphor in "Pegasian" is that of the muse turned horse, Pegasus. The question is how this horse can "take wing," how the muse can lift humankind. Does this happen through dressage? By putting on the right clothes? Or out of the blue, suddenly, whenever the horse feels like it? The whole story is an unfurling of images related to the horse: riding breeches, horseback riding, the carrousel, cavalry, and so on. A structuralist approach would try to classify these images in order to obtain a clear answer to the questions posed. Postmodern narratology, by contrast, would show how the images affect and enrich each other, precluding any unambiguous answer. It remains an open question: is there a right way to reach the goal – to go up in the air?

This openness surfaces in the discussion between the riding master and the rider. The problem is put in terms of metonymic images, which present parts of a larger whole. The flaps of the riding breeches (as parts of the rider), for instance, are supposedly necessary to reach the goal. The books on cavalry and the background information are parts of the lesson, and the fat that would take the place of fat ladies' riding breeches is part of the body. These elements all refer to the right method in a figurative or indirect way. But they also slow down the story and the lesson. This effect is expressed by means of a new metaphor: "These horses are moving around like turtles."

The end of the story combines the metonyms with the metaphors, which leads to insight and understanding. "Finally she understands: the riding breeches give the horse wings, and the horse gives those wings to you." The riding breeches are a metonymic part of the rider but become metaphors for the horse's wings. In turn, these wings become a part of the rider, allowing her to go up in the air. In other words, the alternation of metaphors and metonyms makes it possible to get off the ground. This can in turn be read as a statement on writing itself: inspiration – metaphorically expressed by the horse Pegasus, which stands for the muse – is a process in which one image leads to another. This results in a flux, a creative rush. In the text, this is the moment when horse and rider go up in the air, which is not a moment of synthesis or choice between the disciplined approach of the riding master or the flexible approach of the rider: "Whatever. As long as you take off."

A similar point can be made about "The Map," which develops the central metaphor of mapping in a variety of related images: the blank map, the earth being covered, the map getting so crammed that it does not show anything anymore. Again, there is no obvious conclusion, but an incongruity shows up instead: the more roads the boy maps, the less they mean to him. As soon as something is mapped, it ceases to hold any interest; truly interesting things do not appear on maps and cannot be represented in such a straightforward fashion.

In these cases, the metaphor does *not* create a dialectical synthesis or a higher integration of opposites. On the contrary, it is the icon par excellence of a "cultural schizophrenia" that is never resolved.[51] It connects different domains without ever reconciling them and is thus in tune with the contradictions that have come to be considered typical of "the cultural logic of late capitalism."[52] Thus, metaphor initiates the step from textual to contextual analysis. The interaction between the parts of a metaphor is in itself limitless. It becomes even more endless through the interplay with other metaphors in the text and through contact with the context. Narratological analysis, therefore, always remains unfinished.

Traces of classical narratology

The extent to which postmodern analysis still makes use of classical terminology varies with each writer. With a little goodwill, one could discern a continuum from near-total rejection to adaptation and cautious acceptance. The left end of the spectrum is taken up by the most combative brand of postmodern narratology that leaves behind classical terminology like *focalizer* and *heterodiegesis* and uses a new arsenal of jargon referring to imagery, contradiction, and the broader cultural implications of the text. One example is Gibson's theory, which explicitly and extensively explains why classical notions will not do, while introducing a terminology of its own. Less negative about classical theory is Mark Currie, who continues to use a number of fundamental classical concepts without clarification while at the same time explicitly resisting the presuppositions that underlie them.

At the right end of the spectrum we find moderate postmodern narratologists like Patrick O'Neill, who retains nearly all the fundamental concepts of Genette, Bal, and Rimmon-Kenan but expands and makes them more flexible in order to make them better suited to typically postmodern concerns such as instability and the paradoxical combination of contradictory textual elements. O'Neill enhances the classical triad of story, narrative, and narration with a fourth level, *textuality*, which connects the narrative text with its communicative context; that is, its author and reader.[53] He studies these four levels using *possible worlds theory* (which we will discuss in more detail later) combined with rudimentary game theory. Both the literary text and narratology are games that make up and at the same time relativize their own rules. This mostly takes place through a confrontation of different rules and players: a text is never one single game and can never be played by a single agent. This is why O'Neill replaces the one-sided structuralist terminology with concepts that refer to composite entities. He replaces the notion of the narrator, for example, with that of a composite, polyphonic narration that he calls *compound discourse*.[54]

Integration classical and postmodern

We feel that a complete rejection of structuralist terminology does more harm than good. Terms such as *focalization* and *consciousness representation* may cause a lot of problems, but at the same time they clarify things that would otherwise remain obscure. Moreover, it is an illusion to think that the new concepts proposed by narratologists like Gibson are free of such pitfalls. When Gibson talks about the laterality and monstrosity of a text, he is still using notions that betray a spatial conception of a text. Even though spatial conceptualization is rejected by postmodernists, laterality is obviously a spatial concept. Moreover, Gibson falls prey to an anthropomorphous view since he regards the monstrous as the non-human. These terms are in fact metaphors and therefore make use of the processes they are meant to study. This is not exactly a way out of the structuralist traps. What is more, the introduction of new terminology does not always lead to drastically different interpretations of narrative texts. Gibson sometimes reverts to precisely the structuralist terminology and methodology he seeks to avoid.[55] So far, the vocabulary and methodology of postmodern narratology have not been systematized enough to warrant abandoning structuralist practices altogether. A combination of classical systematization and postmodern relativization appears to be the best approach right now.

2. NARRATOLOGY AND IDEOLOGY

2.1. *Ethics*

Classical legacy Structuralism cannot be said to be blind to the ideology and the values that are present in a literary text. On the contrary, Greimas's structuralist semantics have always been concerned with the ideological oppositions and preferences that are tied to the organization of the text. Even if ideology is taken in a neutral way – that is to say, as a world-view and a view of humankind – it undeniably comprises a hierarchy and therefore a set of preferences.[56] Greimas-style analyses can clarify these preferences. For instance, in a particular narrative the feminine may always be connected to what is light and good, while the masculine may be associated with what is dark and false.

Nevertheless, such a structuralist approach sharply differs from contemporary ideological analyses. For one, structuralists often reduce the ideology to a code, a system that is thought to be inherently present in the text and that therefore downplays the role of the reader. As opposed to this, contemporary approaches emphasize the importance of the reader. Second, the attention to ideology is almost completely absent from Genette-style narratology.

Let us start with the second point. Genette wants to distinguish focalization types in a technical way and therefore does not take into account the historical development of the subject concept, which nonetheless determines these types and their reception by the reader. Multiple focalization may suggest that the subject is represented in the text as a fragmentary or heterogeneous entity, and this may be connected with a certain view of humankind in the social and historical context. There is little or no room for this insight in classical narratology. Even temporal structure, which may at first sight seem to be value-free, might be ideologically loaded. If Thomas Pynchon in *Gravity's Rainbow* pulls the reader's leg by inspiring confidence in a realistic chronology while at the same time sabotaging it through carefully hidden impossibilities, he unhinges an entire world-view. Genette has set up his tidy temporal categories but hardly pays attention to their ideological dimensions and their content. He limits their concrete meaning to their function in Proust's work.

As to the first point – the reduction of ideology to a semiotic code – we can start with Roland Barthes. According to him a story contains codes that refer directly or indirectly to social values, norms, and beliefs.[57] An example of this is the cultural code, which connects all textual elements referring to the social domains of science, knowledge, and ideas. Textual elements can thus be organized starting from one's psychoanalytical knowledge, which may lead to the connection of all the fragments that refer to an Oedipus complex. In Barthes's concrete analysis, however, the reader disappears and only the codes are dealt with.

The same happens in Philippe Hamon's structuralist study of ideology.[58] The reader's work is minimized, while the urgency of the text is maximized. Ideology is studied as "the ideology-effect," but this effect is not conceived of as the reader's work. On the contrary, Hamon says that the normative aspect of the whole process derives from the formal characteristics inherent in the text.[59] It seems as if the text is a formal package in which norms are wrapped up like a letter in an envelope. Hamon pays much attention to the representation of consciousness: the way in which characters think and talk shows the values and norms that a text displays and imposes.[60] Obviously, these values are not independent of the extratextual value scales and the interpretations of the reader, but Hamon does not focus on either of these two aspects.

Extension of the legacy?

Many attempts have been made to align these two readerly aspects with the structuralist patterns of thought. A good example is the work of Liesbeth Korthals Altes.[61] She studies ideology in *The Ogre*, a novel by the French author Michel Tournier, and tries to reconcile Greimas-style semantics with hermeneutical attention to the reader. Her terminology strongly resembles Hamon's. She talks about "the value-effect" of the text, an effect that according to her is controlled by the text itself. This happens on three levels. The first two are the well-known structuralist layers of narrative and narration. For the analysis of narrative, Korthals Altes uses Greimas's analysis of actions by characters; for the analysis of narration, she builds on M. M. Bakhtin's work, which we will encounter again shortly. The third level, that of reading, seems to be an extension of structuralism, but the description of reading as text-driven programming makes clear that, here as well, the text itself does all the work. The reader is programmed by the system of the text. In later work, Korthals Altes focuses more on the reader's contribution, starting from a critical reading of the work by Paul Ricœur.[62]

A similar attempt to expand classical structuralism can be found in the work of Vincent Jouve, who combines Hamon's views with those of Korthals Altes.[63] He also investigates the "value-effect" and thinks that the text itself is capable of creating that effect or even imposing it. Just like Korthals Altes, Jouve studies the values displayed and imposed by the work on three levels. At the level of narrative, he too uses Greimas's grammar of the characters' actions. He pays much attention to the ethics imposed by the evolution of the events and by the final outcome. Morals on this level are exemplified by the plot, which cannot be isolated from the characters, all of whom are carriers of an ideology. Focalization also receives a heavy ideological load, which is not surprising because it literally and figuratively involves a standpoint, an attitude.

At the level of narration, Jouve shows that consciousness representation and the narrator inevitably demonstrate certain preferences and value judgments. In the representation of the thoughts and feelings of characters, these values especially appear in the choice of words, in the syntax, and in the implicit or explicit orientation toward the other characters. Jouve discusses the narrator's ideology by means of the implied author – a concept that is absent from Genette's classical narratology but that fits Jouve's attempt to expand the text. Moreover, the construct of the implied author can provide an ultimate point of reference that remains indispensable for a structuralist like Jouve. Paradoxically, Jouve uses a problematic and non-structuralist concept in order to safeguard an orderly structure.

Even broader than the implied author is Jouve's third level, which he describes as the level of the reader but which in practice remains a textual domain. In terms reminiscent of Korthals Altes, he talks about the programming of reading by the text. This programming is claimed to come about in addresses to the reader (in which the reader supposedly identifies himself with the narratee) and in all kinds of paratextual and intertextual elements such as the subtitle, the preface, and references to other texts. In a move similar to the strategy of Korthals Altes, Jouve introduces the reader on his third level with the help of a theorist – in this case Michel Picard, who makes a distinction between a reading that remains detached and one in which the reader identifies with characters or actions.[64] Once more, this reference to the reader's expectations and attitudes remains secondary to the text, which is considered to be the driving force.

Steering between classical and post-classical

Perhaps this emphasis on the text is not such a bad idea after all. The attention to ideology might damage narratology's practical applicability and utility. The historical and geographical refinements triggered by this choice of focus may lead to a multitude of options that inevitably constrain applicability and that do not always lead to a better systematization. For narratologists who do not want to give up this systematization, it is crucial to steer a middle course between classical methodology and post-classical ideological interpretation.

This means, first of all, that one reveals the ideological baggage of a text and puts it into perspective and, second, that one estimates the importance of this baggage for one's own theory. The work of M. M. Bakhtin provides an excellent first step in this direction. He considered the novel as a polyphonous genre and showed in his work on Dostoyevsky how every novel is a texture made up of registers and forms of language that each comprise a specific ideology.[65] Bakhtin especially focuses on voice, or in structuralist terms, on the level of narration. Literary theory has to reflect the fact that a literary text is a confrontation of textual layers and ideologies, which means theory has to be many-voiced or polyphonous too. In some post-classical approaches, which we will discuss shortly, the polyphony of theory is regarded as an ethical question, a kind of resistance to the monophony and intolerance of authoritarian ideology.

In the slipstream of Bakhtin's work, Boris Uspensky concentrates on narrators and characters as carriers of an ideology.[66] Uspensky suggests, for example, that a likeable character may be intended as an example of a correct or a good value system, but he instantly adds that this is not necessarily the case. A specific narrative technique – in this case, the favorable presentation of a character – does not always have a consistent ideological meaning. In one story, a likeable character may indeed be the carrier of a positive value system, while in another story likeability may incorporate all kinds of negative values. Moreover, it is obvious that the reader can resist this type of ideological manipulation. The narrator may also anticipate this resistance; and a character may display contradictory ideologies or his ideology may contrast with his actions. As a result, it becomes impossible to identify a clear and compelling relationship between narrative technique X and ideological meaning Y.

Post-classical readers

This implies that narrative texts by themselves are no longer carriers of values – as the structuralists wanted them to be – and that they do not function as compelling programming languages for the reader either. Texts lose their unassailable power. They are no longer at the top of a hierarchical relationship that would condemn the reader to a lower position. They are now integrated into a horizontal interaction between equivalent communication partners: in this case, text and reader. Post-classical ethical narratology uses a frame of reference that differs from the classical one. The central role is not assigned to just one element – the text – but to the interaction. That is why the issue is no longer the ethics of literature but the so-called ethics of reading.

The two frames of reference appearing time and again in this connection are rhetorics and pragmatics. Rhetorics considers a story as an attempt to persuade the reader by means of all kinds of techniques. These techniques themselves are no longer analyzed in their own right – as in structuralism – but they are studied in terms of their orientation to and effects on the reader. An insecure narrator may have different intentions: perhaps he wants to make the reader insecure as well, or he may want to seduce him or make him curious. The nature, meaning, and function of a narrative strategy only become clear when these effects are taken into account. It is no longer sufficient to limit oneself, as a structuralist would, to the relationship between the narrator and the fictional universe. The reader's world now plays a crucial role. This leads directly to pragmatics, which studies a text as a form of communication, with a sender, a message, and a receiver. The classical hierarchy of these three elements is abandoned. The receiver is as important as the other elements: he or she is essential for the construction of the message as well as for the construction of the sender. It is the reader who construes an image of the narrator and perhaps also of other senders – such as the implied author.

Ross Chambers, James Phelan, and Peter Rabinowitz are only a few of the most important narratologists who look for the ideological effects of a narrative text within this rhetorical and pragmatic framework. In their work, they often start from characters and narrators. Phelan, for instance, studies the dubious and ambiguous, almost sexist ideology behind Hemingway's portrait of Catherine Barkley, one of the characters in the novel *A Farewell to Arms*.[67] In his monograph, *Narrative as Rhetoric*, he expands his research domain by also drawing attention to the narrator and the time structure.[68] Following Bakhtin, he does not consider a narrative text as a single-voice monologue that supposedly addresses the reader in a compelling manner but rather as an exchange of voices in which the reader has an active role in weighing one voice against another. When reading a story, a reader hears the voices of all kinds of narrative agents – both inside and outside the story – and tries to distill from this polyphony one harmonious whole. This is precisely the way in which the reader gets actively involved in the story. In this active process, ethical values are shaped. Because of the polyphony, these values often remain ambiguous and go against a simple division in good and evil.

Ross Chambers sees the interaction between text and reader as a form of seduction. Narrative techniques aim to seduce the reader, who adapts these techniques to his own desires. Texts only become readable by the transaction between seduction and desire, a process in which narrative strategies and characterization play a decisive role. In this transaction the text attains its value, and the reader assumes his responsibility with regard to the text by responding appropriately to the seduction strategies. What amounts to an appropriate response is partly thematized in the story, which indicates through characters and narrators what the good listener or reader looks like. Chambers considers, for instance, the character of Félicité from Flaubert's *Un cœur simple* as a role model for the reader.[69] But the 'appropriate' reaction is partly determined as well by what the reader himself finds adequate.

Peter Rabinowitz does not study the interaction between text and reader as a game of seduction and desire but as a game of making and following rules. He distinguishes four rules of reading.[70] First, the rules of *notice*: a reader only pays attention to certain aspects of the text, others are often simply ignored. Second, there are the rules of *signification*, which are used by the reader to assign a (possibly symbolic) meaning to the aspects that attract his attention. This consists of connecting these aspects to the reader's everyday experience by interpreting, for example, characters as if they were actual human beings with a specific psychological profile. Third, the reader also uses the rules of *configuration* to connect different textual fragments to each other. This creates patterns that are neither exclusively textual nor exclusively determined by the reader's expectations, but rather the results of a fusion between the two. Finally, the reader applies the rules of *coherence* to transform the text into a coherent whole that nevertheless leaves room for paradoxes and deviations.

Whether the interaction between reader and text is considered as a polyphonous dialogue, as a game of seduction and desire, or as a process of making and following rules, it always involves an interaction between reader and text. Rabinowitz's rules only work in the text to the extent that they correspond with the rules used by the reader; the seduction by the text as described by Chambers can only be successful if it appeals to the reader's desires; and the text's polyphony can only be heard by a reader who is willing to listen. It is impossible to draw clear boundaries, but post-classical narratologists can generally be said to consider the reader to be as important as the text, while their classical predecessors at least prefer the text to the reader, or even simply ignore the latter.

It is not surprising that many narratological studies of the ethical interaction between text and reader devote much attention to the narrator and the characters. First of all, this preference is in line with the expanded structuralist approach (Jouve, Korthals Altes) and Bakhtin's work. Second, narrators and characters are the most anthropomorphous narrative elements. In view of the fact that ethical judgments nearly always pertain to people and considering that rhetorical and pragmatic approaches focus on the relationship between text and human being, these anthropomorphous entities are the preferred points of departure –

which is not to say, of course, that there is no attention for other narrative elements.

The text as a human being

Structuralist narratology considers the anthropomorphous approach of the text as a mistake – even if it is itself guilty of this mistake. Post-classical narratology, on the other hand, argues that texts do have human characteristics, and it often compares literary stories with everyday communication between human beings. In the case of the ethics of reading, this connection between text and human being is sometimes taken so literally that the text is taken as a human being.

The most famous and influential example of this can be found in *The Company We Keep*, in which Wayne Booth extends his earlier, text-based narratology to an ethics of reading. According to Booth, the narrator of a story presents himself to the reader as a potential friend. Stories are "gifts from would-be friends."[71] Narrators "claim to offer us some moments together that will add to our lives."[72] The reader may feel disappointed when it turns out that the narrator does not live up to these expectations. The story's value and ethical dimension are shaped by the extent to which narrators keep their promise of friendship. Once more, this value judgment is not unidirectional. The text does not impose, but the reader is not totally free either. In his judgment he can adjust and change his already existing criteria. In any case, he not only judges the story but also his own capacity to judge the story: "We judge ourselves as we judge the offer."[73]

The judgment's rigor and accuracy depend on the nature of the friendship. Booth distinguishes different kinds of friendship and hence also different kinds of books. He uses seven criteria in order to do so, including quantity (a friend you see often is more demanding and can be judged better than someone you meet only once a year) and intimacy (the more intimate, the greater the demands and the more accurate the judgment will be).[74] The value of the text and the reading cannot be separated from the friendship: good readers, as well as good books, are like good friends.

A comparable anthropomorphization of the text can be found in Adam Newton's *Narrative Ethics*. He is inspired by the philosophy of Emmanuel Levinas, who considers the presence of others as an appeal to the self. The narrative text similarly appeals to the reader: "Like persons, texts present themselves and expose themselves; the claim they make on me does not begin with dedicating myself to them, but rather precedes my discovery of the claim."[75] Newton studies this ethical appeal on three levels: narration, narrative, and the reader's interpretation. This corresponds perfectly to the expanded structuralist approach we found with Korthals Altes and Jouve. They extended the familiar levels of narrative and narration with a third domain as well, that of the reader and the act of reading.

Just like the other two narratologists, Newton holds on to the text's nearly compelling power. He writes about "the imperative aspect of literature" and argues that an ethical or good reading becomes possible only when the reader heeds that imperative.[76] Only then is the reader's reaction legitimate. Only then does "response as responsibility" function.[77] Newton places this response in the Bakhtinian tradition, as a dialogue between text and reader that is a reflection of the polyphonous, dialogical character of the text itself.[78]

The text as law

This brings us to a curious ambiguity of many reader-oriented approaches. On the one hand, they emphasize the importance of the reader; on the other hand, they often fall back upon characteristics that supposedly form part of the text itself and that supposedly function as compelling entities. They seem to be afraid that the ethics of reading will lapse into an ethics of the subjective reader if the power of the text is rejected. Even a deconstructivist such as John Hillis Miller writes about the law that is supposedly issued by a text. But his approach already makes room for deviations from this law and may hence be used as a theoretical systematization of the ambiguity that has just been observed.

Ethics as transgression

On the one hand, Miller argues that a literary text shapes "the law as such"[79] and that the act of reading should be subjected to this law. On the other hand, the reader can never fully grasp the law, which implies two things. First, every attempt to make the ethical law of a literary genre explicit will deform this law. Every readerly attempt to approach the law constitutes a deviation from the law: "This law forces the reader to betray the text or deviate from it in the act of reading it, in the name of a higher demand that can yet be reached only by way of the text."[80] Second, this law is not "in" the text, as a letter or a message is in an envelope. It constantly escapes the formulations of the story. It is never directly or literally present, it is only there as a manner of speaking – figuratively. Or better, the law is a figure of speech that can only be approached in the story's figures of speech.[81]

That is why narrative ethics has to concentrate on the study of the text's metaphors and metonyms. Stories do not literally say what the law is, but they talk about it in similes. The reader has to respect these similes – he or she should not translate them into simple, literal descriptions such as, "In fact, Mutsaers wants to say that we do not need to follow rules." At the same time, this respect for the figures of speech will always be a betrayal: if one does not want to translate figurative language, one can only try to grasp it in other, new images. As a result, the act of reading becomes an endless unfurling of constantly renewed images. An unstoppable stream of tropes is set in motion, and it is precisely this stream that shapes the reading that does justice to the text. Reading becomes a form of "figuring it out," a development of the figures of speech.[82]

Ethics and morality

For Miller, a good, ethical reading is endless and undecided. In every attempt to approach the law, this reading moves away from it. That is why it never attains the simplicity of a moral or a lesson. Ethics is distinct from morality by remaining undecided. It vacillates between law and transgression, approach and deviation. This uncertainty makes the text literary and makes the reading ethical instead of moralizing. Just like the text itself, the act of reading has to be an infinite unfurling of images. Reading is never finished and in that sense, the text is unreadable. That is why Miller sees "the unreadability of the text" as the outstanding characteristic of the "true ethics of reading."[83]

Ethics and Mutsaers

In Miller's case, the ethics of reading ties in with the postmodern attention to figures of speech. As we demonstrated in the discussion of postmodern narratology, "Pegasian" teems with imagery, and the story literally and figuratively refuses to take a definitive position. Many of these images evoke power, such as the central metaphor of dressage. The riding master tries to discipline the girl, while she tries to train the horse in turn. The end of the story shows that nobody really is in power. The riding master does not manage to subject the girl, and she does not succeed in training the horse. But she goes up in the air all the same. Or better, that is precisely why she goes up in the air. Thanks to the undecidability ("Whatever."), the goal has been reached.

Perhaps this refusal to exercise power is the best way to get things done. And in that way, it really is dressage. This dressage is used explicitly as a metaphor for life: "true dressage, just like real life, doesn't have anything to do with racing." It is not the speed that counts, but "the sensation" you get by riding. The goal is not to arrive as fast as possible but to be on your way. The goal is undecidability, being neither here nor there. The ethical aspect of the text resides in the constant alternation of images and viewpoints and in the refusal to choose a single viewpoint. The ethical aspect of a narratological reading resides in the unfurling of these images and in the suggestion of undecidability.

There is still room for classical narratology here. The undecidability in question is doubtlessly enhanced by the story's variable focalization and free indirect speech. The latter sometimes makes it impossible to figure out who is talking: the riding master, the rider, or the narrator. In this connection, the invisibility of the extradiegetic narrator can also be seen as a means to relinquish his omniscient and moralizing power. He does not want dressage, as the exercise of power, either. In the end, he will not interfere, nor will he choose sides or formulate a moral.

Nevertheless, the reader can ignore the uncertainty and read the ending as a nearly Machiavellian moral: it does not matter how you get there as long as you get there. For Miller, this would reduce ethics to morality. It would stop the narrative pendulum between various views and images, but there is no element in the text that can prevent the reader from such a moralizing interpretation. The images, the focalization, the free indirect speech, and the invisible narrator – none of them can compel the reader. Just about every narratologist working on an ethics of reading agrees with Booth when he says, "Systematic correlations between a given technique, open or closed, and a given ethical (or for that matter aesthetic) effect, are, I now think, always suspect."[84]

Ethics and Krol

What was said about the image of dressage in the story by Mutsaers holds for Krol's image of the map as well. This text also centers on an image of power and a metaphor of life. The boy wants to map his life and discovers that by doing so he brings it to a halt. This is clarified in the story by means of the image of the bike trip, which can be compared to Mutsaers's horse ride. As soon as the boy has gone somewhere and has indicated this location on his map, the trip becomes meaningless. The goal has been reached, the trip has become superfluous. "Some roads (and the number increased) I traveled two times or more, but this did not count. To have been there once is to be there always; my map indicated this."

"Pegasian" shows what the endless movement of the pendulum and of being-on-one's-way can lead to: success. The story shows what you can achieve if you do not exercise any power. "The Map," on the contrary, shows how the endless movement of the pendulum stops when you do want to exercise power. And then even power becomes meaningless. The map becomes uninteresting as soon as it has exercised its power. Once everything has been put on the map, the first-person narrator takes it off the wall: "It had become meaningless. I haven't kept it either." This ending is almost the opposite of the one in the story by Mutsaers, but both stories show that value (in this case, of dressage and the map) lies in being on one's way to this value and not in reaching the goal.

Following Miller, we have emphasized figures of speech as a potential starting point for illustrating the openness of a text. This openness is considered to make up the value of the text and of its interpretation. Many forms of narrative ethics, however, choose a different point of departure that ties in with the already mentioned interest in the text's anthropomorphous centers. We are thinking specifically about the unreliable narrator, whom Booth considers a "pretender" instead of a friend[85] and who is seen by Chambers as a part of the inevitably risky seduction strategy.[86] In Newton's approach, the unreliability would fit into the "shaping of power relations" that, according to him, are inherent in narration as an appeal to the reader.[87]

Ethics and unreliability

James Phelan and Mary Patricia Martin start from the unreliable homodiegetic first-person narrator to draw conclusions on the "ethical positioning" of the reader.[88] The unreliability of such a narrator is triggered by his double role as character and narrator. As a character he may very well come across as a reliable person, while as a narrator he may be unreliable. This ambiguity is often left unresolved in the text and can even contribute to the value of that text.[89] The reader often cannot tell whether the narrator is reliable or not or whether he is good or bad, ethically speaking. Should he want to come to a conclusion, he will have to activate his own ethical values and desires.[90]

People sharing Miller's preference for openness will call this a moralizing rather than an ethical reading. If Monika Fludernik is right when she says that unreliable narration is the essential characteristic of fictional narrative texts, this type of reading could even be considered as a failure to appreciate the core of fiction.[91] If we return to the three levels of classical narratology, we could describe moralizing reading as an evaluation of the story, in isolation from narrative and narration. A novel could be rejected, for instance, on the basis of the events described in it – for example, the adultery in Flaubert's *Madame Bovary* – or because of the allegedly despicable characteristics of the actantial roles – for instance, the negative characteristics of the female figures. This involves an evaluation of elements that are part of the *fabula* and that therefore remain outside the literary organization of the *suzjhet*. In other words, it concerns judgments that disregard the narrative and fictional character of the text – fictional as defined by Fludernik. In this case, one specific ideology (for example, one that is politically correct) would be opposed to another (for example, one that is not politically correct). This hardly would have anything to do with narrative ethics anymore.

2.2. *Gender*

Narrative ethics is not the most famous example of the ideology-related developments in contemporary narrative theory. Undoubtedly, feminist narratology can lay claim to that status. Since the eighties, it has been investigating the relationship between narrative texts and narratological theories on the one hand and sex, gender, and sexual orientation on the other. "Sex" is the term used for the biological distinction between men and women, while "gender" refers to the social construction of the sexes. Most often, this construction is related to sexual orientation. The traditional construction of the roles of men and women includes a heterosexual preference. Gender cannot be disconnected from sex and sexuality even if it does not coincide with them.

Classical exclusion

Feminist narratology shows that gender, sex, and sexuality play a central role in the construction and interpretation of narrative texts, while classical narratology excludes these three aspects. As Susan Lanser observes in her influential essay, "Toward a Feminist Narratology," this exclusion is related to the gender of canonized narratologists and of the texts used by them.[92] Not only does it usually involve male theoreticians (Stanzel, Genette, Chatman, Prince), but usually also male writers. Many so-called universal concepts from classical narrative theory and many allegedly universal characteristics of literary texts are in fact typical of a specific period – for narratology this is usually structuralism, for literature mostly fiction up to and including modernism – a specific culture and a specific predominantly male population.

Narratology is not universal or neutral. It is colored by the context in which it functions, and this context consists of a whole series of factors such as social class, sex, age, economic and professional position, physical condition, and education. Every narratological concept bears traces of this context, and feminist theoreticians argue that these traces are ideological to the extent that they express the power relations of that context. The structuralist desire to classify, survey, and master, for instance, is the expression of a typically Western and male view of knowledge. More generally, Lanser says in her standard work, *Fictions of Authority*, "that even the broadest, most obvious elements of narration are ideologically charged and socially variable, sensitive to gender differences in ways that have not been recognized."[93] By paying attention to the more general and ideological context, feminist narratology is part of the expansion that is typical of nearly all post-classical forms of narratology. Feminist narratologists such as Robyn Warhol and Kathy Mezei join forces with "contextualist narratology," which has to complement and correct classical narratology.[94]

Feminist exclusion?

Obviously, it is impossible to map the entire context of a text and a theory. Following Althusser, the French sociologist Bourdieu talks about an "overdetermination" (*surdétermination*) of contextual factors: human beings are influenced by so many factors that they can never have a complete picture of them, let alone systematize them.[95] This blindness may lead to the illusion of freedom or to the feeling that one can choose one specific factor as the most important one. In reality, no single factor can function without influencing the entire network. Gender functions differently with an old, rich, white academic than with a young, poor Asian immigrant – to say nothing about looks and health. Even though feminist narratology often recognizes this in theory, many concrete text analyses don't pay attention to the entire network and favor the cluster sex, gender, and sexuality. In those analyses, it seems as if being a woman is an autonomous function, one that constitutes the most important influence on text and theory. Lanser argues, for instance, that feminist narratology cannot find definitive correlations between ideology and narrative form, only to claim later that there are causal relations between gender and genre.[96]

In a recent evaluation of feminist narratology, Ruth Page claims that "it is not possible to propose incontestable links between gender and narrative form."[97] According to her, form depends on a large number of factors such as content, function, and context. The selection of one factor inevitably entails an ideological bias. Even with respect to narratives that directly deal with gender-related subjects such as birth, Page argues that narrative strategies are not determined by the speaker's gender. She rejects the feminist presupposition that the speaker's gender can explain the form of the narrative.[98] This can be linked to the qualification in our discussion of narrative ethics: there is no compelling or causal connection between a formal textual element and a contextual, ideological element. A specific narrative strategy is not the direct consequence of a specific ideological position, and neither does it lead directly to a specific ideological reading.

Universality This qualification, however, does not undermine the feminist approach since it does not pretend to design a general and universally valid framework. It rightly emphasizes a factor that has been ignored in traditional theory, and so it does not amount to a new supertheory. Warhol explicitly turns her back on the structuralist illusion that narratology presents universal concepts. Precisely because feminist narratology is interested in the ever-changing context and the constantly renewed construction of the difference between men and women, she rejects every unchanging macrotheory.[99] Nancy Miller says that feminist textual criticism believes in a "poetics of location": she realizes that every text – literary or theoretical – is located in a specific context.[100]

This qualification, made by feminist narratologists themselves, is best kept in mind when reading actual narrative analyses. These often seem to deal with the "typically female" and the "typically male" in an oversimplified and universalizing manner, but in the light of this qualification, such assertions acquire their contextualized value. Teresa de Lauretis emphasizes that feminist literary theory does not work with an essentialist conception of Woman.[101] In Mária Brewer's words: "Women's discourse has little to do with an ineffable or unnamable essence of Femininity."[102] There is no essentially female narrative form either. If Lanser argues that, historically speaking, female writers use narrative forms that are less oriented toward the public domain than the forms used by men, she does not attempt a universal law or a reification of female writing. She tries rather to connect this writing with the specific eighteenth-century context in which letters and diaries were seen as female genres, and speeches and novels as male ones.[103] More than once, Lanser warns the reader that she does not propose a real, authentic, and essentially female way of writing and reading.[104]

Shift in feminist narratology

Perhaps this qualification is partly also the result of a shift in feminist narratology itself. In the beginning, it often seemed as if gender guided the text, while in the meantime the reverse has come to hold. Warhol says that the first feminist narratologists accepted gender as a category that precedes the text, while recent approaches argue that the narrative text shapes gender.[105] A good example can be found in Sally Robinson's study *Engendering the Subject*, which starts with the sentence: "I am concerned with how gender is produced through narrative processes, not prior to them."[106] More generally, the text is no longer considered to be the reflection of a given ideology, but to be its construction. Obviously, this construction is not free; it is influenced by the context. This results in a nearly dialectical relationship between narrative technique and ideology. As Lanser puts it, narrative technique is not so much a product of ideology but rather the ideology itself.[107]

These introductory remarks on qualification and shift are not meant to downplay the results of feminist narratology. On the contrary, there is probably no other post-classical narrative theory that has analyzed, influenced, and modified so many aspects of narratology.[108] As a pragmatic approach to the text, feminist research has concentrated on the sender of the text (the author), the message (the narrative form), and the receiver (the reader). In all these domains, it pays attention to aspects that have mostly been ignored in the structuralist approach and that here assume the status of leitmotifs: experience and desire; the struggle for authority; ambiguity; the corporeal. We will deal with these points in the different domains of pragmatic narratology.

Ambiguity and struggle

The most striking pattern in feminist analyses is probably the combination of resistance and complexity. Female authors, narrative strategies, and readers are often represented as critical actors in the struggle against an existing male tradition. In this struggle, women often use the male weapons and transform them. This move makes not only these weapons ambiguous – for example, the traditional narrator – but the female fighters as well. They are supposed to absorb as well as transform the male counterpart. In simple terms, this pattern comes down to, first, the assertion of an opposition (man versus woman) and, second, the conflation of the opposite extremes in one of the poles; that is, the female one. Many feminist analyses associate the male pole with unequivocality: well-delineated traditions, pursuits, and identities. The female pole, on the contrary, is characterized by ambiguity: vague traditions, camouflaged (because repressed) pursuits, transgressive identities. This association of "female" with "ambiguous" is often already advertised in the titles, for example in the reader *Ambiguous Discourse*, edited by Kathy Mezei.

Gender and author

With *The Madwoman in the Attic*, Sandra Gilbert and Susan Gubar published an early and influential study on female authors in the nineteenth century. Their analysis clearly features the mechanism of struggle and ambiguity. The writers in question are supposed to be united by a common struggle against the male establishment, "a common, female impulse to struggle free from social and literary confinement through strategic redefinitions of self, art, and society."[109] At the level of the author, this struggle amounts to a clash with the paternalistic tradition, which (etymologically as well) identifies the author with the paterfamilias, a human version of God, our Father. This tradition functions as an order: the woman is presented with a mirror in which she has to recognize herself. She has to subject herself to the image man has made for her: that of the subjected angel who puts her creativity at the service of man and, more specifically, at the service of his procreation. A woman who resists this is a monster. She displays male traits such as assertiveness and aggression. The female author is such a monster: a sick hybrid, a she-man, not dissimilar to the postmodern monster discussed above.

For the female author, this ambiguous status is a struggle between experience and tradition. The male narrative tradition never lends a voice to the female experience except through the male stereotypes of angel and monster. A woman who wants to write must come to the conclusion that there are no prestigious narrative forms or genres in which she can express her subjective experience. She may occupy herself with marginal genres such as children's books and fairy tales but not with real literary work, the novel. If she wants to write novels anyway, she will do this out of the "anxiety of authorship," the female version of Bloom's "anxiety of influence."[110] A man who wants to become a writer fears and transforms his great models and influences. He struggles with certain authors. A woman who wants to write struggles with authorship itself, with the literary creativity that, according to tradition, she does not possess and must not appropriate.

The female author's solution for this fear lies in all kinds of ambiguous strategies such as irony, parody, self-mockery, name change (George

Eliot and George Sand are the most famous examples), hidden meanings, and secret messages. Gilbert and Gubar underscore "the duplicity that is essential" to the literary strategies they describe.[111] Male literary conventions are used and abused to express the female experience by means of various detours. Behind the apparent docility, the anger smolders; behind the application of convention, sabotage lurks. The angel hides a monster. And the many female characters who have supposedly gone astray in the novels of authors like Jane Austen, Charlotte Brontë, and George Eliot are bitter parodies of man's image of women who did not subject themselves to the stereotypes. According to Gilbert and Gubar, these madwomen are the literary doubles of the female author: "By projecting their rebellious impulses not into their heroines but into mad or monstrous women . . . female authors dramatize their own self-division, their desire both to accept the structures of patriarchal society and to reject them. [The madwoman] is usually in some sense the *author's* double, an image of her own anxiety and rage."[112]

Humankind and reality

In traditional literary theory, this direct link between character and author is rejected as a kind of naiveté, a confusion of fiction and reality, a misjudgment and reduction of literariness. Feminist narratology, on the other hand, embraces this so-called referentialism and anthropomorphism. It looks in the text for references to social reality and the author's subjective experience, as opposed to the structuralists who considered the text to be an independently functioning system of signs. The emphasis on the personality of the authors distinguishes feminist narratology from the poststructuralist approach as well, which proclaims the death of the author and the impersonality of the literary text.[113] Feminist narratology shares its anthropomorphism with narrative ethics, which also pays much attention to the human agents of literary communication (the writer and the reader) and the anthropomorphic aspects of the literary text. As we observed in the discussion of narrative ethics, this is not surprising for an ideological approach.

In this connection, Lanser talks about the text as "mimesis" instead of "semiosis."[114] "Mimesis" is assumed to have a much broader meaning than in traditional narratology. Traditionally, mimesis refers to a textual procedure, but in feminist narratology it becomes a political strategy, an attempt to assume the authority of traditional narrative art by imitating and manipulating it. This ambiguous appropriation of tradition is a form of mimicry, described by Luce Irigaray as a disrespectful imitation, a playful repetition, and generalized by Tania Modleski as "a time-honored tactic among oppressed groups, who often appear to acquiesce in the oppressor's ideas about it, thus producing a double meaning: the same language or act simultaneously confirms the oppressor's stereotypes of the oppressed and offers a dissenting and empowering view for those in the know."[115] To the extent that mimesis is traditionally seen as a kind of reflection, this vision ties in perfectly with Gilbert and Gubar's ideas, which imply that the female author needs to pass through the looking glass that reflects the male stereotypes.[116]

Gender and reader

The female reader encounters a kind of mimicry, struggle, and ambiguity that is similar to that of the female author. Modleski rejects theories of the reader that conceive of feminist interpretations as a complement to existing male literature rather than as a critique of this literature. According to her, there is a desire for power in this critique. This desire may imitate the existing reading strategies, but it also transforms them, notably by connecting them to the female experience. While this experience is no more than a hypothesis for the male reading tradition, it is a compelling point of departure for feminist readings. Once more, the combination of the male hermeneutic tradition with the female experience leads to ambiguity in the sense that this reading implies both identification and rejection. The singularity of the female reading lies precisely in this ambiguity, and this is where the female reader seizes power. The interpretation of a text is an attempt to gain power over the text. Tradition would like such a reading to be unequivocal; a feminist reading, on the contrary, sees the recognition of ambiguity as a recognition of the female position and therefore also as a form of "female empowerment."[117]

The double nature of female readings is itself redoubled by the difference between male and female texts. The male canon distorts the female experience and at best makes that experience tangible for the female reader through the distortion. Such texts evoke a negative and a positive reading: it is negative to the extent that the reading resists male distortion; it is positive to the extent that resistance functions as an access to authentic experience. In this connection, Patrocinio Schweickart talks about "a dual hermeneutic."[118] The point of reading female texts is not resistance but rather embracement, an empathic reading with three crucial characteristics. First of all, the reader is a sympathetic witness, "a witness in defense of the woman writer"; second, the reader connects the text with the context in which it came into existence; and third, the reader recognizes her own subjectivity as the inevitable road to the so-called objectivity of the text.[119] With a feminist reader, a male text triggers resistance: she wants to control that text; a female text, on the contrary, triggers "intersubjective communication" in which the reader fuses with the subjectivity of the author, the text, and the context, which are all colored by gender. The male model of distance is in opposition to the female model of dialogue, "the dialogic model of reading."[120]

Gender and character

This feminist reading model pays much attention to the character as a carrier of gender ideology. Not only the image of a male or a female character comes under scrutiny but also the narrative techniques used in character presentation. An early example of this is *The Heroine's Text*, in which Nancy Miller analyzes the female characters in eighteenth-century English and French novels. She combines a structuralist focus on the narrative sequence with a feminist interest in the female life story. In the novels she studies, the narrative sequence is driven by the "logic of the faux pas": the life of a woman is an insecure road that may lead to disaster by a single wrong choice.[121] Woman, therefore, is an extremely vulnerable creature, and this vulnerability has to do with her sexual desires. Two fundamental narrative developments are possible: the euphoric one, which leads to the integration of woman in society, and the dysphoric one, which leads to disaster.

Novels from the Enlightenment often choose the epistolary form. According to Miller, the rhetoric a man uses in his letters is a form of double play. On the one hand, a man wants to seduce his female addressee, which appeals to the woman's so-called dangerous sexual desires. On the other hand, he wants to subject her to the patriarchal order, which makes female desire subordinate to domestic peace. The narrative is shaped by the woman's wavering reactions to the man's paradoxical strategy. The ending – positive or negative – must remove the doubt.

A similar story of uncertainty and relief can be found in many Biblical stories about women. In *Lethal Love*, Mieke Bal aims to compensate for the absence of the subject in Genettian narratology.[122] She does this by studying how Biblical stories construe the female subject. She calls this construction a collocation, an idiomatic connection between body and morality. In the stories, the woman's body is staged as impure and imperfect. It signifies a lack. This is immediately interpreted as a moral danger.[123] Bal emphasizes that the Bible is not a purely patriarchal text and that it does not simply oppose male omnipotence to female subordination. The male subject is often insecure and powerless. What is more, it is precisely this uncertainty that is externalized and incorporated in the narrative construction of woman. In Adam and Eve's story of the Creation, assigning to the woman the position of the mother ultimately counteracts the woman's impurity and the man's uncertainty. This position domesticates the body, integrates woman into a process of education, and alleviates man's uncertainty. It is a position that is sealed in Eve's name, "a name that means, as her mate says, 'the mother of all living.' "[124]

The confrontation of male stereotypes and female subjects is an ever-present theme in feminist character studies. In the already mentioned monograph, *Engendering the Subject*, Sally Robinson shows that the work of Doris Lessing, Angela Carter, and Garyl Jones stages women who do not at all correspond to the classical pattern and who cannot be reduced to a simple reversal or rejection of that pattern either. These authors produce complex, often contradictory images undermining the dominant image of women. By means of all kinds of narrative strategies, these texts resist the homogenizing images of Woman that dominate a certain culture at a certain time.

Gender and narration

Gender studies of the narrator are also characterized by ambiguity and conflict. According to Susan Lanser, the female voice is polyphonic. At one level, it seems to conform to male rhetoric; at another level it undermines it. Just as in narrative ethics, Lanser refers to Bakhtin's polyphony. What was considered to be a general characteristic of the literary text is now seen as a typically female characteristic. Lanser argues that "polyphony is more pronounced and more consequential in women's narratives and in the narratives of other dominated peoples."[125] The female voice hovers between subordination and authority, between private and public. The undecidability and ambiguity of the literary text, which is underscored in many post-classical approaches as a characteristic of literature at large, is often interpreted in feminist work as a characteristic of femininity – which may be employed by male narrators.[126]

Authority

These narrative strategies fit in the power struggle inherent in the conflict feminist narratology wants to focus on. Lanser considers every narration as "a quest for discursive authority," and obviously this quest is ambiguous: on the one hand, the struggle for power is a male desire, on the other hand it attempts to overthrow male dominance.[127] This attempt is realized by exposing the traditional male rhetorical techniques that lend power to the speaker. According to Lanser, this is why female narrators often demonstrate a high degree of self-awareness. In other theories, this self-awareness is seen as a general characteristic of literariness (fiction is supposedly always a form of metafiction); in feminist theories, it is considered a sign of female narration. The fictionality of male authority is exposed, and in this way, female narration tries to gain its own authority.[128]

Starting from this ambiguous attempt to lend authority to narration, Lanser discusses three fundamental forms of narration. First, there is the *authorial voice*, which is mostly heterodiegetic, extradiegetic, self-conscious, and oriented toward the public realm. This is the cliché of the male narrator. Often his sex is not indicated explicitly, but the reader simply supposes the narrator is a man. A female narrator appropriating this position has important consequences. The reader may feel so disappointed in his expectations, that he may consider the female narrator as unreliable.[129] Once again, unreliability does not derive from the text itself (and certainly not from a correspondence with such a problematic concept as the implied author) but rather from the reader's expectation patterns. It turns out that gender plays a fundamental role in these patterns.

Unreliable narration

The *personal voice* is the second kind of narrator that Lanser studies from the gender angle. It refers to all forms of autodiegetic narration. Since it is personal, the reader often considers it to be less objective and more intimate or private. Moreover, if the voice belongs to a woman, it is easily seen as indiscrete – a transgression of the law saying that women have to remain silent on subjects men can definitely talk about.[130] The mere transgression of the silence imperative may lend authority to the female voice here. Moreover, the image of women in this personal narration may clash with the dominant images. Finally, this narration can clarify which gender-related presuppositions constitute the basis of the belief that these personal narratives – certainly in the case of women – are small-scale and subjective reports without any general validity. Such a self-conscious exposure of conventions may transform them into weapons in the struggle for authority.

Finally, there is the *communal voice*, which Lanser thinks is typical of marginal and repressed groups and "therefore" of women.[131] There is no structuralist definition of this type of narration. Lanser uses the term to refer to "a practice in which narrative authority is invested in a definable community and textually inscribed either through multiple, mutually authorizing voices or through the voice of a single individual who is manifestly authorized by a community."[132] Precisely because of the female and communal aspect, this narrative strategy is the most natural form of resistance against the male and individual authorial mode of narration. It contributes to the construction of "a female body politic"[133] – the feminist politics of the collective that opposes the male politics of the individual. As we will see later, the term "body politic" also has direct bodily connotations that play an important role in feminist discourse.

Gender and narratee The collective is often associated with the female and confronted with the individual, which is supposed to be more male. Robyn Warhol shows in *Gendered Interventions* that at the level of the narratee as well the female narrative strategy is more oriented toward the realization of togetherness and collectivity than the male voice.[134] In this study of the Victorian novel, Warhol concentrates on the passages in which the narratee is addressed directly. In these passages, male authors (William Thackeray, Charles Kingsley, Charles Dickens, Anthony Trollope) try to get the reader to distance himself from the events, while female authors (George Eliot, Elizabeth Gaskell, Harriet Beecher Stowe) attempt to get the reader involved in the events. Warhol realizes that the reader can always distance himself from suggestions addressed to the narratee, but in any case, her evidence quite convincingly shows that female authors writing in English in the middle of the nineteenth century are more didactic than their male colleagues. They aspire to change the world more than their colleagues. It is clear from George Eliot's essays that she saw didactic disposition as an intrinsic part of her program of realism, which obviously corroborates Warhol's hypothesis.[135]

Crossdressing Warhol easily accommodates counterexamples as expressions of cross-dressing: male ideologies are disguised as female narrative strategies and vice versa.[136] This is probably too facile a solution because such an explanation does not fully account for the possibility that the canonization of the texts in her corpus is the consequence of a socially constructed concept of femininity that gives priority to care and affection. According to Warhol, these are the values that the female Victorian authors have wanted to convey to their readers. However, these values, as well as Warhol's view itself, are not neutral: they are themselves dependent on a social conception of "femininity" and on a specific canonization process that has decided who the so-called representative Victorian writers are. Warhol's corpus is probably too small to justify the generalizations she makes. Nevertheless, her book is a creative attempt to relate the influence of gender to a narratological interpretation grounded in historical knowledge.

Gender and genre

According to feminist narratology, the use of genre conventions is colored by gender as well. Female authors, narrators, and characters sometimes take advantage of those genre patterns to claim authority conventionally associated with them. By doing this, they not only undermine the male authority that is traditionally attached to certain genres, but they also reform the genre conventions. Sally Robinson interprets Doris Lessing's four Martha Quest novels as a female manipulation of the male ideal of self-realization described in the Bildungsroman. Lessing seems to choose the traditional Bildungsroman, a genre reflecting the "male" goal-oriented system, in which elements such as progress, career, and reputation are central. In the beginning of the tetralogy, it looks as if Martha is after this form of so-called self-realization. But she clashes with the system, so that her classical quest fails. Her story progressively deviates from the male values that are inherent in the genre. Instead of efficiency, Martha discovers an "absence of movement."[137] Thanks to this absence, she arrives at a critical conclusion about her ambiguous situation. As a white colonial woman in Central Africa before and after the Second World War, she is, on the one hand, part of the "male" system in which *Bildung* is defined as civilization and progress. On the other hand, she comes to realize that this so-called improvement is an illusion.

Gender and plot

The development of a personality is only one of the many potential plots in a narrative text. Nevertheless, considering the goal-oriented evolution, the self-expansion, and the desire to dominate the environment, this development of personality can function as a typical example of what traditional narratology calls a plot. According to Mária Brewer, these traditional plot definitions are strongly informed by male desire that is oriented toward separate, individual development and dominance and that is mostly expressed in stories full of adventures, undertakings, and projects.[138] From that perspective, many female stories seem hardly to have a plot at all. Supposedly, they are static contemplations or descriptions of lives in which nothing happens. Feminist narratology counters this allegation by saying that the narration itself is the plot. That is where the adventure and desire hide. Communication not only provides the form but also the content, the plot of the narration.[139] Only from a male, androcentric perspective can these texts be discarded as being "plotless" or as having a "weak plot."

Ruth Page locates the identification of "female plots" and "weak narrativity" within the canonization process. The canon has a preference for male texts and plots.[140] At the same time, she indicates that other factors apart from gender come into play, that female authors can unfold well-designed plots as well, and that male narrations can just as frequently be plotless. According to her, a binary opposition between male and female plots is untenable.

Gender and desire

The interpretation of the plot as a form of desire is only one of the many ways in which feminist narratology imports that desire into theory. Writing, story-telling, and reading cannot be separated from the many shapes of desire such as, for instance, the desire for communication, understanding, and authority. Lanser explicitly interprets the introduction of desire as a critique of the so-called rational and scientific approach of structuralism. Desire is variable and therefore goes against the classical quest for fixed and universal categories. Desire is impure; it does not care for neat structuralist classifications. And desire is ungraspable; it cannot be reduced to what theory can tell us about it.[141]

Nevertheless, feminist narratology attempts to introduce desire into theory. Early on Teresa de Lauretis contributed to this effort in her essay, "Desire in Narrative."[142] She reproaches the structuralists for treating narration exclusively as a product, an entity, and not as a process, a movement. As a product, a narrative text is reduced to a system of building blocks such as narration and focalization. Viewed as a process, a narrative text is a development through which a subject tries to design itself. This subject is not an abstract category such as the subject role in Greimas's actantial model but an actual person anchored in a historical and a psychological context. In this context, gender plays a crucial role. On the one hand, the story is the expression of a desire that is strongly inspired by gender; on the other hand, the story precisely produces that desire. In this sense, the desiring subject is created by the stories it creates. It is "a subject engendered, we might say, precisely by the process of its engagement in the narrative genres."[143]

Desire's dynamic is realized through narrative development, which often consists of some sort of quest. De Lauretis analyzes different structuralist approaches to narrative development – for instance in the work of Propp, Lotman, and Girard – and connects this with the Freudian view on subjective development, which also contains narrative elements. According to Freud, the child develops into an adult in a sequence of phases in which the Oedipal conflict marks the fundamental transition. De Lauretis argues that Oedipus as a mythical figure is exemplary of narrative heroes: he wants to know and to reign. Woman simultaneously appears as an obstacle (the sphinx's riddle puts Oedipus to the test) and an object (Oedipus wants to possess the sphinx's knowledge and ultimately desires his mother). Woman is a necessary detour, a phase of transition as part of the transformation into a man. The hero in fiction and the child in psychoanalysis share the male desire to transgress the boundary, to occupy and dominate woman's space.

Desire and difference

Since the oedipal vicissitudes are "paradigmatic to all narratives,"[144] narrative developments have to be associated with the conflict between, on the one hand, the male hero as the active subject and, on the other hand, the female obstacle as the passive object. Narratives are endless movements between these two poles. They create the differences, bridge them, and reproduce them. Therefore, "the work of narrative . . . is a mapping of differences, and specifically, first and foremost, of sexual difference into each text."[145] The desire to tell, live, and read stories must be seen from the perspective of this mapping of differences. Stories tempt the reader to identify with the subject, a man. For the female reader, this temptation leads to an ambiguous identification, on the one hand, with male desire and, on the other hand, with its female counterpart. This "double identification"[146] is an example of the typical form of reasoning we have already encountered a number of times in feminist narratology: first, an opposition is set up between man and woman and, second, woman is shown to harbor this opposition in herself, which means that she is ambiguous.

To the extent that the double identification involves an identification with male desire, woman subjects herself to that male narrative template. In this way, she can desire to be desired in the masculine way. But to the extent that she combines this with the female position of object and obstacle, she undermines the male position of subject and aspiring agent. This ambiguity too we have repeatedly noted in feminist discussions of narrative forms: on the one hand, there is complicity and subordination, on the other hand, there is resistance and undermining. According to de Lauretis, narratology should not resolve this ambiguity nor ignore it, but simply map it.

Desire, language and body

In narrative texts, this "mapping" occurs through language that translates desire and the body. Oedipal narratives give both of them an ideological form. They point to locations of desire, erogenous zones, or danger zones – the gaze, for instance, which as the myth of Medusa shows can kill the hero. Only by means of this translation, the female body seems to be truly defined. It seems as if only now it receives its essence. "The essence of femininity, is then a product of discourse," a discourse that is propelled by "male pleasure."[147] Here as well, woman is seduced; she is invited to adopt and stage that discourse – literally, to embody it. The narrative expression of the body is one of the most obvious program points for a feminist narratology. Or, as Teresa de Lauretis militantly puts it: "The stakes, for women, are rooted in the body." Not only is the body the seat of desire and sexual difference, it is also "the supreme object of representation for the visual arts, the medical sciences, the capitalist media industry."[148]

Traditional narrative language offers a representation of the body that does not fit the female experience. She is forced to look for a language of her own. Many feminist studies call this language "performative" because it does not translate a given identity but rather produces a subjectivity that is never entirely finished or fixed.[149] This *écriture féminine*, a term canonized by Hélène Cixous, is supposed to give to the female body a voice that counteracts the male language of abstraction and subordination of that body.[150]

The traditional (psychoanalytical) view sees language as a process that installs boundaries and thereby divides and organizes the body. Only in this way does a human being receive an identity. As a child, he or she supposedly lives in a boundless symbiosis with the environment; thanks to language, this symbiosis is replaced by a well-delineated identity. *Ecriture féminine* rejects this dichotomy and evolution: it wants to be a language of transgression and corporeality, a language in which identity is not fixed but in which it is always being sought. This quest is the movement of desire that never stops. In that sense, the feminist subject is nomadic and escapes the conventional male categorization.[151] The same holds for the body, which must not be trapped in definitions.

The language of narratology – and, more generally, of literary criticism – has to take into account this dynamic corporeality and subjectivity, and therefore it has to distance itself from the rigid, impersonal, and abstract discourse of structuralists and poststructuralists. In Nancy Miller's words, the theory has to find a way "to reembody the author."[152] This theoretical attention to the corporeal must not lead to a new version of the traditional discourse that aims to master and subject everything. On the contrary, it must demonstrate its own dependence on the context in which it came into existence – including its preferences, predecessors, and backgrounds. For the narratologist, this means that he or she has to take his or her own stories into account. In this connection, Rosi Braidotti says, "I want to practice a set of narrations of my own embodied genealogy."[153] Feminist analysis is, according to Miller, localized; that is, positioned in and by the context, but it refuses to settle down. This makes a general theory undesirable, which brings us back to the start of our discussion of feminist narratology.

Feminism and Mutsaers

Mutsaers's story ties in with a number of the feminist points of attention discussed above. For one, there is the female protagonist who is indeed characterized by resistance and ambiguity. The girl resists the authoritarian riding master, but she wants power herself, more specifically the power to fly. The character of the riding master too is more ambiguous than a first reading would suggest. At first sight, the authoritarian behavior of the riding master evokes the old-fashioned image of man repressing woman. This image is strengthened by one of the meanings of the Dutch word *pikeur*, a "womanizer." In any case, the riding master is an authoritarian figure who wants the girl to wear real riding breeches, but his pupil has her own thoughts concerning this rather resolutely expressed wish.

However, this sketch of the situation does not take into account the fact that the riding instructor may be a woman. This character is never referred to as "he." In Dutch, it is current practice to use the masculine word for an official in function even if it refers to a woman, and perhaps the narrator of this text follows this practice. There might not even be a feminine word in this case, because *pikeuse* does not seem to be correct Dutch. If the riding master is female, her words about the heavenly sensation that little girls have not yet experienced suggest that she is an adult who *has* had that experience. The fact that it is possible to see the riding master as a woman has another important consequence. It unmasks the "spontaneous" presupposition that the riding master has to be a man and thereby exposes the projection of an outdated prejudice, an idea about the hierarchy – evoked by Mutsaers in the shape of the whip – in the relationship between man and woman. This reading is not farfetched for a text in which the wearing of certain trousers is a central motif. In Dutch, *de broek dragen*, ("to wear the pants") is said of women who are in control of their husband.

Moreover, we must not forget that, at the end of the text, the girl "understands" why it is better to wear real riding breeches. The fact that the riding master's sex cannot be determined conclusively enables at least two readings of this ending. In the conventional interpretation, in which the riding master is a man, his words turn out to be correct, and this appears to confirm or even strengthen his position of power. However, when the reference to "wearing the pants" is picked up, a reading in which Mutsaers at the same time undermines this power becomes possible as well. In the less straightforward interpretation in which the riding master is a woman, she may establish her authority only to show the girl the pleasure of the real riding breeches. This pleasure may even be taken as a metaphor for power in relation to men. In this context, riding the horse with the right pants, together with the wings this gives to the rider, may even invite an erotic reading: the woman "mounts" the man and reaches an orgasm in this dominant position. This may be a little fanciful, but characterization and focalization do invite the reader to interpret this story in a feminist-narratological way. The acceptance of this invitation turns "Pegasian" into a text on sex and power, and especially on the conventional images evoked by the interplay of these themes.

This feminist reading puts character and themes into perspective, and additionally the ambiguous narration and representation of consciousness tie in with the polyphonous female narration as characterized by Susan Lanser. This relates not only to the use of free indirect speech, which sometimes makes it impossible to distinguish the narrator's voice from that of the character's. There is also the girl's voice, which as an ironic echo transforms the riding master's words into questions. Literally as well as metaphorically, this transformation calls into question the discourse of authority. This questioning continues until the last lines of the story. The question, "Is it the idea or is it the sensation?," is followed by a new question, this time without a question mark: "Whatever." The absence of the question mark suggests that this "response-question" is the conclusion: One shouldn't look for unequivocal answers to questions. Questions *are* answers. The answer to the story's uncertainty – is it discipline or a game, an idea or sensation? – lies in the acceptance of that uncertainty. And it is precisely this acceptance that leads to transgression and thus to taking off. This is the girl's desire as well as the riding master's, a desire that constitutes a bridge not only between the characters but also between opposites such as discipline and game, or idea and feeling.

Feminism and Krol

"The Map" also deals with a female character and authority. Mrs. Paalman from the bookshop wears the pants. Her name seems to carry a double sign of her manliness: *paal* (pole) can easily be seen as a phallic symbol, and "man" is simply part of her name. That she is in control at home is suggested ironically by describing the bookstore as a living room: "It wasn't any bigger than a large living room." This transfers the traditional male traits to the woman, but apparently it does not imply an undermining of the existing stereotypes in the rest of the fictional world. The village (or the customer) accepts that literary preferences strongly depend on the sex of the reader. People ask for "a light novel for a girl of seventeen."

The village seems to cherish other ideological stereotypes as well. The Christian ideology turns Sundays into days of rest. The shop is closed and shuttered: "Closed off from the world." The first-person narrator is nonetheless allowed to look at a map and thus violates the stereotypical closed-off world. It calls on him to "bike" all places on the map. This desire is much more individualistic and much more aimed at mastery than Mutsaers's Pegasian desire, which builds bridges. "What excited me was the thought that it now made sense *to have been everywhere*. The prospect I was going to cover the earth with my body. To be everywhere . . ." The self does not break free from the earth as in Mutsaers's story, but it covers the earth, subjects it. The body becomes an instrument of power to conquer the earth by biking.

As soon as this conquest has taken place, and everything has been mapped, the map is "meaningless" to the narrator. His desire has been satisfied and disappears. This stands in sharp contrast to the desire of Mutsaers's girl, who does not disappear in her flight but precisely lives on. With some hesitation, one could see the individualistic, goal-oriented and finite desire of Krol's first-person narrator as an illustration of so-called male desire, while the transgressive and infinite desire of Mutsaers's girl could be called feminine.

Focalization and narration could be connected to these two types of desire. In Krol's text, the story is told in retrospect. Just like the desire it features, the narrated period is definitively over. There is a distance in time between the narrator and the boy, which by itself suggests that the narrator has distanced himself from infantile desire. Mutsaers's text features simultaneous narration and eagerly looks forward to the moment when "you take off." There is no distance – not in perception, not in narration, and not with regard to the desire in question. Krol's story may be felt to establish boundaries and breaks, while Mutsaers's story can be seen as building bridges and crossing boundaries.

By way of illustration, we have consciously opposed the two stories in a radical manner. This is of course a simplification that runs the risk of making essentialist claims about "male desires" and "female narrative forms." Nevertheless, this reading also demonstrates that gender does play a role, even in stories that do not explicitly deal with the relations between men and women. Undoubtedly, this role can be described better or more easily in stories that do tackle these relations directly,[154] but it is hard to claim that the use of a feminist reading has to depend on the importance of gender in the plot. This is not an objective criterion. To a certain extent, the reader can decide for himself or herself how important gender is for interpretation, and this decision will inevitably be influenced by the importance he or she attaches to the gender question *outside* the text. Even in a text that at first sight has little to do with gender, the reader may look for this ideological issue. There is no doubt that he or she will "discover" a number of things. The ideology found in a text is influenced by the ideology to which a reader adheres outside the text and vice versa: this "external" ideology is also influenced by the act of reading the text. In fact it only plays a role to the extent that it is activated by the text. The reader cannot step out of this hermeneutic circle by saying that literature objectively contains certain gender aspects.

3. NARRATOLOGY AND POSSIBLE WORLDS

The "possible worlds" concept, which was introduced in narratology relatively recently, derives from modal logic. This discipline investigates the possibility, impossibility, contingency, or necessity of propositions. Especially Thomas Pavel,[155] Lubomir Doležel,[156] and Marie-Laure Ryan[157] have pointed out the usefulness of this concept for literary theory. We start from *Possible Worlds in Literary Theory* in which Ruth Ronen covers the various uses of the concept and shows how it may benefit the analysis of a literary text.[158] In order to characterize the modal structure of a literary text in a more concrete way, we will rely on Doležel. Finally, we will discuss one specific application of the theory of possible worlds – David Herman's work on hypothetical focalization.[159]

As we already suggested in our discussion of cybernarratology, the "possible worlds" concept can be related to "virtual reality," a concept that often appears in the study of hypertext. According to Ryan, *virtuality* has three dimensions. First, the term can be used as a synonym of "illusory." Virtual reality is a feigned reality that gives us the illusion it is real. Second, the concept refers to computer technology. Virtual reality is the world evoked by technology, for instance the worldwide web. Third, virtuality may be synonymous with possibility or potentiality. In that reading, virtual reality becomes a potential or possible world, and in this way cybernarratology can be related to modal logic and the narratology of possible worlds it has given rise to.[160] Just as cybernarratology sees the textual world as a palimpsest that comprises different layers of virtual realities, the theory of possible worlds envisages the world as a composite complex of potential and existing realities.

Truth and reality

From Plato to Bertrand Russell, conventional theories of truth determined the truth value of a proposition by looking at the correspondence with a situation in the world. Therefore, propositions in fictional texts did not have any truth value whatsoever. Nevertheless, literary texts often do refer to reality. In order to characterize this type of reference, the philosopher John Searle described fictional speech acts as making it seem as if they refer to reality. They do not have to meet all the requirements of a normal referential speech act. In this way, Searle lifted the usual rules of truth for literary texts, and in a certain sense he thereby rehabilitated this type of text.[161]

In pragmatic theory, truth is no longer considered as the result of the connection between language and world. Moreover, truth is no longer seen as a matter of everything or nothing. To the reader or hearer, statements can be acceptable and plausible, and in that sense, they can be truthful. According to this theory, a proposition can be true in one way or another, even if that which the proposition refers to does not exist. For a certain utterance to be true, the state of affairs that is referred to does not have to exist in reality. Even if one does not know whether the state of affairs is real, the utterance can be considered true. This depends on the extent to which the utterance is judged to function well in its context. If utterances "work," they are accepted as true. Utterances in a novel that contribute to the plausibility or impressiveness of the book could be considered true. They work perfectly within their context, and that is enough.

Truth and fictionality

This conception of truth corresponds nicely with the current anti-mimetic theory of fictionality, which argues that fiction creates its own discursive universe in which propositions can be true or false. Internal criteria are sufficient to reach a decision. The world evoked by the literary text may deviate from reality, but this does not mean that it is an untrue world. Of course, this perspective on fictionality does not imply that literature is irrelevant for extratextual reality. Fictional texts always function in relation to non-fictional texts and, therefore, can tell us much about these so-called realistic texts as well as about so-called reality. For example, the relationship between historical novels and historiography can teach us much about the ways in which we deal with the past (the so-called extratextual reality).

Reality and possibility

The use of the "possible worlds" concept is rooted in the pragmatic theory of truth and reinforces the accompanying conceptions of fictionality. The theory of possible worlds starts from the simple insight that certain situations could have developed differently or, to put it plainly, that the world could have been different. There are various opinions on the assignment of actuality to these possible worlds, but all philosophers who use this concept agree that non-actual possibilities can constitute perfectly coherent systems about which coherent utterances can be made.

As Marie-Laure Ryan indicates, a triadic model is often used to represent the actuality of possible worlds.[162] The theory of possible worlds considers reality as a universe consisting of three different levels or worlds. The center is the actual world, the existing state of affairs. Possible worlds circle this center as satellites, and at the outer limit we find the impossible worlds. The difference between satellites and periphery lies in the so-called accessibility relation that they have with the center. Possible worlds have access to the existing worlds: they could at one point become real. How this is determined differs from one theoretician to another, but often the laws of logic and time are used as criteria to decide whether the literary world can gain access to the real world or not. A world in which the logical law of the excluded middle is not respected (for example, when a character is at the same time dead and alive) will be called peripheral or impossible. In this view, a story in which an old man suddenly becomes a child would create an impossible world as well.

This approach considers fiction as a possible or an impossible world – as one of the modal options available to us. The fact that fiction as a possible world constitutes an autonomous, closed system means that it can be compared without any problem to another possible world (such as dreams) and that it can even be described by referring to that other ontological system, the existing world on which it is based. Following Umberto Eco, many literary theorists tend to interpret the existing world as a cultural construction.[163] Fictionality is then conceived as the result of the interplay between the system constructed by a literary text and the system available to authors and readers in the form of knowledge of the existing world. The world created by a novel is called fictional because it is seen as an alternative to the existing state of affairs.

Advantages of possible worlds

For narratology, the most general advantage of this theory is the presentation of a philosophically based framework that considers the narrative text as a system that has its own laws and is at the same time related to the context. In a classic detective novel, the resurrection of a character that has been murdered is impossible. In this case, the definition of what is possible corresponds rather well to what is considered to be possible in the human experience of reality. In a non-classic detective novel like Atte Jongstra's *The House M.* (*Het huis M.*), such a resurrection turns out to be perfectly possible.[164] The murder in question is committed over and over again as well. What is possible in this novel clearly deviates from what is possible in everyday reality.

Apart from this general and context-oriented relevance, the possible worlds theory also makes it possible to envisage the narrative world *within* the literary text as a collection of possible worlds. The construction and evolution of the story are seen as the interaction between

Modality

those worlds. Every possible world within a single text is in principle defined by means of a specific modality such as probability, possibility, or necessity. In "The Map," the boy sees the desire to map everything and to have been everywhere as one of the possibilities. For the adult narrator, this desire forms part of the impossible world and the failure of this desire is a necessity. The interaction between the different possible worlds appears to be essential for the development of the character and the story.

The interaction and the relationship between the worlds differ from story to story. In a naturalist text, that which is possible mostly has to surrender to that which is necessary: dreams clash with unchangeable reality. In Willem Brakman's novels, this hierarchy is often reversed since the main characters prefer impossible dreams to achievable realities. Coercive reality is a horror, possibility leads to disaster, and only the impossible is interesting. The main character in *The Wreckage of Things (De sloop der dingen)* aims for the impossible suspension of time. The demolition of his village entails a modal statement: "I consider it a disaster that this Duindorp will be demolished, and therefore it is possible."[165] Reality is the result of this demolition – that is, degeneration and death – "which would make everything lethally real."[166] The different modalities alternate infinitely, without there ever being a final victory or resolution. So the interaction of fictional worlds in Brakman's novel does not lead to the completion found in Krol or the naturalists. The reader is offered a story without a straightforward plot or clear ending. The endless alternation of possible worlds lies at the basis of this seemingly directionless story that nonetheless aims to put off the necessary ending and the real demolition as much as possible.

Alethic modality

In order to study the different kinds of modality in a novel's narrative or fictional world, Doležel has developed a four-dimensional system.[167] He characterizes every dimension by means of three terms. First of all, the narrative world can be described from the perspective of *alethic modality* – from the Greek word *aletheia* meaning "truth." Alethic modality refers to everything that is necessary, possible, or impossible according to the laws of nature and logic. Necessity, possibility, and impossibility constitute the decisive criteria for alethic modality.

The clearest examples of this are causality and spatio-temporal specificity. A fictional world in which people can fly violates the laws of nature and therefore constitutes a supernatural world. Physically speaking, this world is impossible. However, it may very well be logically coherent and, in that sense, logically possible. The world becomes logically impossible only if logical laws are violated in this supernatural world as well. A fairy tale in which people can fly does not have to be a logically impossible world. Moreover, alethically speaking, many intermediate forms are possible. Between the natural and the supernatural world there are intermediate worlds – such as dreams and hallucinations – that may be explained in a perfectly logical and natural manner, for instance, when hallucinations are triggered by the use of drugs. That which is impossible in one world and for one character may be possible in another world for another character. This situation plays an important role in the definition of the hero, who in most cases is capable of doing things other characters are not capable of.

Deontic modality

A second form of modality in the narrative world has to do with norms. In a fictional world certain things are prohibited, others are obligatory and yet others are permitted. Prohibition, obligation, and permission are the three building blocks of *deontic modality*. According to Doležel, the deontic marking of actions is the richest source of narrativity.[168] An action – for instance, a trip – can appear perfectly neutral in and by itself, but deontically speaking it may turn out to be a violation of a prohibition that may trigger an entire system of counteractions. Typical narrative patterns such as the test, the initiation, and the fall can be analyzed from the perspective of this modality.

Of course, these norms may change in the course of the story, and characters may play an important role in this. Their importance and status often even depend on their contribution to the transformation of dominant norms. The hero may demonstrate his power by imposing what is permitted and what is obligatory. The world of norms is in constant development because norms are the stakes of a constant struggle. The struggle between personal and general norms forms the basis of stereotypical narrative patterns such as forbidden passion or liberation from a stifling environment.

Axiological modality

The third modality, *axiological modality*, that can be used to describe the fictional world is moral judgment. In this case as well, there are three possibilities: good, bad, or indifferent. There is a constant interaction between subjects (the characters) and their environment. That which a character thinks of as good can be bad according to his environment. Just like deontic modality, the axiological dimension forms an important source of narrative actions. In most cases, axiological modality leads to actions via the detour of desire or repulsion. The traditional hero will desire what is good, and this desire will stir him into action. A nihilistic character here appears driven by indifference: he finds the values of his environment neither good nor bad, he does not care for them.

Epistemic modality The fourth and final modal building block of the fictional world is the *epistemic modality*, which consists of three possibilities: knowledge, ignorance, and belief. The latter refers to presuppositions of characters that are not based on the real state of affairs in the story. Knowledge is mostly distributed unevenly in the characters, and this forms an important source of narrative actions. A detective is the best example of a character starting from ignorance to arrive at knowledge. A schemer can be said to exist thanks to the ignorance of his victims. Misunderstandings and false presuppositions are at the basis of typical narrative patterns such as the comedy of errors. More generally, the interaction between knowledge, ignorance, and belief is central in narrative patterns such as the quest, deception, and disappointment.

Interaction The action of a story can easily be studied as the interaction between the four modalities discussed above. What is possible may be, for instance, forbidden and bad. As long as this possibility does not penetrate a character's consciousness and knowledge, there is no problem. But when the character learns of this possibility and starts seeing it as valuable or good, all kinds of narrative possibilities crop up. A character facing an explicitly formulated prohibition may become conscious of something related to that prohibition, which may paradoxically result in a violation of the latter. An extreme example of this can be found in the following promise: "You can have the treasure that is buried under this tree, but you must not think of the big bad wolf while digging for it." Without the prohibition, the thought of the wolf would probably never have entered the hearer's consciousness, and the prohibition would never have been violated.

Modality and plot The interaction between the four modalities can explain many aspects of narrative development and plot. This way, the functionalist conception of plot can be improved. Classical narratology usually determines narrative structure starting from the knowledge of the ending. This structure therefore tends to be described by referring to events that have actually happened in the fictional world. Nevertheless, things that have not really happened (for instance, dreams and plans) are often essential for narrative structure. If the narrative text is considered as an interaction of possible worlds, so-called non-events come to the fore. In this kind of interpretation, modal aspects are taken into account that do not occur as real events in the story but that are very important for the meaning of the story as we have described it in the second chapter of this book.[169] The continuous impossibility of a certain situation cannot be ignored, because it can be of vital importance for the things that are possible or even real during that period. *Madame Bovary* is largely driven by the main character's unfulfilled desires, so that the conflict between the possible world and the actual situation she finds herself in has to be part of the narratological interpretation of Flaubert's narrative structure.

Possible worlds and reader

Ruth Ronen shows that some literary theorists use the possible worlds concept in a more metaphorical way than others. For David Herman, a possible world comes down to the context the reader uses to interpret (problematic) elements of the narrative text so that they become meaningful, acceptable, and therefore quite possible. At the beginning of Louis Ferron's novel *The Fichtenwald Stonecutter (De keisnijder van Fichtenwald)*, the character Friedolien sees the environment as peaceful and comforting, while the reader immediately notices that it is a concentration camp. His or her knowledge of these camps will gradually reveal Friedolien's problematic observation as a lie.[170] David Herman gives the example of a statement concerning Brussels. If a character in a text says that Brussels has many interesting museums, this does not automatically mean the character asserts that the capital of Belgium has interesting museums. A reader who knows that Brussels is the capital will, however, probably interpret the remark in this way, and thus he will create a possible world that may very well deviate from the character's possible world. Every reader has a different kind of knowledge and therefore constructs his or her own possible world.[171]

Possible worlds and focalization

In this construction of a possible world, focalization plays an important role: Friedolien's misleading observation is very important for the reader's interpretation. A certain type of focalization implies a certain degree of (un)certainty and (im)possibility. If the observation of the camp as a resort came from a reliable narrator instead of from a mendacious character such as Friedolien, the reader would consider the observation to be more trustworthy. Perhaps he would conclude that in this novel other things are possible than in his world. When a reader accepts a novel's non-realistic world as real or possible, Marie-Laure Ryan talks about "recentering." Normally, the actual world is the world of which I am the center; I cannot move outside it, and, therefore, I cannot consider it just a possibility.[172] If a reader is convinced – or carried away – by the text he is reading, he surrenders his outsider position and places himself in the center of the narrative world, which is thus moved from (im)possibility to reality. The text's focalization is one of the elements directing this change in the reader's viewpoint.[173]

But such a form of recentering does not always lead to a long-term or permanent acceptance of the textual world as real. In many cases, one recentering follows another, just as one focalization follows another. An unequivocal conclusion about the reality of the represented world is not always within reach. Narrative texts show different degrees of certainty with regard to what is being narrated, and sometimes it is impossible to draw a clear boundary between what the text sees as actual and what is conceived of as a possible world. This is certainly the case in what David Herman calls *hypothetical focalization*. The term refers to an impossible center of observation. Inanimate things such as stones and books become centers of experience in Edgar Allan Poe's "The Fall of the House of Usher." In *A Fabulous View*, IJlander lets a stuffed squirrel tell and observe the story. What is made up and told by the dead animal becomes reality in the life of Zaalman, the main character who as a taxidermist prepared the animal. Hypothetical observation is not always tied to a non-actual observer but can be built in via conditional constructions as well, as in Rushdie's *Haroun and the Sea of Stories*: "Miss Oneeta was standing on her upstairs balcony, shaking like a jelly; and if it hadn't been raining, Haroun might have noticed that she was crying."[174]

Hypothetical focalization

David Herman combines possible worlds with focalization by placing the structuralist focalization types on a continuum. At one end there is total certainty about what is being communicated, and at the other, there is total doubt. External focalization implies a distance that can be interpreted by the reader as a signal of certainty. He or she may be wrong, for instance, when an uncertain or unreliable narrator uses a so-called omniscient perceiver. Internal focalization moves in the direction of doubt. In the case of a fixed internal focalizer, attitudes and opinions are in most cases rooted in a single possible world, and this may induce a feeling of uncertainty in the reader, especially when the character's observations do not correspond to what the reader thinks is normal.

Nevertheless, a fixed center of observation generally raises less doubt than variable and multiple internal focalization. These focalization types respectively produce a pair or a whole series of possible worlds, often without any clear coherence or systematization.

David Herman places hypothetical focalization closest to the pole of doubt. With this type, the existence of the observer is uncertain, which inevitably raises doubts concerning his or her observations. However, in our opinion a reader may also recognize this type as a very conventional way for a narrator to introduce new elements without raising doubts as to their value. Eighteenth-century novels are crammed with omniscient narrators who, from time to time, try to make their omniscience more credible by introducing reservations about their own statements. The repeated use of words like "perhaps" and "probably" gives the reader an impression of reliability rather than doubt. Hypothetical focalization can create this impression as well. Fragments with observations by an alter ego, a double or a phantom may confirm rather than undermine the main character's experiences.

Possible worlds and Mutsaers

"Pegasian" sketches a fictional world in which human beings can fly on a horse. This feature is a possibility that is not really put into question in this fictional world. The question posed by the story is not, Can a human being go up in the air on a horse? The question is rather, Do the riding breeches contribute to this form of transcendence? This problem is the focal point in the struggle between the girl and the riding master. The conflict does not in the first place concern the truth or falsity of a world in which people can fly; it concerns the way in which this world can be reached. Nowhere does the riding master deny that one can go up in the air on a horse. He merely denies that this is possible without the necessary discipline.

The riding breeches play a crucial role in this self-training. The discussion on the importance of the trousers is emphasized by a variable focalization that remains close to the spoken dialogue. The riding master is convinced of the utility of the riding breeches, while at least in the first part of the text, the girl thinks they are superfluous. The difference between the two figures can be described using Doležel's modalities. With respect to the axiological dimension, the riding master thinks the riding breeches are good, but the girl does not. At the deontic level, the riding master maintains that the breeches are obligatory, but this does not hold true for the girl. Alethically speaking, the breeches are necessary according to the riding master, but in the girl's opinion, they are not. In the end, the battle moves to the third pole of the dimensions. Axiologically, the pole of indifference wins out: it does not matter whether one wears those breeches or not. At the deontic level, the pole of "permission" wins out: the riding breeches may be worn, but "a simple straightforward denim pair" works equally well. Alethically speaking, the riding breeches are part of what is possible; they do not belong to that which is necessary. Looking at the resolution from the perspective of the shifts at these three levels, the story eventually chooses the greatest openness possible: the "winning" poles are "possible," "allowed," and "indifferent." In this way, the struggle between the two characters demonstrates that many things are possible in the fictional world of this story – probably more than in the world the reader considers to be real.

There is yet a fourth modality: the epistemic one. Looking at it from this dimension, the story starts from the struggle between a character pretending to know how things ought to be done – the riding master – and a character that apparently knows nothing and constantly asks questions – the girl. At the end, the girl does know how things work ("Finally she understands"), but this knowledge turns out to be a form of ignorance. She does not know at all whether ideas or sensations are at stake, but she does know that does not matter. Her knowledge does not amount to a servile acceptance of the insights offered by the riding master, who seems to know everything and who would be able to choose between idea and sensation ("it's rather the sensation that matters"). The girl's knowledge consists of an acceptance of a certain kind of ignorance.

All things considered, the elusiveness of Mutsaers's story could be explained from this perspective as a combination of modalities that are usually kept separate: knowledgeable and ignorant; good and indifferent; obligatory and permitted; necessary and possible. This combination makes a variety of things possible in the story, and it also explains why many elements are left up in the air – literally as well as figuratively. The confrontation of different opinions about what is possible and what is not leads to a combination rather than a selection or a choice.

The "struggle" pertaining to this confrontation is not a noncommittal or abstract display of different possible worlds. The possibilities are not totally free or God-given at all. They come about and they are imposed in a context of authority. The riding master has an authoritative position, perhaps thanks to his age (he is, in any case, older than the girl), perhaps also because of his experience and knowledge. The possible worlds of the two characters are strongly influenced by the riding master's position.

In the first part of the text, the two characters not only differ with respect to their attitude toward the riding breeches but also in their views on authority. The riding master considers his authority self-evident. This shows through in the quiet self-confidence with which he tries to persuade his pupil to wear the breeches: "The riding master would appreciate it if she'd remember. . . ." The pupil, on the contrary, is not impressed and has doubts concerning the riding master's recommendations, partly perhaps out of an adolescent dissatisfaction with the power of people who are older. When the riding master sticks to his opinion more rigidly and behaves more condescendingly, the girl becomes more reckless. It does not look as if their ideas about what is possible and what is impossible will ever coincide. The end is not the final outcome of the struggle between the riding master's authoritarian attitude and the anti-authoritarian manner of the girl. It is very well possible that both attitudes allow one to take off. At the level of authority, all possibilities remain open as well, and the story refuses to promote one possibility to the status of the "real" state of affairs.

Simplifying a little, we could say that classical narratology could be said to limit itself in most cases to that real state of affairs. It nearly exclusively pays attention to the so-called factual building blocks of the narrative world such as events, characters, and setting. The non-factual can never be approached in a concrete way. Possible worlds narratology provides a theoretical framework in which the non-factual can be analyzed in a detailed manner; that is, as the interaction between various modalities.

Possible worlds and Krol

In "The Map," the title object constitutes a world in itself. It opens up an almost infinite possibility that is opposed to the actual world of the village dominated by constraints and prohibitions. There are mechanical and ritual regulations for the purchase of a book, and there is a prohibition on the purchase of the map on Sunday. And on Monday, the boy could not buy the map either: "I did not have enough money, so that I had to wait until Saturday." Obligation and non-permission are the crucial modalities in the world of the village. Deontic modality pushes everything else to the background.

The map intensifies the experience of the first-person narrator to such an extent that he adapts his experience of reality to it. He wants to make his world coincide with the map, first with that of the village, later with "a blank map of the Netherlands." Literally and figuratively, he transgresses the village borders. Deontic modality is not so important here, since the boy does not seem to be interested in the violation of a prohibition. He is driven rather by an epistemic desire, a pursuit of knowledge. He wants to get to know the world and map it. Thus, the map becomes "[a] whole table full of *new things*." This world is literally an outside world, a domain outside the realm of the village. The boy aims to integrate the outside world into a system, a map. That is what he thinks is good. At the axiological level, one could say that "good" is linked to "knowledge," and this knowledge would then be a question of mapping.

The first-person narrator does not always perceive this overlap of two possible worlds – the map and the areas he wants to visit – in the same way. When he is telling his story, the map has lost much of its significance, and his world is no longer oriented to coincide with this map. The narrator has imported the outside world almost entirely into a system, and this is precisely the reason why that world has lost so much of its attraction. The interiorization of the outside world is a desire the young experiencing I pursued only temporarily. The map led to an expansion of his horizon and his knowledge. The young boy's dream starts to fade, however, as soon as he travels to further destinations more easily and the dreamed-of expansion starts to belong to his actual world. Knowledge is no longer identified with "good," but rather with "indifferent": "It had become meaningless."

It is important to keep track of the narrative situation in this interpretation. When he tells his story, the first-person narrator has already been through the whole process of the expansion of his horizon, and this undoubtedly colors his representation of the world before that expansion. His focus on the shading of the Christian shops' windows, for example, is directly linked to liberation, which is one of his central themes. The quotation of the opinion on the Paalman couple suggests a normality propelled by gossip. Their routine interaction with a customer indicates the absence of excitement. The actual world of the young boy is clearly distorted by retrospection; that is, by the actual world of the adult narrator. To formulate matters in strictly narratological terms: his focalization as a young member of the village community is determined by his focalization as an adult. The possible worlds of the map and the desire to expand his domain can be seen as the result of the projection to which the adult first-person narrator surrenders in his memories.

4. NARRATOLOGY AND THE READER

In our feminist interpretation of "Pegasian," much depended on the willingness of the reader to accept the fact that the riding instructor may be a woman. In our feminist and in our modal interpretation of "The Map," we used a certain view on Christian ideology that is probably not shared by everyone. The narratological interpretation differs from reader to reader and the most progressive type of narratology is the one that takes into account the interpretive variants in the theory formation. In structuralist narratology, the reader was officially excluded, but whenever the abstract categories and types were actually applied, their effect on the reader was implicitly referred to. Delay and acceleration, omniscience and reliability can only be grasped in terms of impressions on the reader. This is no coincidence: the structuralists may have isolated the text, but they still worked with the well-known communication triad of sender, message, and receiver in which the audience obviously plays a central role.

Reader and structuralism

From the end of the nineteen sixties onwards, Wolfgang Iser and Hans Robert Jauss started to develop, respectively, *reception esthetics* and *reception history* – two theories that for the first time included the reader in literary criticism in a systematic way.[175] Jauss wanted to rewrite literary history by considering it as a sequence of ways in which a literary text confirms and breaks with patterns of expectation. Iser, on the other hand, wanted to design a theory describing the effect of the literary text in general. He started from the assumption that the text pushes the reader into the direction of a certain interpretation. In analogy to the implied author – the concept introduced by Wayne Booth, which we commented on extensively in the first chapter – Iser opted for the somewhat misleading term "implied reader" for the text-driven role of the reader. According to Iser, the turning points in the development of this role are the "gaps" that result from the fact that the text can never fully meet the expectations that the reader cherishes based on his experience of reality.[176] Gaps derive not only from the imperfect overlap with reality as it is experienced but also

Reader and reception theory

from the structure of the text. They can for instance result from abrupt transitions in the story or sudden changes in narration or focalization.

Iser's theory is discussed for a reason in the last chapter of Rimmon-Kenan's survey *Narrative Fiction*. She realized all too well that narratology had to take the reader into account more systematically, and at the time she was writing her textbook, Iser's work provided a natural supplement in this respect. Rimmon-Kenan also paid attention to other reader-oriented approaches such as psychology and semiotics.[177] In the afterword she added in 2002 to her now classic book, she emphasizes the importance of these approaches even more. She appreciates the expansion brought about by post-classical narratology, which no longer limits analysis to literature itself but also pays attention to the context. According to her, this expansion is largely due to various reader-oriented approaches.[178]

Reader and cognitive paradigm

Ever since reception esthetics, the reader has been integrated into narratology in many different ways, especially in the context of the cognitive paradigm, which has acquired an important position in the human sciences and which stresses the processing of information.[179] The terms "cognitive" and "information" may create the impression that a predominantly mental perspective on the reading experience is at issue, but this is not necessarily the case. Psychologists such as Richard Gerrig and Victor Nell study the emotional identification and far-reaching immersion that give the reader the impression he is carried away by the text.[180] In their empirical tests, narratologists working within this paradigm mostly limit themselves to the concrete interpretation of texts, but in our opinion, this does not diminish the value of their contributions.

Some cognitive approaches come very close to cognitive psychology and adopt some of its positivistic presuppositions. Peter Dixon and Marisa Bortolussi start from a rigid distinction between, on the one hand, so-called objective characteristics in the text and, on the other hand, subjective effects of those characteristics on the reader.[181] As we saw in our discussion of postmodern narratology and narrative ethics, most post-classical approaches reject this traditional and dualistic view of the objective text and the subjective reader. So-called objective characteristics are construed by the reader as well. The exact points of contact and the differences between text and reader can probably not be determined in any straightforward way – as became clear in the discussion of other post-classical approaches above. For those approaches, a rigid distinction between object and subject is certainly no solution.

Frame theory

A cognitive approach that has proven useful for literary theory is *frame theory*. This approach was developed by, among others, Marvin Minsky in the study of artificial intelligence.[182] It assumes that, when confronted with a new situation, people select a structure from memory, which helps them to deal with this new situation. For Minsky, this frame consists of a network of nodes and relations that can be applied quite easily to the new situation. The theory also allows for some flexibility in this application: on the one hand, the network consists of representations that are perfectly valid for the situation; on the other hand, it also contains a number of slots to be filled with specific details that are only valid for the situation at hand and that thereby augment the frame's relevance for that situation. These details can be worked out to fit the new situation in a concrete way. When in a foreign country one notices a sign on the edge of the road, its location, shape, size, and the material it is made of will immediately trigger the insight that this is a traffic sign. For the precise meaning of the sign, the icon and text on the sign will be as important as the concrete environment.

Frame and the unreliable narrator

Manfred Jahn defines a frame as "the cognitive model that is selected and used (and sometimes discarded) in the process of reading a narrative."[183] Both Jahn and Ansgar Nünning[184] have applied frame theory to narratology. As we mentioned in the discussion of the structuralist characteristics of narration, Nünning argues that the unreliable narrator is often a psychological projection of the reader who aims to clarify ambiguities or contradictions in the narrator's utterances. This, however, does not capture all meanings of the concept. It is necessary to anticipate a whole gamut of reader reactions. In any case, textual features are not sufficient to argue against the trustworthiness of a narrator. One always has to investigate the framework leading to the observation that the narrator lies or that he is morally unstable.

Traditionally, narratology reserves the term "lie" for a lack of correspondence between a narrator's utterance and a situation that occurs in another part of the text. If the reader accepts the situation as an actual one, the utterance is called unreliable. At first sight, this is an intersubjectively valid method to distinguish truth from falsity, and yet even this method must take into account cultural and epistemological nuance. What about white lies and formulations that can be interpreted in different ways? Judgments concerning moral instability imply a general norm that, at least in our society, can hardly be defined. Every interpretation of a narrator's unreliability has to be linked to the specific norm one uses as a reader.

Krol and the unreliable narrator

We have noted before that the first-person narrator in Gerrit Krol's story does not offer an impartial representation of the period before he acquires the map. He misrepresents that phase because of the influence the map has had on him. He was liberated by it, and therefore he is no longer capable of representing the time before the liberation in any objective way. In other words, the first-person narrator in "The Map" is not entirely reliable when he is talking about his youth. He does not lie, but his selection of data gives rise to a biased image. In the construction of that image, the reader plays a role as well. He or she may interpret the first paragraph ideologically as the description of an unfree world dominated by the Christian world-view. Sunday is the day of the Lord and people have to rest. This frustrates a number of desires related to consumption, which nicely illustrates the hold of Christian ideology on society. If no connection is made between the shaded shop windows and Christian morality, the entire first paragraph is much less likely to be interpreted ideologically. As a result, the paragraph will appear less of a distortion originating from the narrator's evolution, an evolution that may be described as a distancing from or even a rejection of the original ideology. Perhaps these descriptions are in fact too strong, and in any case they only make sense within the ideological cognitive frame some readers use.

Frame and the third-person narrator

Manfred Jahn uses frame theory for the analysis of third-person narrative situations. Following Mieke Bal,[185] he reduces narrative texts to the formula, "X tells R that Y sees that Z does." According to Jahn, this formula is the most complete description of the model a reader can use to process a third-person narrative text. There are three typical models, the so-called defaults. First, there are texts for which the entire formula holds. Second, there are texts without an internal focalizer;[186] these correspond to the formula "X tells R that Z does." And third, there are texts with a nearly invisible narrator: "(X tells R that) Y sees that Z does." Every model brings along its own expectations. A visible narrator who does not participate in the story is believed to be omnipresent, omniscient, and reliable. From an internal focalizer, we expect an especially subjective presentation of the events that could as it were be seen to originate in the focalizer's mind.

As we have indicated in our brief presentation of the theory, the concept of frame is flexible enough to adapt defaults to texts that do not immediately conform to the typical expectations. In the course of reading, the selected frame is developed further and refined at the level of the details that have to be filled out.[187] Only if the text completely clashes with one's basic expectations – for instance, when a first-person narrator disrupts the third-person model – the initial frame is dropped. The choice for a new frame not only depends on the solution it can offer to the reading problem but also on the extent to which it provides a better interpretation of the text read so far.

Jahn argues, however, that some narratological terms and concepts have to be made more flexible if they are to be used as efficiently as possible in the processing of narrative texts. A sentence such as "The room was dark" may lead to the application of the well-known frame "description," a mode of narration Seymour Chatman describes as stopping the narrative clock so as to let the narrator present the environment.[188] However, this frame is too narrow for this sentence since it may also be the result of an internal focalizer's observation. In that case, time does not stop at all: the character's observation implies a certain duration.

Frame and free indirect speech

Another concept that, according to Jahn, has to be made more flexible is that of free indirect speech. His frame version of free indirect speech emphasizes the context in which this form of representation occurs. A sentence recognized as free indirect speech (frame 1) can be part of a character's observation (frame 2), and frame 1 as well as frame 2 may fit into a quotation of the character's thoughts by the narrator or in a summary of those thoughts also provided by the narrator. An example from *Madame Bovary*: "Would she never escape? She was every bit as good as all the women who lived happy lives."[189] Frame 1 consists of the sentence "Would she never escape?"; frame 2 is Emma Bovary's observation (she asks herself this question); the narrator quotes her thoughts. In the second sentence ("She was every bit as good. . . ."), it is very well possible that the narrator summarizes her thought.

In order for a sentence to be recognized as free indirect speech, Jahn develops a general description listing three characteristics. First, a sentence that can be read as free indirect speech is a non-subordinated construction: it is not a subclause introduced by "that," but an independent main clause. Second, tense and person are adapted to the existing narrative situation. "Would he see her tomorrow?" is the free indirect version of "He wondered, 'Will I see her tomorrow?' " in which the first person shifts to a third person, and the future tense changes to the conditional mood. Third, the sentence represents thoughts, utterances, and writings of a character. Because of this general description, the literary standard model of free indirect speech (third person, past tense) loses its focal status in narratology. Nevertheless, Jahn does not go as far as Fludernik, who as we mentioned above thinks that free indirect speech should be studied as a form of typification.[190]

Frame, free indirect speech, and Mutsaers

"Pegasian" is a third-person narrative with a reclusive, invisible narrator, which makes the reader's task slightly more difficult. The riding school itself does not become the subject of a description and neither does the appearance of the riding master and the girl. Only the girl's jeans are mentioned. This scanty information slightly frustrates the reader's elementary expectations. Nevertheless, it can be assumed that the story is told by a traditional narrator, which means that this is an example of the first formula, and as such it answers to the most complete formulation of the framework: X tells R that Y sees that Z does something. Once this is accepted, the narrator's invisibility and parsimony can be seen as an indication of the distance he keeps with regard to his characters. The invisible narrator presents the conversation between the riding master and the girl in a mostly indirect way. He avoids a simple dialogue, perhaps to add an ironic note to the whole event. This irony may lend the girl's opinions a pathetic overtone that is further intensified by the triviality of the topic, a pair of riding breeches.

Moreover, the indirect presentation in this text allows for a mixture of utterances and thoughts that especially undermines the riding master's authority. It is not always clear whether the riding master has actually voiced a certain thought, but the accumulation of nagging opinions demonstrates the extent to which the narrator has a hold on the character and is able to humiliate him (or her). A flexible and contextual understanding of free indirect speech, as Jahn proposes it, attaches more importance to the function of this mode of presentation than to its grammatical properties. It clarifies the uses of free indirect speech and demonstrates how it ties in with the meaning of the story and the central theme of authority.

Not only does free indirect speech generate the detached depiction of the riding master, the girl too is represented rather ironically in the first part of the story especially when her behavior is considered to be a teenage whim. In the last paragraph, however, free indirect speech causes empathy rather than irony. The narrator recedes in favor of the character, which makes it slightly harder to use the third-person frame. The girl's eventual insight is honored with a positive thought ("As long as you take off.") in which the narrator and the girl seem to come to an agreement.

In this interpretation, the reader encounters two versions of free indirect speech in this story: an ironic version and an empathic version. It is not necessary to drop one in favor of the other. The specific succession of distance and empathy nicely ties in with the girl's development in relation to the riding master: at first, she completely disagrees with him, but this changes later. Since free indirect speech follows the girl's development, the narrator – who is responsible for the choice of speech – could be said to be more sympathetic to the girl, in spite of his relative detachment in the first part. His ironic treatment of the riding master might suggest he shares her negative attitude toward him.

David Herman published an important part of his cognitive contributions to narratology in the flagship American journal PMLA, which underscores the current prestige of this approach.[191] Herman wants to know how to define a narrative text. He uses the term *script*, which, just as *frame*, derives from artificial intelligence. A script is an expectation concerning the specific sequence of a series of events.[192] Both in the case of frame and script, the reader draws on his memory to interpret the reading experience by means of structures acquired earlier. However, contrary to frame, which is a static structure, script emphasizes development. This makes it more suitable as a theoretical tool for the interpretation of a narrative text, which is always dynamic. *Script*

According to David Herman's general hypothesis, a story, much like a greeting or a quarrel, is a way of joining existing knowledge with new data. This can only work if we really possess the existing knowledge in question. What knowledge leads a reader to view a text as a narrative text? Herman starts from the structuralist suggestions concerning the minimal story as a temporal and causal sequence of events. He goes on to claim there are many textual characteristics that contribute to the reception of a text as a story – such as the indication of new information in a recognizable context and the suggestion of an action structure. *Script and story*

Nevertheless, a text only really becomes a story when the reader sees a connection between the text and an existing script. The sentences, "Mary was invited to Jack's party. She wondered if he would like a kite,"[193] can easily be taken as a story or as part of a story because we all know how birthday parties are organized and prepared. In this example the preparation is crucial.

Activation of scripts

A specific sequence of sentences seems to constrain the number and type of activated scripts, but it is hard to deduce the exact nature of this constraint from the characteristics of the sentences themselves. In another context and for other readers, the sentences about the party can be part of a story about a retirement party of a colleague who uses kites to study the weather. This context can be imagined on the basis of the text, but the full range of potential scripts can never be exhaustively considered. It does seem feasible to say of a certain sequence of sentences that they resemble a story more than another sequence might. Herman therefore defines a text's narrativity as the extent to which this text activates scripts urging the reader to consider the text as a story.[194] According to him, the degree of activation is higher when the activated knowledge is more complex and comprehensive. The more scripts a text activates, and the more refined these scripts are, the faster the text will be considered as a story.

Herman links the activation of scripts to a hypothesis about literary history. He argues that narrative innovation often implies the explicit rejection of old scripts, which forces the reader to use another kind of world knowledge in the interpretation of a text with a seemingly familiar subject. The subject is familiar, but the scripts that are normally used to interpret it do not seem to function anymore. At the beginning of *Don Quixote*, Cervantes makes the reader give up his or her idealized knowledge of the development of a quest in favor of what Herman describes as "scripts grounded in an awareness of human potential and limitations."[195]

Script and genre

According to Herman, the diachronic study of reader activation has to be linked to a synchronic analysis of the various ways in which different genres deal with scripts in the same period. He gives three examples from the 1920s and '30s: children's literature, autobiography, and the experimental novel. In that period as well, children's literature wanted to activate morally virtuous scripts such as the postponement of satisfaction. Of course, this presupposes a target audience that recognizes these scripts. In this context, activation implies the consolidation of existing scripts or perhaps the production of larger action structures by the combination of scripts young readers already are familiar with.

A passage from the autobiography of Maud Gonne, an Irish nationalist, demonstrates that this genre places much higher demands on the reader especially when it comes to scripts about identity and self. Gonne activates but also undermines the scripts in which heroism is related to masculinity. This forces the reader to revise his or her preconceived ideas on female development. Herman takes his last example from *Nightwood*, an experimental novel by Djuna Barnes. She confronts the reader with a great variety of activated scripts and reduces the action structures to a few movements, so that the application of familiar action sequences becomes very difficult. This forces the reader – even more so than in the case of Gonne – to call his own scripts into question and to make adjustments.

Herman avoids exaggerated statements on the differences between the genres to which his examples belong, and quite rightly so. A novel does not need to be more demanding than an autobiography, and authors of children's literature may be less than serious with respect to their didactic assignment. Nevertheless, this synchronic approach provides more insight into the position of a narrative text within the genre system. The combination of synchronic and diachronic enables post-classical narratology to contribute to literary history.

Scripts and Mutsaers

Which scripts do Mutsaers and Krol activate and how do they use them? "Pegasian" immediately invokes our expectations about a conversation. Conversations can develop in many directions, but in this case, the possibilities are limited by the fact that one of the participants seems to be in a position of power. All of us have at one time been addressed by an insistent and authoritarian figure, so that we are familiar with this kind of conversation. Our knowledge about its ending will partly depend on our own experiences – people who have suffered because of powerful people may find it hard to imagine a good result – and, in our opinion, script theory allows the use of these experiences. This could mean that important aspects of the text are neglected to the benefit of personal projection. Nevertheless, a lot of narrative prose possesses a power of activation that, at least partly, runs counter to this projection. This is also the case in "Pegasian." The girl's first utterance already indicates that she will put up some resistance, and so we immediately have to integrate this element with our expectations. How do conversations between an authoritarian figure and a younger assertive person develop? It is unlikely that the person in power will simply back down, but it is clearly possible that he (or she) might have recourse to other than verbal instruments. The younger person may give in after a while, but her resistance may also continue, especially if the authoritarian figure's irritation shows through and if the younger person notices that in spite of her subordinate position she has reached some results.

The first part of "Pegasian" largely conforms to the conventional development of an argument between an authority figure and a pupil. The text's first sentences call for such a script. The riding master slowly loses his patience but eventually takes out his frustration on the horses instead of the girl: "These horses are moving around like turtles. Time to bring out the whip." She, on the contrary, enjoys resisting the riding master and stands her ground. With respect to script theory, it is interesting that the text strongly plays down the argument script in the second part. In order to understand the girl's eventual insight, the reader can turn to scripts on adolescent behavior, some more condescending than others. Perhaps the riding master has convinced the girl after all, and perhaps her resistance was simply due to the idea that this is the way one reacts when one is young. Or perhaps her eventual insight suggests that it would have been better not to put up resistance at all instead of making a scene like a typical teenager. These interpretations obviously depend on the reader's conception of a teenager or adolescent.

The argument part of the script is activated by the conversation, the reconciliatory part by the story's ending. Of course, the text's formal aspects influence the application of the activated scripts. Multiple focalization and a reclusive narrator make it hard to interpret the word "finally" in the second part: "Finally, she understands." If "finally" expresses the narrator's evaluation, the latter seems to share the disdain that is part of the condescending script about willful teenage behavior. If the word must be assigned to the girl, this triggers the slightly disarming suggestion that she was willing to understand the usefulness of the riding breeches but that she simply was not convinced.

Scripts and Krol

The first paragraph of "The Map" describes Mr. and Mrs. Paalman's bookstore in the village of Dorkwerd. A spatial description may trigger expectations as to the events to come in the environment at hand. In Krol's story, the bookstore, as an example of the blinding effects of

Christianity, can be used as the starting point for a number of different scripts. Perhaps the main character will try to steal books in the shop. Perhaps Mr. and Mrs. Paalman will have an adventure inspired by their contact with books. Perhaps the world of books will liberate the couple's imagination, which might lead to a clash with their environment. On the basis of the sentence, "he's nice, she is wearing the pants," the reader may suspect that the bookstore will be the scene of a battle between the sexes.

The fact that so many scripts are imaginable indicates that the text has a high degree of narrativity. Aspects of these scripts can be integrated with the scripts evoked by the second paragraph. At the beginning of this paragraph, the first-person narrator introduces himself and emphasizes the importance of the shop window being shaded. He sees the map when he is not supposed to see it, which gives the object an extraordinary value. Will there be a confrontation between the first-person narrator and the ideology symbolized by the shutters? Will the map show him the way out of the community dominated by Christian prohibitions? The adventure suggested by these scripts is, however, limited to trips to places that are on the map but that had not been visited by the main character before. Liberation will not come as fast as might have been expected, because the experiencing I keeps returning home during his map period. The end of his narration reinforces this qualification since the first-person narrator tells us the map had become superfluous and that therefore he did not keep it. The liberation script, which was evoked by, among other things, the windows being shaded on Sunday, vanishes together with the map. The undermining of this script leads the reader to reinterpret the first-person narrator's entire development along the lines of a much less adventurous script. This disappointing development is also a script that appears to be inherent in growing up. The child cherishes dreams and imagines scripts that can in fact be realized only very partially. Krol's choice of a first-person narrator intensifies the reader's identification with the boy, which frustrates the reader's expectations even more. This disillusionment can contribute to the insight that the reconstruction of the past is distorted by relativization and disappointment.

Fludernik's constructivism

Just like Manfred Jahn and Ansgar Nünning, Monika Fludernik places her work in the context of constructivist theory, which is a very explicit example of the cognitive paradigm. The constructivists claim that communication cannot simply be represented as the transfer of information from a sender to a receiver but argue that the receiver autonomously produces information in his own cognitive domain.[196] For the "natural" narratology proposed by Fludernik,[197] this means that her theory does not so much involve texts or their technical aspects but rather the frames or scripts by means of which these texts are interpreted.

Natural narratives Fludernik starts from so-called natural narratives; that is, narratives coming up spontaneously in a conversation. She observes that these enable us to construe our experience in a way that corresponds to the manner in which we construe our "normal" experience outside of the stories. "Experience" must here be understood in the broadest possible sense, signifying everything that happens to a human being. The processing of this experience in natural narratives as well as in life itself is governed by principles we also use in the interpretation of written and even literary texts. These involve cognitive principles of organization such as actions, observations, projections of a communicative frame, quests for explanations, and so on.[198]

Narrativity Taking these observations into account, Fludernik formulates an original definition of the central narratological concept of "narrativity." *Experientiality* According to her, a reader will see a text as a story when it implies experientiality; that is, when it evokes "real" experiences that the reader recognizes, or assumes that he recognizes, and that enable him to relate to the story. According to Fludernik, a text does not need to have a plot to count as a narrative. It suffices to encounter on any textual level an anthropomorphous agent who has certain experiences. Such an agent displays emotional involvement and evaluates his or her experiences, which urges the reader to interpret the text as a narrative. Of course, narrativity can also result from the experience-oriented representation of successive actions, but an anthropomorphous representation of a specific consciousness will suffice.

Narrativization Fludernik uses the term "narrativization" to refer to the reading strategy that "naturalizes" texts as narratives by connecting them to natural narratives and the concomitant experientiality and narrativity.[199] When a reader is confronted with a text that at first sight seems to be incomprehensible, he will often have recourse to the narrative concept he is familiar with because of his knowledge of natural narratives. Since, according to Fludernik, these narratives use the same cognitive principles of organization as the ones we use in our experience of everyday reality, "realism" is a central concept in her definition of narrativization.

This does not concern the mimetic characteristics of a text as in most conventional definitions of literary realism. It rather refers to the natural frame the reader uses in his construction of reality as well as in his literary interpretation. Chronology, causality, and outcome are three well-known aspects of this frame. According to Fludernik, readers apply realist parameters like space and time in a very flexible way, allowing them to process the experimental distortions of a text as well, at least if these "unnatural" aspects tie in with their natural frames. If an experimental text tampers with the concept of character, the reader may still use the existence of psychologically disturbed people to relate such a text to his natural experience. Nevertheless, narrativization sometimes fails, for example, when a text no longer consists of grammatically correct sentences and does not seem to have a theme, or when sentences hardly seem to make sense to the reader and their succession raises questions he or she cannot answer.

Constructivist perspective on story/narrative/narration

This constructivist model enables Fludernik to demonstrate that the traditional distinction between story on the one hand and narrative plus narration on the other is by no means as absolute as most narratologists think. This distinction is largely based on a realist conception of narration that stipulates that an event precedes its representation. However, it is extremely difficult to isolate an event from the way in which it is represented. Fludernik no longer defines the narrative text by linking it to a sequence of facts. She does not need to look for the "real story" or the bias involved in representation. In this way, she puts into perspective the eccentricity of many twentieth-century texts in which hardly anything happens. These are only eccentric for classical narratologists who cling to the story as a norm.

Of course, the conceptualization of the story remains useful as one of the realist parameters to read a text. When a narrator describes events from the past, the reader will "naturally" be inclined to read his report as the representation of successive events. This merely demonstrates, however, that classical narratological theories are based on a realist frame. Therefore, it seems inevitable that they interpret texts on the basis of anthropomorphic and psychologizing concepts. This insight need not undermine the theory, but it does stimulate reflection on the structuralist concepts, even when dealing with an extremely simple text that fully allows realist projection. According to Fludernik, anthropomorphization is not a problem in itself, because it constitutes the essence of processing narrative text.

Fludernik's scope

Fludernik's theory is very general and broad. Her concept of experientiality covers concepts such as script and frame. Even ideology and David Herman's conception of the possible world as the context a reader imports into his interpretation may be subsumed under this heading. But this generality does not exclude concrete interpretations. In "Pegasian," nothing much happens, but because of its orientation toward human experience, the reader will inevitably interpret it as a story. The two characters feel strongly about the topic of the conversation, and the narrator makes an effort to dramatize this involvement by using free indirect speech. The narrator himself remains in the background but, as we have suggested before, he is not neutral either. His manipulative representation of the characters' thoughts and utterances may lead the reader to develop a negative or positive view of either of these figures.

Fludernik and Mutsaers

Even if the thoughts and utterances may blend in refined ways, the reader will face few problems in interpreting this text. He or she recognizes a conversation and connects it with everyday, natural conversations. The application of realist parameters would probably be easier without the confusing use of free indirect speech, but the circumstances of the conversation become clear rather quickly. A riding master and a girl are talking to each other in a riding school. After a small time lapse at the end of the first part, the girl comes to an insight while riding. This insight may be a little unexpected, certainly considering the girl's stubborn resistance earlier, but as a positive and clear ending of the story, it perfectly fits the expectations of a reader with realist tendencies. In a realist frame, one or more characters undergo an evolution that is nicely wrapped up at the end of the story.

Fludernik and Krol

At first sight, "The Map" seems to invoke the realist frame even more than "Pegasian." Krol's narrator clearly tells his story in retrospect, and the importance of the map makes it possible to make a clear distinction between "authentic" reality and its cartographic representation. As he gets older, the narrator's emotional attachment to the map diminishes, but this does not prevent him from devoting a separate narration to this object. This paradox may be an obstacle to readers using realist parameters. Does the narrator claim that he no longer considers the map to be important, or does he suggest that the map exerts a permanent influence on him? Is there a clear distinction between present and past?

Is "authentic" reality not as artificial as the reality of the map? Is this map really so irrelevant, given the fact that the narrator devotes an entire story to it? Since "The Map" does not fully correspond to the average reader's expectations, this story, more than "Pegasian," seems to invite an antirealist reading. In both cases, however, the text has a relatively unexpected ending that may raise all kinds of additional questions with respect to, for instance, the narrator's attitude.

In responding to these questions, the reader will undoubtedly be drawn into the game. The answers will be colored by his or her ideology, his or her views on possibility and actuality, his or her frames and scripts, and his or her knowledge of natural narratives. Post-classical narratology has the merit that it has incorporated all these inevitabilities into a theory that, because of its structuralist legacy, had tried to ignore these questions for too long. This does not mean that classical narratology is pushed aside, but rather that it is qualified and enhanced by the more recent approaches. Our post-classical readings of "Pegasian" and "The Map" demonstrate this as well: they show potential interpretations and make clear that these depend on the reader and the context. Perhaps, narratology is now based on fewer certainties than structuralism had hoped for, but this is probably the reason why narrative theory has such great potential.

Appendix A

Pegasian

Charlotte Mutsaers

The riding master would appreciate it if she'd remember that when horse riding you might best be wearing a real pair of riding breeches, those with side flaps.

She asks why, since a simple straightforward denim pair goes well too. What are those flaps for, in fact?

The riding master answers that you catch a very special kind of wind in them.

Do they make you go faster?

No, not faster – as a matter of fact, true dressage, just like real life, doesn't have anything to do with racing – it's rather the sensation that matters. Little girls who have never personally experienced this heavenly sensation did well not to shoot off their mouths. And it wouldn't hurt to consult a few books on cavalry. Horse riding without background information doesn't make sense for anyone. And this here is no club for amateurs.

And the women who wear their own riding breeches, in the form of fat, can they perhaps ride like that?

Now the riding master doesn't feel like explaining anything anymore. Sometimes your patience simply runs out. Furthermore, all this questioning ruins the class, notably for the other ladies. These horses are moving around like turtles. Time to bring out the whip.

When the carousel is back in full swing, she hears the rustle of the riding breeches over the cracking of the whip. Finally she understands: the riding breeches give the horse wings, and the horse gives those wings to you. Is it the idea or is it the sensation? Whatever. As long as you take off.

Appendix B

The Map

Gerrit Krol

On Sundays the Christian shops had their shades drawn. Their windows would be hidden by shades, mostly of lightbrown paper, to avoid that man would be seduced on Sunday to buy something on Monday. On the corner of little Brouwerstreet and Ebbingestreet, for instance, you had the Paalman bookshop. It wasn't any bigger than a large living room. There was a counter behind which ("he's nice, she's wearing the pants") Mr and Mrs Paalman operated as if it were a grocery store. The shop was especially busy towards the feast of Saint Nicholas. One waited one's turn, and when it was finally there, one uttered one's wishes, in the manner of "a light novel for a girl of seventeen" or "a historical novel, preferably illustrated," and then racks and piles would be searched for such a book. It was found, opened on the first page, and shown to the customer who, with his glasses on, would read the title, the name of the author, and the publishing house; then he would take off his glasses and nod the way one approves of a wine in a restaurant.

This bookstore's shades were drawn on Sundays. Closed off from the world. But one of these Sundays, on my way to the children's church, I saw, because the shades didn't close completely (they had stuck somewhere, leaving a mere two-inch gap), precisely in those two forbidden inches part of a folded tourist map or biking map which, perhaps because of the Sunday light, had slightly curled so that, on my haunches now, I could be surprised by the degree of detail and especially by the name I read: Dorkwerd. The village I knew so well and which I had never seen on a map! And further to the right the northern part, indicated with red, of the city of Groningen: the Heights and a small stretch of railroad track, the New Canal and the bike path alongside. Everything clear and close, everything enlarged. Never had I seen such a map, with such minute detail.

Monday afternoon, in the bookshop, I pointed to it. I did not have enough money, so that I had to wait until Saturday.

That Saturday . . . At one-thirty I brought it home with me and opened it on the table.

"Even the stone works are on it," I cried out, moved as I was.

A whole table full of *new things*. Later that afternoon I sat on the floor with it on my knees in front of the stove. What excited me was the thought that it now made sense *to have been everywhere*. The prospect I was going to cover the earth with my body. To be everywhere . . .

The feeling didn't go away. On the contrary. I had drawn a blank map of the Netherlands and indicated the roads where I had biked; and the roads I had not had yet, that is where I went, I biked them so that I could draw them. Some roads (and the number increased) I traveled two times or more, but this did not count. To have been there once is to be there always; my map indicated this.

When I had to recognize that I occasionally traveled somewhere by train, so not really by myself and neither in direct contact with the road, my dream would fade away in the sense that I did not keep track of these trips. The area around the city was covered, but because I had had all roads, nothing was added anymore, and one day I would remove the map from the wall. It had become meaningless. I haven't kept it either.

Notes

INTRODUCTION

1. The English translations of these stories are ours. The originals are taken from Charlotte Mutsaers, *Paardejam* (Amsterdam: Meulenhoff, 1996), 187; and from Gerrit Krol, *De oudste jongen* (Amsterdam: Querido, 1998), 120–21.

2. "Riding master" (which comes closest to the Dutch *pikeur*) is not a gender-neutral term. We will address this problem in our discussion of feminist narratology in chapter 3 of this handbook.

3. Franz Kafka, "Up in the Gallery," in *The Complete Stories*, ed. Nahum N. Glatzer, trans. Willa and Edwin Muir (New York: Shocken Books, 1946), 401–2.

Chapter 1

BEFORE AND SURROUNDING STRUCTURALISM

1. E. M. Forster, *Aspects of the Novel* (Harmondsworth: Penguin, 1990), 87.

2. Shlomith Rimmon-Kenan, *Narrative Fiction: Contemporary Poetics* (London: Methuen, 1983), 17.

3. José Angel García Landa and Susana Onega, *Narratology: An Introduction* (London: Longman), 3.

4. Gerald Prince, *A Dictionary of Narratology* (Lincoln: University of Nebraska Press, 1987), 53.

5. "I would like to argue that temporal succession is sufficient as a *minimal* requirement for a group of events to form a story" (Rimmon-Kenan, *Narrative Fiction*, 18).

6. Rimmon-Kenan, *Narrative Fiction*, 106–8.

7. As can be derived from James Miller's edition of the writings on poetics (*Theory of Fiction: Henry James*, ed. James E. Miller [Lincoln: University of Nebraska Press, 1972]), James's statement "that the *scenic* method is my absolute, my imperative, my *only* salvation" (180) did not imply at all that the author's personality had to be erased. It remains present in the way it shows reality and therefore *showing* is not an objective method. James writes in "The Art of Fiction": "The deepest quality of a work of art will always be the quality of the mind of the producer" (43). Narratorial invisibility must not be confused with a neutral representation of social reality.

8. Percy Lubbock, *The Craft of Fiction* (London: Jonathan Cape, 1968), 110–23.

9. Philippe Lejeune, *Le pacte autobiographique* (Paris: Seuil, 1975), 15: "In order for a text to be an autobiography (or, more generally, an instance of intimate literature), author, narrator, and character have to coincide" (our translation).

10. "We might better speak of the 'inferred' than of the 'implied' author" (Seymour Chatman, *Coming to Terms: The Rhetoric of Narrative in Fiction and Film* [Ithaca: Cornell University Press, 1993], 77).

11. Gérard Genette, *Narrative Discourse Revisited*, trans. Jane E. Lewin (Ithaca: Cornell University Press, 1988), 150.

12. Ansgar Nünning, " 'But why *will* you say that I am mad?': On the Theory, History, and Signals of Unreliable Narration in British Fiction," *Arbeiten aus Anglistik und Amerikanistik* 22, no. 1 (1997): 83–105. We will return to this important article in chapter 3. See also Nünning, "Unreliable, Compared to What? Towards a Cognitive Theory of *Unreliable Narration*: Prolegomena and Hypotheses," in *Grenzüberschreitungen: Narratologie im Kontext / Transcending Boundaries: Narratology in Context*, ed. Walter Grünzweig and Andreas Solbach, 53–73 (Tübingen: Gunter Narr Verlag, 1999).

13. Chatman, *Coming to Terms*, 74.

14. Ansgar Nünning, "Renaissance eines anthropomorphisierten Passepartouts oder Nachruf auf ein literaturkritisches Phantom? Überlegungen und Alternativen zum Konzept des 'implied author.' " *Deutsche Vierteljahresschrift für Literaturwissenschaft und Geistesgeschichte* 67, no. 1 (1993): 1–25, (especially 9–11).

15. Chatman, *Coming to Terms*, 81.

16. Chatman, *Coming to Terms*, 87.

17. Genette, *Narrative Discourse Revisited*, 145. Only in very exceptional circumstances does Genette think it is useful to distinguish between the image the reader has of the author (that is, the implied author) and the real author. These circumstances include forgery (for example, a fake Rimbaud), ghost writing (where the name on the cover is not that of the real author), and collective authorship. Genette admits that the reader always develops an image of the author, but he believes it is wrong to turn that image into a narratological concept. For him, the image of the author no longer belongs to narratology: "In my opinion, narratology has no need to go beyond the narrative situation and the two agents 'implied author' and 'implied reader' are clearly situated in that 'beyond' " (137).

18. P. D. Juhl, *Interpretation: An Essay in the Philosophy of Literary Criticism* (Princeton: Princeton University Press, 1980), 186. The following statement goes in the same direction: "If the work expresses certain beliefs, then the author is committed to those beliefs and to their truth" (178).

19. See Nünning, "Renaissance," 11–16.

20. Edgar Allan Poe, "The Masque of the Red Death," in *Poetry and Tales*, ed.

Patrick R. Quinn (New York: Literary Classics of the United States [Library of America], 1984), 485.

21. Seymour Chatman, *Story and Discourse: Narrative Structure in Fiction and Film* (Ithaca NY: Cornell University Press, 1978), 145–95. Chatman speaks about absent narrators such as the collector and the stenographer on e.g. 169 and 173.

22. Rimmon-Kenan, *Narrative Fiction*, 88.

23. Wayne Booth, *The Rhetoric of Fiction* (Chicago: University of Chicago Press, 1961), 138.

24. Gibson's article is entitled "Authors, Speakers, Readers, and Mock Readers." It appeared in *College English* 11 (1950): 265–69, and is mentioned by Booth, *Rhetoric of Fiction*, 138.

25. Wolfgang Iser, *The Implied Reader: Patterns of Communication in Prose Fiction from Bunyan to Beckett* (Baltimore: Johns Hopkins University Press, 1974). We will return to this in chapter 3.

26. Nünning, "Renaissance," 8–9.

27. Gerald Prince, "On Readers and Listeners in Narrative," *Neophilologus* 55 (1971): 117–22. See also "Notes towards a Categorization of Fictional Narratees," *Genre* 4 (1971): 100–105 and "Introduction à l'étude du narrataire," *Poétique* 14 (1973): 178–96. Prince also discusses the concept in his monograph, *Narratology: The Form and Functioning of Narrative* (The Hague: Mouton, 1982).

28. Charlotte Mutsaers, *Zeepijn* (Amsterdam: Meulenhoff, 1999), 20–28.

29. Chatman, *Story and Discourse*, 254.

30. See also Wallace Martin, *Recent Theories of Narrative* (Ithaca NY: Cornell University Press, 1986), 154. Martin further divides the mock reader into a model reader and an authorial reader, so that there are just as many kinds of receivers as there are kinds of senders. Chatman saves the symmetry between producers and consumers in a different way. On the sender side, he lists the author, the implied author, and the narrator (who combines the dramatized author, the dramatized narrator, and the undramatized narrator proposed in our figure). On the receiver side, he mentions the narratee, the implied audience, and the real audience. See Chatman, *Story and Discourse*, 267.

31. Mary-Louise Pratt, *Toward a Speech-Act Theory of Literary Discourse* (Bloomington: Indiana University Press, 1977), 3–78. Monika Fludernik, whose work we will focus on in chapter 3, incorporates this concept in her encompassing theory of narrative.

32. "Speaker and Audience are present in the literary speech situation . . . they have commitments to one another as they do everywhere else, and those commitments are presupposed by both the creator and the receiver of the work. Far from being autonomous, self-contained, self-motivating, context-free objects which exist independently from the 'pragmatic' concerns of 'everyday'

discourse, literary works take place in a context, and like any other utterance they cannot be described apart from that context" (Pratt, *Toward a Speech-Act Theory*, 115).

33. In theoretical terms, the literary speech act is a performative. This type of utterance does not merely represent a specific situation – in that case it would be a constative – but it rather brings something about. As a performative, literature creates a world. The performative's success depends on certain felicity conditions that derive from and can only be met thanks to the communicative context. These conditions subject literary communication to a series of conventions (such as genre) shared by sender and receiver. The literary text precisely derives its illocutionary force – that is, its power to make the reader believe in the world it evokes – from these conventions, which it uses and activates. (Sandy Petrey, *Speech Acts and Literary Theory* [New York: Routledge, 1990], 4–21.) According to Susan Sniader Lanser, the world evoked by the literary text is an "alternative world" (*The Narrative Act: Point of View in Prose Fiction* [Princeton: Princeton University Press, 1981], 291), and the literary utterance amounts to a special kind of illocutionary act, which she calls a "hypothetical" (289). Richard Ohmann speaks in this connection of the "imaginative construction of a world" ("Speech Acts and the Definition of Literature," *Philosophy and Rhetoric* 4 (1971): 1–19). The hypothetical, alternative, and imaginary qualities of the literary world will resurface in chapter 3, during our discussion of possible worlds theory.

34. Thomas Mann, *Der Tod in Venedig*, *Gesammelte Werke* (Frankfurt am Main: S. Fischer Verlag, 1960), 8: 493–94. The translation is taken from Dorrit Cohn, *Transparent Minds: Narrative Modes for Presenting Consciousness in Fiction* (Princeton: Princeton University Press, 1978), 27.

35. James Joyce, *Ulysses*, ed. Hans Walter Gabler (New York: Vintage Books, 1986), 132.

36. Gustave Flaubert, *Madame Bovary*, trans. Geoffrey Wall (Harmondsworth: Penguin, 1992), 172.

37. Harry Mulisch, *Voer voor psychologen. Zelfportret* (Amsterdam: Bezige Bij, 1961), 21.

38. A. F. Th. van der Heijden, *Asbestemming. Een requiem* (Amsterdam: Querido, 1994), 239.

39. Jeroen Brouwers, *Sunken Red*, trans. Adrienne Dixon (London: Peter Owen, 1990), 49.

40. Brouwers, *Sunken Red*, 57.

41. Willem Brakman, *Een weekend in Oostende* (Amsterdam: Querido, 1982), 39–40.

42. Point-of-view is an ambiguous concept. Gérard Genette and Mieke Bal, who will both be dealt with extensively in chapter 2, have solved this problem by

treating the activities of narration and perception separately. As we will see immediately, Franz Stanzel's perspective scale is less ambiguous than Friedman's point of view but still more ambiguous than the solution proposed by Genette and Bal. For a summary of the tradition, see Jaap Lintvelt, *Essai de typologie narrative: Le "point de vue"* (Paris: José Corti, 1981), 111–76.

43. In an earlier essay, Friedman distinguished eight points of view. See "Point of View in Fiction: The Development of a Critical Concept," PMLA 70, no. 5 (1955): 1160–84. Our presentation is based on a reworked version as it appeared in Friedman's book *Form and Meaning in Fiction* (Athens: University of Georgia Press, 1975), 134–65.

44. Hugo Claus, *De Geruchten* (Amsterdam: Bezige Bij, 1996).

45. "The next step toward the objectification of the story material is the elimination not only of the author, who disappeared with the 'I' as witness frame, but also of any narrator whatsoever. Here the reader ostensibly listens to no one; the story comes directly through the minds of the characters as it leaves its mark there" (Friedman, *Form and Meaning*, 152–53).

46. "Having eliminated the author and then the narrator, we are now ready to dispose of mental states altogether" (Friedman, *Form and Meaning*, 155).

47. Stanzel's two most important books have been translated into English: *Narrative Situations in the Novel:* Tom Jones, Moby-Dick, The Ambassadors, Ulysses, trans. J. Pusack (Bloomington: Indiana University Press, 1971) and *A Theory of Narrative*, trans. Charlotte Goedsche (Cambridge: Cambridge University Press, 1984).

48. We offer Stanzel's circle as reproduced in Landa and Onega, *Narratology*, 162.

49. Dorrit Cohn, "The Encirclement of Narrative. On Franz Stanzel's *Theorie des Erzählens*," *Poetics Today* 2, no. 2 (1981): 157–82.

50. Franz K. Stanzel, "A Low-Structuralist at Bay? Further Thoughts on *A Theory of Narrative*," *Poetics Today* 11, no. 4 (1990): 805–16. Stanzel refers (808) to the *Ulysses* chapter we quote here, but the interpretation of the fragments is our development of Stanzel's suggestions.

51. Joyce, *Ulysses*, 150.

Chapter 2

STRUCTURALISM

1. The issue also appeared as a book: *Communications, 8: L'analyse structurale du récit* (Paris: Seuil, 1981).

2. Tzvetan Todorov, *Grammaire du Décaméron* (The Hague: Mouton, 1969), 10 (our translation).

3. Vladimir Propp, *Morphology of the Folktale*, 2nd ed., trans. Laurence Scott,

rev. by Louis A. Wagner (Austin: University of Texas Press, 1968). The original Russian edition appeared in 1928. Claude Bremond begins his classic study, *Logique du récit* (Paris: Seuil, 1973) with a long chapter entitled "The Propp Legacy" (9–128) in which he shows how Propp has influenced the narrative theories developed by Greimas, Todorov, and of course Bremond himself.

4. Oswald Ducrot and others, *Qu'est-ce que le structuralisme?* (Paris: Seuil, 1968), 102.

5. A summary description of the three levels is available in Gérard Genette, *Narrative Discourse*, trans. Jane E. Lewin (Ithaca NY: Cornell University Press, 1980), 27.

6. A. J. Greimas, *On Meaning: Selected Writings in Semiotic Theory*, trans. Paul J. Perron and Frank H. Collins (Minneapolis: University of Minnesota Press, 1987), 121 ff.

7. Rimmon-Kenan criticizes Greimas for reducing the entire literary productions by the French authors Bernanos and Maupassant to such a square (*Narrative Fiction*, 12–13).

8. Jonathan Culler, *Structuralist Poetics: Structuralism, Linguistics and the Study of Literature* (Ithaca NY: Cornell University Press, 1975), 20–24.

9. Roland Barthes, "Introduction to the Structural Analysis of Narratives," in *Image-Music-Text*, ed. Stephen Heath, 79–124 (Glasgow: Fontana/Collins, 1977), 81.

10. We will illustrate these reproaches in our discussion of the separate textual levels. A general critique of structuralist spatialization is offered by Andrew Gibson, *Towards a Postmodern Theory of Narrative* (Edinburgh: Edinburgh University Press, 1996), 1–8.

11. The most important narratological works by Genette are *Narrative Discourse* (originally published in French in 1972) and *Narrative Discourse Revisited* (originally published in French in 1983), and *Fiction and Diction*, trans. C. Porter (Ithaca NY: Cornell University Press, 1993), which originally appeared in French in 1991. Mieke Bal's *Narratology: Introduction to the Theory of Narrative*, 2nd ed. (Toronto: University of Toronto Press, 1997) is the revised version of the English translation (by Christine Van Boheemen) of her Dutch monograph, *De theorie van vertellen en verhalen*, 2nd ed. (Muiderberg: Coutinho, 1980). Finally, Rimmon-Kenan's main contribution is *Narrative Fiction*, a second, slightly extended edition of which came out in 2002.

12. See for example Boris Tomashevsky, "Thematics," in *Russian Formalist Criticism: Four Essays*, ed. Lee T. Lemon and Marion J. Reis, 61–95 (Lincoln: University of Nebraska Press, 1965). Originally published in Russian in 1925.

13. Tomashevsky, "Thematics," 66–78.

14. Barthes, "Introduction to the Structural Analysis, 87ff."

15. Roman Jakobson, "Two Aspects of Language and Two Types of Aphasic Disturbances," in Roman Jakobson and Morris Halle, *Fundamentals of Language*, (The Hague: Mouton, 1956), 67–96.

16. Ian Fleming, "From a View to a Kill," *For Your Eyes Only* (London: Hodder and Stoughton, 1989), 7–37.

17 Fleming, "From a View to a Kill," 7, 9.

18. Propp, *Morphology of the Folktale*, 25–83.

19. Umberto Eco, "Narrative Structure in Fleming," in *The Poetics of Murder. Detective Fiction and Literary Theory*, ed. Glenn Most and William W. Stowe, 93–117 (San Diego: Harcourt Brace Jovanich, 1983).

20. Bremond, *Logique du récit*, 33.

21. Bremond, *Logique du récit*, 135.

22. A. J. Greimas, *Structural Semantics: An Attempt at Method*, trans. D. McDowell, R. Schlefier, and A. Velie (Lincoln: University of Nebraska Press, 1983).

23. Cok van der Voort, "De analyse van verhalend proza," in *Literatuur en context: Een inleiding in de literatuurwetenschap*, ed. Peter Zeeman, 24–58 (Nijmegen: Sun, 1991), 41. Mieke Bal translates *destinateur* as "power" (*Narratology*, 198–201), but we prefer Van der Voort's more neutral term.

24. See for example Martin, *Recent Theories of Narrative*, 117.

25. Forster, *Aspects of the Novel*, 73.

26. Rimmon-Kenan, *Narrative Fiction*, 41.

27. Chatman, *Story and Discourse*, 126 ff.

28. M. M. Bakhtin, "Forms of Time and of the Chronotope in the Novel," in *The Dialogic Imagination: Four Essays*, ed. Michael Holquist, trans. Caryl Emerson and Michael Holquist (Austin: University of Texas Press, 1981), 84–258.

29. "Thus the chronotope, functioning as the primary means for materializing time in space, emerges as a center for concretizing representation, as a force giving body to the entire novel. All the novel's abstract elements – philosophical and social generalizations, ideas, analyses of cause and effect – gravitate toward the chronotope and through it take on flesh and blood, permitting the imaging power of art to do its work" (Bakhtin, "Forms of Time," 250).

30. Chatman, *Story and Discourse*, 26.

31. Fleming, "From a View to a Kill," 37.

32. "The chronotope in literature has an intrinsic *generic* significance. It can even be said that it is precisely the chronotope that defines genre and generic distinctions" (Bakhtin, "Forms of Time," 84–85). After an overview of historical developments in the novel and its concomitant chronotopes, Bakhtin concludes, "The chronotopes we have discussed provide the basis for distinguishing generic types; they lie at the heart of specific varieties of the novel genre, formed and

developed over the course of many centuries" (Bakhtin, "Forms of Time," 250–51).

33. Bakhtin, "Forms of Time," 165, 225.

34. Bal, *Narratology*, 214–17.

35. See Christel Van Boheemen-Saaf, "Deconstructivisme," in *Vormen van literatuurwetenschap. Moderne richtingen en hun mogelijkheden voor tekstinterpretatie*, ed. R. T. Segers, 229– 47 (Groningen: Wolters-Noordhoff, 1985), 243–44.

36. Genette, *Narrative Discourse*, 33–160.

37. The article, "Erzählzeit und erzählte Zeit," appeared for the first time in 1948 in *Festschrift Paul Kluckhohn und Hermann Schneider* (Tübingen: J. C. B. Mohr), 195–212. It was also incorporated into Günther Müller, *Morphologische Poetik: Gesammelte Aufsätze* (Tübingen: Max Niemeyer, 1968), 269–86.

38. Bal, *Narratology*, 102.

39. Gerard Reve, *Het Boek Van Violet En Dood* (Amsterdam: Veen, 1996), 7.

40. Multatuli, *Max Havelaar, or the Coffee Auctions of the Dutch Trading Company*, trans. Roy Edwards (London: Penguin Books, 1987), 64.

41. Multatuli, *Max Havelaar*, 133.

42. Bal, *Narratology*, 100.

43. Gérard Genette, "Discours du récit," in *Figures III* (Paris: Seuil, 1972), 90. The Lewin translation (*Narrative Discourse*, 48 ff.) uses "first narrative," which creates the wrong impression of enumeration.

44. See for example Meir Sternberg, *Expositional Modes and Temporal Ordering in Fiction* (Baltimore: Johns Hopkins University Press, 1978).

45. Eberhard Lämmert, *Bauformen des Erzählens* (Stuttgart: Metzler, 1955).

46. Marcel Proust, *Remembrance of Things Past: Swann's Way*, trans. Scott Moncrieff (New York: Knopf, 1982), 3.

47. Fleming, "From a View to a Kill," 10–11.

48. Gijs IJlander, *Een fabelachtig uitzicht* (Utrecht: Veen, 1990), 167–73 and 212–13.

49. Rimmon-Kenan, *Narrative Fiction*, 59–70. See our note 55.

50. Bal calls this type "explicit" characterization (*Narratology*, 129–31).

51. Gerard Reve, *Het hijgend hert* (Amsterdam: Veen, 1998), 32.

52. William Faulkner, "A Rose for Emily," *Selected Short Stories of William Faulkner* (New York: Modern Library, 1961), 49–61. Pierre Bourdieu connects the misleading characterization in this story with the socially constructed expectations of the reader. See Bourdieu, *The Rules of Art: Genesis and Structure of the Literary Field*, trans. Susan Emanuel (Stanford: Stanford University Press, 1995), 322–30.

53. Bal calls this type "implicit" characterization (*Narratology*, 129–31).

54. Willem Brakman, *Ansichten uit Amerika* (Amsterdam: Querido, 1981), 25, 21, 74.

55. Here we depart from Rimmon-Kenan. She considers characterizations on the basis of name and environment as a form of analogy, whereas we see name and environment as elements contiguous to the character. For us, these descriptions therefore belong to metonymic characterization.

56. Theodor W. Adorno, "Notes on Kafka," in *Prisms*, trans. Samuel and Shierry Weber (Cambridge: MIT Press, 1981), 243 ff.

57. Rimmon-Kenan, *Narrative Fiction*, 68–69.

58. Bal, *Narratology*, 132.

59. For an extensive formulation of this criticism, see Gibson, *Towards a Postmodern Theory*, 69–104, 236–44.

60. "The person is no more than a collection of semes . . . Sarrasine is the sum, the point of convergence, of: *turbulence, artistic gift, independence, excess*" (Roland Barthes, *S/Z: An Essay*, trans. Richard Miller [New York: Hill and Wang, 1974], 191). The same opinion is expressed by Philippe Hamon in his classic study of character, "Pour un statut sémiologique du personnage," first published in 1972 and reprinted in Roland Barthes and others, *Poétique du récit* (Paris: Seuil, 1977), 115–80.

61. In "Structuralist Approaches to Character in Narrative: The State of the Art," *Semiotica* 75, nos. 1–2 (1989): 1–24, Uri Margolin offers an elucidating summary of the various structuralist views. He tries to compensate for "the lack of a developed structuralist-semiotic theory of character" (9) by resorting to "possible worlds semantics" (20), which we will discuss in chapter 3.

62. Bal, *Narratology*, 146–47.

63. In *Narrative Discourse Revisited*, Genette writes, "Mieke Bal seems to have – and sometimes to attribute to me . . . – the idea that every narrative statement includes a *focalizer* (character) and a *focalized* (character). . . . For me, there is no focalizing or focalized character. . . ." (72–73).

64. Genette's and Bal's views on focalization are discussed in Pierre Vitoux, "Le jeu de la focalisation," *Poétique* 51 (1982): 359–68. Vitoux rightly mentions "the double necessity" (362) not only of distinguishing between the subject and object of focalization for the sake of analysis but also of studying them together to see how they interrelate.

65. Apart from internal and external focalization, Genette also conceives of "zero focalization" (*Narrative Discourse*, 189). In this respect, we prefer to follow Bal and Rimmon-Kenan, who show such a triad confuses the focalizer with the focalized. External focalization in Genette is in fact the perception that limits itself to the outside of things, and according to Bal and Rimmon-Kenan, this is a matter of the focalized rather than of the focalizer. The latter can be internal in the case of Genette's external focalization since a character too can limit his or her perception to the outside of things. (See Rimmon-Kenan, *Narrative*

Fiction, 74 and Bal, *Narratology*, 142–61.) In order to avoid the confusion between external focalizer and externally focalized object, Vitoux proposes to describe the external focalizer as the "non-delegated" agent of perception (who is situated on the highest level in the narrative) and the internal focalizer as the "delegated" one (perception is delegated to a "lower" agent, a character). (See Vitoux, "Le jeu de la focalisation," 360.) For a lucid presentation of the various views and problems in connection with focalization, see Manfred Jahn, "Windows of Focalization: Deconstructing and Reconstructing a Narratological Concept," *Style* 30, no. 2 (1996): 241–67.

66. Edgar Allan Poe, "Metzengerstein," *The Complete Works of Edgar Allan Poe. Volume II: Tales-Volume I*, ed. James Harrison (New York: AMS Press, 1965), 188.

67. Brakman, *Een weekend in Oostende*, 39.

68. Brakman, *Een weekend in Oostende*, 44.

69. Brakman, *Een weekend in Oostende* 46.

70. Huub Beurskens, *Suikerpruimen gevolgd door Het lam* (Amsterdam: Meulenhoff, 1997), 9–10.

71. See William Edmiston, "Focalization and the First-Person Narrator: A Revision of the Theory," *Poetics Today* 10, no. 4 (1989): 729–44. This article contains an excellent summary of the views developed by Genette, Bal, Cohn, and Rimmon-Kenan in connection with focalization. In his book, *Hindsight and Insight: Focalization in Four Eighteenth-Century French Novels* (University Park: Pennsylvania State University Press, 1991), Edmiston develops his suggestions and provides an interesting overview in "The Evolution of the Concept of Focalization" (147–69).

72. Beurskens, *Suikerpruimen*, 45.

73. Genette, *Narrative Discourse*, 189–90.

74. Beurskens, *Suikerpruimen*, 49.

75. Beurskens, *Suikerpruimen*, 70–71.

76. Rimmon-Kenan, *Narrative Fiction*, 77–82.

77. Malcolm Lowry, *Under the Volcano* (London: Picador, 1990), 3.

78. Louis Paul Boon, *Minuet*, trans. Adrienne Dixon (New York: Persea Books, 1979), 9.

79. Rimmon-Kenan, *Narrative Fiction*, 77–78. Vitoux submits that an internal focalizer may well speculate about the thoughts and feelings of others but that such a speculation in fact amounts to a transgression of the norm since it is normally reserved for the non-delegated focalizer; that is, the one who perceives from the highest level of the narrative ("Le jeu de la focalisation," 363). He is followed in this suggestion by Edmiston, who uses Genette's term "paralepsis" (*Narrative Discourse*, 207–11) "for this type of infraction, in which the narrating self says more than he could possibly know" ("Focalization and the First-Person

Narrator," 741). Note that Edmiston describes this special case of focalization in terms of narration. As we will see, the distinction between narrating self and experiencing self is not as rigorous as the structuralists would wish.

80. Poe, "Metzengerstein," 186.

81. Brouwers, *Sunken Red*, 54–55.

82. Rimmon-Kenan (*Narrative Fiction*, 81–82) does not connect the ideological and psychological aspects. Since we conceive of the psychological aspect in its broadest sense, we incorporate the cognitive, emotional, and ideological aspects into this category. In all three cases, perceptions reflect the inner world of the focalizer, while in the case of the spatio-temporal aspects, the emphasis was on the outside world.

83. Louis Ferron, *De Walsenkoning. Een duik in het autobiografische diepe* (Amsterdam: Bezige Bij, 1993), 83.

84. In "Narrative Structure in Fleming," Umberto Eco connects this Manichean ideology to the Cold War.

85. Mulisch, *Voer voor psychologen*, 104.

86. See Vitoux, "Le jeu de la focalisation," 365. In "Narration et focalisation," *Poétique* 76 (1988): 487–98, Gérard Cordesse systematizes the "articulation of narration and focalization" (489) by distinguishing between focalization under a heterodiegetic regime and focalization under a homodiegetic regime – these terms will be defined in the following section on narration. As a result, focalizer types are usefully connected with narrator types.

87. See for example Genette, *Narrative Discourse*, 212.

88. See for example Gibson, *Towards a Postmodern Theory of Narrative*, 143–78. The reproach cannot only be leveled at structuralist narrative theory but also at a number of more encompassing approaches that study literary narration as part of human communication. Jonathan Culler too has criticized the anthropomorphism of such theories and especially of speech-act narratology ("Problems in the Theory of Fiction," *Diacritics* 14, no. 1 [1984]: 2–11).

89. Ivan Turgenev, "Asya," *First Love and Other Stories*, trans. Richard Freeborn (Oxford: Oxford Paperbacks, 1999), 100.

90. Edgar Allan Poe, *Selected Tales*, ed. Julian Symons (Oxford and New York: Oxford University Press, 1982), 278.

91. Louis Paul Boon, *Chapel Road*, trans. Adrienne Dixon (New York: Hippocrene Books, 1972), 257–58.

92. Kurt Vonnegut, *Slaughterhouse-Five* (London: Jonathan Cape, 1969).

93. Genette, *Narrative Discourse*, 234–37.

94. Rimmon-Kenan, *Narrative Fiction*, 92; Genette, *Narrative Discourse*, 227–34.

95. Lucien Dällenbach, *The Mirror in the Text*, trans. Jeremy Whiteley with Emma Hughes (Cambridge: Polity Press, 1989), 35.

96. Brakman, *Een weekend in Oostende*, 52.

97. Genette, *Narrative Discourse*, 245.

98. Van der Voort, "De analyse van verhalend proza," 44.

99. Cohn, "The Encirclement of Narrative," 159–60.

100. Brakman, *Een weekend in Oostende*, 50.

101. Genette, *Narrative Discourse*, 216–23.

102. Mulisch, *Voer voor psychologen*, 89–231.

103. Rimmon-Kenan, *Narrative Fiction*, 96.

104. Ansgar Nünning defines unreliability as "the discrepancy between the intentions and value system of the narrator and the fore-knowledge and norms of the reader" (" 'But why *will* you say that I am mad?,' " 87).

105. Lanser, *The Narrative Act*, 86.

106. Lanser, *The Narrative Act*, 166.

107. Lanser admits this: "I expect that other theorists will be able to supplement these 'status symbols,' and I would caution against any premature closure of the system." (Lanser, *The Narrative Act*, 173) Lanser also believes status does not suffice to characterize the narrator and therefore adds two other categories: contact (the type and form of the relationship between narrator and narratee) and stance (the type and form of the relationship between the narrator, his or her characters, and the narrated world).

108. Rimmon-Kenan, *Narrative Fiction*, 106–16.

109. Beurskens, *Suikerpruimen*, 76.

110. Beurskens, *Suikerpruimen*, 78.

111. Brian McHale, "Free Indirect Discourse: A Survey of Recent Accounts," *PTL: A Journal for Descriptive Poetics and Theory of Literature* 3 (1978): 249–87.

112. Joyce, *Ulysses*, 197.

113. Meir Sternberg uses the term "direct-speech fallacy" to describe the mistaken prejudice that direct speech would be a faithful and exact representation of words and thoughts: "From the premise that direct speech (unlike the indirect and other kinds of quotation, let alone the narrative of events) *can* reproduce the original speaker's words, it neither follows that it must perforce do so nor that it ought to do so nor, of course, that it actually does so" ("Point of View and the Indirections of Direct Speech," *Language and Style* 15, no. 2 [1982]: 67–117 [68]).

114. Monika Fludernik, *The Fictions of Language and the Languages of Fiction: The Linguistic Representation of Speech and Consciousness* (London: Routledge, 1993), 17, 19.

115. Fludernik, *The Fictions of Language*, 389–433.

116. Fludernik, *The Fictions of Language*, 446–53.

117. Beurskens, *Suikerpruimen*, 10

118. Beurskens, *Suikerpruimen*, 70.

119. The term is somewhat misleading since "the original" does not refer to a reality that exists prior to representation but to the created impression that we are dealing with the representation of an original reality. Originality is the effect of a strategy instead of its point of departure.

120. The term was coined by Roy Pascal, *The Dual Voice: Free Indirect Speech and Its Functioning in the Nineteenth-Century European Novel* (Manchester: Manchester University Press, 1977). A fine summary of the dual-voice approaches is available from Fludernik, *The Fictions of Language*, 322–56.

121. See M. M. Bakhtin, "Discourse in the Novel," *The Dialogic Imagination: Four Essays*, ed. Michael Holquist, trans. Caryl Emerson and Michael Holquist (Austin: University of Texas Press, 1981), 259–422.

122. Ann Banfield, *Unspeakable Sentences: Narration and Representation in the Language of Fiction* (Boston: Routledge & Kegan Paul, 1982).

123. This view derives from the idea that every form of personal expression inevitably includes impersonal patterns: "One can even go on to consider the linguistic expression of emotionality, or of consciousness itself, to be of an intrinsically pre-patterned nature. It then becomes possible to identify both lexical and syntactic expressivity as a strategy of typification or symbolization, employed to symbolize the non-linguistic ([free] indirect) discourse of emotion within the boundaries of *linguistic* consciousness" (Fludernik, *The Fictions of Language*, 426).

124. Genette uses *Hunger* by Knut Hamsun as his example of quoted monologue. After a critical discussion of the position such a monologue occupies in Cohn and Stanzel, he develops a diagram in which this form of consciousness representation appears as extradiegetic, homodiegetic, and internally focalized. See *Narrative Discourse Revisited*, 128.

125. Genette, *Narrative Discourse*, 174.

126. Cohn's letter and Genette's answer appeared under the title "A Narratological Exchange" in *Neverending Stories: Toward a Critical Narratology*, ed. Ann Fehn and others, 258–66 (Princeton: Princeton University Press, 1992).

127. Genette says, "My point is not that it belongs to hetero- rather than to homodiegesis; I simply refuse to 'assign' it to either, i.e. to say that it belongs to one form rather than to another" ("A Narratological Exchange," 264).

128. "In the 'Penelope' section of *Ulysses*, for example, the ruminations are totally those of Molly Bloom, in her own words (or sounds). She is not functioning as narrator, not telling anyone a story after the fact, but simply carrying on normal thinking processes in the present story moment. The thought stream is simply quoted by a totally effaced narrator" (Chatman, *Coming to Terms*, 147).

129. As an example of a second-degree narrative with an intradiegetic narrator, Genette mentions "any kind of recollection that a character has (in a dream or not)" (*Narrative Discourse*, 231).

Chapter 3

POST-CLASSICAL NARRATOLOGY

1. We borrow the term "post-classical" from David Herman, whose introduction to *Narratologies: New Perspectives on Narrative Analysis*, ed. David Herman (Columbus: Ohio State University Press, 1999, 1–30) provides an excellent overview of recent developments in narratology.

2. See for example the research reported on in the journals *Journal of Memory and Language*; *Journal of Experimental Psychology: Learning, Memory and Cognition*; and *Poetics*.

3. Gordon H. Bower and Daniel G. Morrow, "Mental Models in Narrative Comprehension," *Science* 247 (1990): 44–48; Richard Gerrig, *Experiencing Narrative Worlds: On the Psychological Activities of Reading* (New Haven: Yale University Press, 1993).

4. The seminal article in this respect is William Labov and Joshua Waletzky, "Narrative Analysis: Oral Versions of Personal Experience," in *Essays on the Verbal and the Visual*, ed. June Helm, 354–96 (Seattle: University of Washington Press, 1967).

5. A prime example of anthropological narratology can be found in *The Great Code: The Bible and Literature* (London: Ark, 1981) in which Northrop Frye considers Biblical metaphors and narrative procedures as the starting points for (literary) narratives.

6. René Girard, *Deceit, Desire, and the Novel: Self and Other in Literary Structure*, trans. Yvonne Freccero (Baltimore: Johns Hopkins University Press, 1965); *The Scapegoat*, trans. Yvonne Freccero (London: Athlone Press, 1986); and *Things Hidden Since the Foundation of the World*, trans. Stephen Bann and Michael Metteer (Stanford: Stanford University Press, 1987).

7. For Freudian narratology, see Peter Brooks, *Reading for the Plot: Design and Intention in Narrative* (Oxford: Oxford University Press, 1984) and also *Psychoanalysis and Storytelling* (Oxford: Blackwell, 1994). For Lacanian narratology, see for example Robert Con Davis, ed., *Lacan and Narration: The Psychoanalytic Difference in Narrative Theory* (Baltimore: Johns Hopkins University, 1983).

8. Gérard Genette, *Palimpsests: Literature in the Second Degree*, trans. Channa Newman and Claude Doubinsky (Lincoln: University of Nebraska Press, 1998). For a recent study of postmodern rewriting, see Christian Moraru, *Rewriting: Postmodern Narrative and Cultural Critique in the Age of Cloning* (Albany: State University of New York Press, 2001). Moraru makes the link with cybernarratology in the chapter entitled, "The Pleasure of the Hypertext" (117–23).

9. George Landow's most influential publication is *Hypertext: The Convergence of Contemporary Critical Theory and Technology* (Baltimore: Johns Hopkins University Press, 1992).

10. Jaron Lanier and Frank Biocca, "An Insider's View of the Future of Virtual Reality," *Journal of Communications* 42, no. 4 (1992): 150–72. Marie-Laure Ryan says, "Though *virtual reality* is the term that has captured the imagination of the general public, arguably because of the poetic appeal of its built-in oxymoron, the scientific community prefers terms such as *artificial reality* (the physico-spatial equivalent of artificial intelligence) or *virtual environments*. The official technical journal of the field, *Presence*, is subtitled *Teleoperators and Virtual Environments*" (*Narrative as Virtual Reality: Immersion and Interactivity in Literature and Electronic Media* [Baltimore: Johns Hopkins University Press, 2001], 358).

11. See Marie-Laure Ryan's articles, "Cyberage Narratology: Computers, Metaphor, and Narrative," in *Narratologies*, ed. David Herman, 113–41 (Columbus: Ohio State University Press, 1999); and "Cyberspace, Virtuality, and the Text," in *Cyberspace Textuality: Computer Technology and Literary Theory*, ed. Marie-Laure Ryan, 78–107 (Bloomington: Indiana University Press, 1999).

12. "I wish to challenge the recurrent practice of applying the theories of literary criticism to a new empirical field, seemingly without any reassessment of the terms and concepts involved. This lack of self-reflection places the research in direct danger of turning the vocabulary of literary theory into a set of unfocused metaphors" (Espen J. Aarseth, *Cybertext: Perspectives on Ergodic Literature* [Baltimore: Johns Hopkins University Press, 1997], 14).

13. "I refer to the idea of a narrative text as a labyrinth, a game, or an imaginary world. . . . The problem with these powerful metaphors, when they begin to affect the critic's perspective and judgment, is that they enable a systematic misrepresentation . . . a spatiodynamic fallacy where the narrative is not perceived as a presentation of a world but rather as that world itself. . . . The study of cybertext reveals the misprision of the spaciodynamic [*sic*] metaphors of narrative theory. . . . It seems to me that the cybertexts fit the game-world-labyrinth terminology in a way that exposes its deficiencies when used on narrative texts" (Aarseth, *Cybertext*, 3–5).

14. Ryan, *Narrative as Virtual Reality*, 347–55. "Literary texts can thus be either self-reflexive or immersive, or they can alternate between these two stances through a game of in and out . . . but they cannot offer both experiences at the same time" (284). Roland Barthes introduces the term "writerly" text in *S/Z*, 4.

15. A schematic representation of this synthesis is available from Ryan, *Narrative as Virtual Reality*, 192.

16. "The critical discourse that will secure the place of interactive texts in literary history may still remain to be invented, but it is not too early to derive from the hypertext some cognitive lessons about the nuts and bolts of the reading process" (Ryan, *Narrative as Virtual Reality*, 226).

17. Janet Murray, *Hamlet on the Holodeck: The Future of Narrative in Cyberspace* (New York: The Free Press, 1997).

18. See for example Hans Bertens, *The Idea of the Postmodern: A History* (London: Routledge, 1995). In this section, we are primarily dealing with the postmodernism that is closely connected to poststructuralism and deconstructionism.

19. Jean-François Lyotard, *The Postmodern Condition: A Report on Knowledge*, trans. Geoff Bennington and Brian Massumi (Minneapolis: University of Minnesota Press, 1984).

20. Mark Currie, *Postmodern Narrative Theory* (London: MacMillan, 1998).

21. Currie means that a narratological analysis must take in the political and cultural context. We will elucidate this widely accepted suggestion with reference to feminist narratology.

22. See for example Jacques Lacan, "The Insistence of the Letter in the Unconscious," in *Modern Criticism and Theory*, ed. David Lodge, trans. Jan Miel, 79–106 (London: Longman, 1988); Hayden White, *Metahistory: The Historical Imagination in Nineteenth-Century Europe* (Baltimore: Johns Hopkins University Press, 1973); and Homi Bhabha, ed., *Nation and Narration* (London: Routledge, 1989). An overview of the disciplines that turn narratology into a general method to analyze culture is available from Christopher Nash, ed., *Narrative in Culture: The Uses of Storytelling in the Sciences, Philosophy and Literature* (London: Routledge, 1990). Along the same lines, see Steven Cohan and Linda Shires, *Telling Stories: A Theoretical Analysis of Narrative Fiction* (London: Routledge, 1988).

23. Daniel Punday sees this embeddedness as the materiality of the text with which he not only means language but also material reality as evoked in the stories told about it. If a novel brings up a Victorian woman or uses a cathedral as its setting, this woman and this cathedral are already embedded in other narratives, for instance for the reader. Punday considers "this extra-textual object of reference as always already involved in other narratives" (*Narrative after Deconstruction* [Albany: State University of New York Press, 2003], 143).

24. Punday says about the tension between the text's openness and totality: "The tension between these two qualities of discourse is an inherent part of the post-deconstructive turn to narrative. As I have suggested, what attracts critics to narrative is its ability to be ambiguously deconstructive. Deconstruction is seen by critics variously as too much concerned with textual slippage or too much enamored with inescapable textual laws. . . . Narrative seems to accept both textual indeterminacy and totality while bringing this conflict to the surface and – most importantly – suggesting that these two might be resolved productively" (*Narrative after Deconstruction*, 7). As Punday repeatedly shows (25–26), this tension is also inherent in deconstruction itself. His so-called post-deconstructive theory of narrative is in fact "loosely deconstructive" (140); it proves a seamless fit for

a deconstruction that does not see reality as a text but rather as a continuous tension between reality and text. Only Punday's emphasis on re-integration and a new totality could somehow be called post-deconstructive.

25. Gibson, *Towards a Postmodern Theory of Narrative*, 212–35.

26. Currie, *Postmodern Narrative Theory*, 54–61.

27. Paul de Man, *Blindness and Insight: Essays in the Rhetoric of Contemporary Criticism* (London: Methuen, 1971).

28. Gibson, *Towards a Postmodern Theory of Narrative*, 236–74.

29. Currie, *Postmodern Narrative Theory*, 113. This theoretical attention for derailment fits the concrete narrative deregulation that is often called typical of postmodern narrative strategies. See for example Michael Roemer, *Telling Stories: Postmodernism and the Invalidation of Traditional Narrative* (Boston: Rowman & Littlefield, 1995).

30. Ursula K. Heise, *Chronoschisms: Time, Narrative, and Postmodernism* (Cambridge: Cambridge University Press, 1997), 40.

31. Heise, *Chronoschisms*, 23–47.

32. Heise, *Chronoschisms*, 26; Joseph Francese, *Narrating Postmodern Time and Space* (Albany: State University of New York Press, 1997), 107–9.

33. Punday refers to Lyotard, among others, when he is talking about "simultaneous and heterogeneous temporalities" (*Narrative after Deconstruction*, 54).

34. Gibson, *Towards a Postmodern Theory of Narrative*, 179–84.

35. Following Derrida, postmodern narratology holds that repetition precedes the sign and that therefore there is not first an abstract sign (for example, a phoneme) that is then approached and staged in endless repetitions. See for example Jacques Derrida, *Speech and Phenomena and Other Essays on Husserl's Theory of Signs*, trans. David B. Allison (Evanston IL: Northwestern University Press, 1973). In the literary theory of American deconstruction, this view on repetition has been developed by J. Hillis Miller, *Fiction and Repetition: Seven English Novels* (Oxford: Basil Blackwell, 1982).

36. Punday, *Narrative after Deconstruction*, 113–15.

37. This view can be traced back to Derrida's concept of "dissemination" (the spatial dispersion of meanings), which is inherent in "*differance*" (the endlessly delayed attribution of meaning). See for example Jacques Derrida, "Differance," *Margins of Philosophy*, trans. Alan Bass (Chicago: University of Chicago Press, 1982), 1–28.

38. Punday describes postmodernist space as "the ongoing transformation of one space into another" (*Narrative after Deconstruction*, 76). He relies on Edward Soja's famous *Postmodern Geographies: The Reassertion of Space in Critical Social Theory* (London: Verso, 1989), 222–48.

39. The rhizome is an underground stem that puts out lateral shoots and thus

produces a network without a center and without a fixed starting point. See Gilles Deleuze and Félix Guattari, "Introduction: Rhizome," in *A Thousand Plateaus*, trans. Brian Massumi (Minneapolis: University of Minnesota Press, 1987), 3–25. For an application within the postmodern interpretation of narrative, see Punday, *Narrative after Deconstruction*, 129–30.

40. Francese, *Narrating Postmodern Time and Space*, 107, 155.

41. Punday, *Narrative after Deconstruction*, 39.

42. Punday, *Narrative after Deconstruction*, 80–81.

43. Punday develops this idea with the help of Derrida's views on "the rhetorical topos and the physical site" as geographical and physical space (*Narrative after Deconstruction*, 33).

44. Punday, *Narrative after Deconstruction*, 128–31.

45. See for example Barry Smart, *Postmodernity* (London: Routledge, 1993).

46. David Harvey, *The Condition of Postmodernity: An Enquiry into the Origins of Cultural Change* (Oxford: Blackwell, 1989), 155–58.

47. See for example Lyotard, *The Postmodern Condition*; Jean Baudrillard, *The Consumer Society: Myths and Structures* (Thousand Oaks CA: Sage Publications, 1998); Fredric Jameson, *Postmodernism, or, The Cultural Logic of Late Capitalism* (Durham: Duke University Press, 1991). Punday offers a brief summary of these theories and connects them with postmodern time-space (*Narrative after Deconstruction*, 87–106).

48. See for example Jacques Derrida, "White Mythology," *New Literary History* 6 (1974): 527–64; Paul de Man, *Allegories of Reading: Figural Language in Rousseau, Nietzsche, Rilke, and Proust* (New Haven: Yale University Press, 1979); Harold Bloom, *A Map of Misreading* (New York: Oxford University Press, 1975). For a brief overview of the deconstructionist's attention to metaphor, see Vincent B. Leitch, *Deconstructive Criticism: An Advanced Introduction* (London: Hutchinson, 1983), 45–54.

49. Edgar Allan Poe, "Berenice," in *Selected Tales*, ed. Julian Symons (Oxford and New York: Oxford University Press, 1982), 18–25. See also Lacan's abovementioned essay "The Insistence of the Letter in the Unconscious."

50. Marie Bonaparte, *The Life and Works of Edgar Allan Poe: A Psychoanalytic Interpretation*, trans. John Rodker (London: Imago, 1949), 213–19.

51. Mark Currie uses the term "cultural schizophrenia" in *Postmodern Narrative Theory*, 96–113. His analysis is based on Gilles Deleuze and Félix Guattari, *Anti-Oedipus: Capitalism and Schizophrenia*, trans. Robert Hurley, Mark Seem, and Helen R. Lane (Minneapolis: University of Minnesota Press, 1983) and Deleuze and Guattari, *A Thousand Plateaus*.

52. Jameson, *Postmodernism*, 1–54.

53. Patrick O'Neill, *Fictions of Discourse: Reading Narrative Theory* (Toronto: University of Toronto Press, 1994), 23–26, 107–31.

54. O'Neill, *Fictions of Discourse*, 58

55. Thus Gibson's readings of Stevenson and Beckett sometimes remain very traditional. When dealing with *The Strange Case of Dr Jekyll and Mr Hyde*, Gibson speaks about "the voice of a third person narrator in a first person narrative." His conclusion is, "Another opposition has broken down: that between narrator and narrated, I and he" (*Towards a Postmodern Theory of Narrative*, 140). Such a reading perfectly fits Genette's theory. When Gibson analyzes the monster in Beckett, he largely reduces it to a classical reading of the textual image of the body. He discusses Beckett's preference for the crippled and aging body as an attack on traditional "anatomo-politics" (262), but this is saying little more than that the body in Beckett's work deviates from the dominant body image.

56. See David Hawkes, *Ideology* (London: Routledge, 1996) for an excellent overview of the various definitions of ideology.

57. Barthes, *S/Z*, 18–20.

58. Philippe Hamon, *Texte et idéologie: Valeurs, hiérarchies et évaluations dans l'œuvre littéraire* (Paris: PUF, 1984).

59. Hamon, *Texte et idéologie*, 20.

60. More generally, Hamon speaks of four crucial domains in which the text's ideological effect takes shape: the character's gaze, language, work, and ethics (Hamon, *Texte et idéologie*, 19–22).

61. Liesbeth Korthals Altes, *Le salut par la fiction? Sens, valeurs et narrativité dans "Le Roi des Aulnes" de Michel Tournier* (Amsterdam: Rodopi, 1992).

62. Liesbeth Korthals Altes, "Le tournant éthique dans la théorie littéraire: impasse ou ouverture," *Etudes littéraires* 31, no. 3 (1999): 39–56.

63. Vincent Jouve, *Poétique des valeurs* (Paris: PUF, 2001).

64. Jouve, *Poétique des valeurs*, 143–48.

65. See for example Bakhtin, *The Dialogic Imagination* and also his *Problems of Dostoyevsky's Poetics*, ed. and trans. Caryl Emerson (Minneapolis: University of Minnesota Press, 1984). The Russian original of the latter was published in 1929.

66. Boris Uspensky, *A Poetics of Composition*, trans. Susan Wittig and Valentina Zavarin (Berkeley: University of California Press, 1973). The Russian original was published in 1970. The translators used a manuscript revised by the author.

67. James Phelan, "Narrative Discourse, Literary Character, and Ideology," in *Reading Narrative: Form, Ethics, Ideology*, ed. James Phelan, 132–46 (Columbus: Ohio State University Press, 1989).

68. James Phelan, *Narrative as Rhetoric: Technique, Audiences, Ethics, Ideology* (Columbus: Ohio State University, 1996). For the discussion of Hemingway, see 59–104. In his early work as well, Phelan emphasized temporal evolution

and characterization. See *Reading People, Reading Plots: Character, Progression, and the Interpretation of Narrative* (Chicago: University of Chicago Press, 1989).

69. Ross Chambers, *Story and Situation: Narrative Seduction and the Power of Fiction* (Minneapolis: University of Minnesota Press, 1984), 146.

70. Peter Rabinowitz, *Before Reading: Narrative Conventions and the Politics of Interpretation* (Columbus: Ohio State University Press, 1987). The four rules are summarized on 42–46.

71. Wayne Booth, *The Company We Keep: An Ethics of Fiction* (Berkeley: University of California Press, 1998), 175.

72. Booth, *The Company We Keep*, 176.

73. Booth, *The Company We Keep*, 178.

74. Booth, *The Company We Keep*, 179–201.

75. Adam Zachary Newton, *Narrative Ethics* (Cambridge: Harvard University Press, 1995), 22.

76. Newton, *Narrative Ethics*, 22.

77. Newton, *Narrative Ethics*, 21.

78. Newton, *Narrative Ethics*, 47–50.

79. J. Hillis Miller, *The Ethics of Reading: Kant, de Man, Eliot, Trollope, James, and Benjamin* (New York: Columbia University Press, 1987), 20.

80. Miller, *The Ethics of Reading*, 120.

81. "But if Kant cannot tell you exactly what the law is, where it is, or where it comes from, he can nevertheless tell you to what it is analogous. . . . [T]he law as such . . . is displaced by metaphor or some other form of analogy" (Miller, *The Ethics of Reading*, 20).

82. Miller, *The Ethics of Reading*, 23.

83. Miller, *The Ethics of Reading*, 38–39.

84. Booth, *The Company We Keep*, 75. In this connection, J. Hillis Miller speaks of "baseless positing" (*The Ethics of Reading*, 55). The reader's value judgment does not rest on a foundation made up of the text's narrative procedures; it is a judgment that creates its own grounding. Ross Chambers too says that the authority of a narrative strategy does not reach any further than the readiness of the reader to recognize that authority (*Story and Situation*, 213–14). There is no direct connection between a specific narrative strategy and a specific ethical stance. This derives not only from the reader but also from the text itself. A specific strategy only works via the detour of the whole text of which it is a part. James Phelan says that "the relation between ideology and a particular element of narrative technique is always mediated by the relation of that element to the rest of the narrative" (*Reading People*, 145).

85. See Booth, *The Company We Keep*, 169–200.

86. Chambers, *Story and Situation*, 50–72.

87. Newton, *Narrative Ethics*, 58.

88. James Phelan and Mary Patricia Martin, "The Lessons of 'Weymouth': Homodiegesis, Unreliability, Ethics and *The Remains of the Day*," in Herman, *Narratologies*, 88–109. The term "ethical positioning" is mentioned for the first time on 88 and elucidated on 100–104. Phelan also discusses the unreliable narrator in *Narrative as Rhetoric*, 105–18.

89. "The more general conclusion, then, is that homodiegesis allows the lack of full coherence between the roles of character and of narrator when that lack both serves the larger purpose of the narrative and when it is registered only after the incoherence operates" (Phelan and Martin, "The Lessons of 'Weymouth,' " 93).

90. "Because the homodiegesis blocks our access to conclusive signals from Ishiguro and so transfers the responsibility for disambiguating the scene to the flesh-and-blood reader, the deciding factor in how we carry out that responsibility is our individual ethical beliefs as they interact with our understanding of [the first-person narrator] as a particular character in a particular situation" (Phelan and Martin, "The Lessons of 'Weymouth,' " 103).

91. Monika Fludernik, "Fiction vs. Non-Fiction: Narratological Differentiations," in *Erzählen und Erzähltheorie im 20. Jahrhundert: Festschrift für Wilhelm Füger*, ed. Jörg Helbig, 85–103 (Heidelberg: Carl Winter Universitätsverlag, 2001). Fludernik writes, "Only in fictional narrative do we have true cases of unreliability. It is only in fiction that we assume that the narrator's contradictions have an ulterior purpose, that of alerting us to the author's intentions. Since we cannot check out the author's intentions, this thesis will remain an assumption on the part of the reader" (100).

92. Susan S. Lanser, "Toward a Feminist Narratology," *Style* 20, no. 3 (1986): 341–63.

93. Susan Sniader Lanser, *Fictions of Authority: Women Writers and Narrative Voice* (Ithaca NY: Cornell University Press, 1992), 23.

94. Robyn Warhol, "Guilty Cravings: What Feminist Narratology Can Do for Cultural Studies," in Herman, *Narratologies*, 342; Kathy Mezei, ed., *Ambiguous Discourse: Feminist Narratology and British Women Writers* (Chapel Hill: University of North Carolina Press, 1996), 4–5.

95. Pierre Bourdieu, *Distinction: A Social Critique of the Judgment of Taste*, trans. Richard Nice (London: Routledge, 1984), 101–14.

96. Lanser says first, "Because literary form has a far more uncertain relation to social history than does representational content, even a fully materialist poetics would be hard-pressed to establish definitive correspondences between social ideology and narrative form. I have nonetheless considered it fruitful to venture speculations about causal relationships that others may be able to estab-

lish or refute" (*Fictions of Authority*, 23). Slightly later Lanser's reader witnesses such a causal speculation, when she reproaches Ian Watt's traditional treatment of the novel for being blind to "causal relationships between gender and genre" (37).

97. Ruth E. Page, "Feminist Narratology? Literary and Linguistic Perspectives on Gender and Narrativity," *Language and Literature* 12, no. 1 (2003): 43–56.

98. Page, "Feminist Narratology?" 53.

99. See Warhol, "Guilty Cravings," 342.

100. Nancy K. Miller, *Subject to Change: Reading Feminist Writing* (New York: Columbia University Press, 1988), 4–5.

101. Teresa de Lauretis, ed., *Feminist Studies/Critical Studies* (London: Macmillan, 1986), 9.

102. Mária Minich Brewer, "A Loosening of Tongues: From Narrative Economy to Women Writing," *Modern Language Notes* 99, no. 5 (1984): 1141–61.

103. See Lanser, "Toward a Feminist Narratology," 353–54.

104. For example Susan Sniader Lanser, *Fictions of Authority*, 8, 35.

105. "For the feminist narratologists working a decade ago, gender is a category that preexists the text, an entity, that shapes the text's production and reception" (Warhol, "Guilty Cravings," 347).

106. Sally Robinson, *Engendering the Subject: Gender and Self-Representation in Contemporary Women's Fiction* (Albany: State University of New York Press, 1991), 4.

107. Lanser, *Fictions of Authority*, 5.

108. Lanser, "Toward a Feminist Narratology," 341.

109. Sandra M. Gilbert and Susan Gubar, *The Madwoman in the Attic: The Woman Writer and the Nineteenth-Century Literary Imagination* (New Haven: Yale University Press, 1979), iii. From the end of the eighties onward, Gilbert and Gubar produced a three-part sequel, *No Man's Land*, in which they discussed twentieth-century women writers against the same background of the "battle of the sexes." See Sandra M. Gilbert and Susan Gubar, *The War of the Words* (New Haven: Yale University Press, 1988); *The Place of the Woman Writer in the Twentieth Century: Sexchanges* (New Haven: Yale University Press, 1991); and *The Place of the Woman Writer in the Twentieth Century: Letters from the Front* (New Haven: Yale University Press, 1994).

110. Gilbert and Gubar, *The Madwoman in the Attic*, 49–52.

111. Gilbert and Gubar, *The Madwoman in the Attic*, 73.

112. Gilbert and Gubar, *The Madwoman in the Attic*, 78. Nancy Miller rejects this direct connection between character and author: "I hope it is understood that I am not suggesting we read a heroine as her author's double" (*Subject to Change*, 39).

113. Nancy Miller therefore resists Roland Barthes's famous view about the death of the author. See her essay, "Changing the Subject: Authorship, Writing, and the Reader," in de Lauretis, *Feminist Studies/Critical Studies*, 102–20 (especially 104–7).

114. Lanser, "Toward a Feminist Narratology," 343–44.

115. Tania Modleski, "Feminism and the Power of Interpretation: Some Critical Readings," in de Lauretis, *Feminist Studies/Critical Studies*, 121–38 (especially 128–29). Modleski refers to Luce Irigaray, *This Sex Which Is Not One*, trans. Catherine Porter with Carolyn Burke (Ithaca: Cornell University Press, 1985).

116. Gilbert and Gubar, *The Madwoman in the Attic*, 16–17.

117. Modleski, "Feminism and the Power of Interpretation," 136.

118. "A negative hermeneutic that discloses [the texts'] complicity with patriarchal ideology, and a positive hermeneutic that recuperates the utopian moment – the authentic kernel – from which they draw a significant portion of their emotional power" (28) (Patrocinio P. Schweickart, "Reading Ourselves: Toward a Feminist Theory of Reading," in *Speaking of Gender*, ed. Elaine Showalter, 17–44 [New York: Routledge, 1989]).

119. Schweickart, "Reading Ourselves," 30–31. More generally, this sympathetic reading would have to enhance female integration: "Feminist readings of female texts are motivated by the need 'to connect,' to recuperate, or to formulate – they come to the same thing – the context, the tradition, that would link women writers to one another, to women readers and critics, and to the larger community of women" (32).

120. Schweickart, "Reading Ourselves," 39.

121. Nancy K. Miller, *The Heroine's Text: Readings in the French and English Novel 1722–1782* (New York: Columbia University Press, 1980), x.

122. Mieke Bal, *Femmes imaginaires: L'ancien testament au risque d'une narratologie critique* (Paris: Nizet, 1986), 15. This book was translated in a thoroughly revised version (reducing and abridging the theoretical sections) as *Lethal Love: Feminist Literary Readings of Biblical Love Stories* (Bloomington: Indiana University Press, 1987). The page mentioned in this note did not make it into the translation.

123. Bal, *Lethal Love*, 111.

124. Bal, *Lethal Love*, 128.

125. Lanser, "Toward a Feminist Narratology," 350.

126. Lanser, *Fictions of Authority*, 8, 35.

127. Lanser, *Fictions of Authority*, 7.

128. Lanser, *Fictions of Authority*, 8.

129. Susan S. Lanser, "Sexing the Narrative: Propriety, Desire, and the Engendering of Narratology," *Narrative* 3 (1995): 85–94. The unreliable female heterodiegetic narrator is discussed on page 88. Lanser recapitulates this argu-

ment in "Sexing Narratology: Toward a Gendered Poetics of Narrative Voice," in *Grenzüberschreitungen: Narratologie im Kontext / Transcending Boundaries: Narratology in Context*, ed. Walter Grünzweig and Andreas Solbach, 167–83 (Tübingen: Gunter Narr, 1999). Unreliability is discussed on page 178.

130. The things that may be talked about depend not only on sex and gender but also on sexual preference. Thus it is easier to talk about heterosexual love than about homosexual love. See Lanser, "Sexing the Narrative," 91.

131. Lanser, *Fictions of Authority*, 21–22.

132. Lanser, *Fictions of Authority*, 21.

133. Lanser, *Fictions of Authority*, 22.

134. Robyn Warhol, *Gendered Interventions: Narrative Discourse in the Victorian Novel* (New Brunswick: Rutgers University Press, 1989).

135. See Luc Herman, *Concepts of Realism* (Columbia: Camden House, 1996), 19–23.

136. Warhol, *Gendered Interventions*, 18.

137. Robinson, *Engendering the Subject*, 20.

138. Brewer relies on Annie Leclerc, who sees "the adventure story" as "a model for narrative in general" (Brewer, "A Loosening of Tongues," 1150). The language of such a story is "the discourse of male desire recounting itself through the narrative of adventure, project, enterprise, and conquest" (1151) and that is always "the discourse of desire as separation and mastery" (1153).

139. Lanser, "Toward a Feminist Narratology," 357.

140. Page, "Feminist Narratology?" 46.

141. Lanser, "Sexing the Narrative," 93; Lanser, "Sexing Narratology," 180–81.

142. This essay constitutes the fifth chapter of Teresa de Lauretis, *Alice Doesn't: Feminism, Semiotics, Cinema* (London: Macmillan, 1984), 103–57.

143. De Lauretis, *Alice Doesn't*, 106. See also Robinson, *Engendering the Subject*.

144. "The Oedipus story . . . is in fact paradigmatic to all narratives" (de Lauretis, *Alice Doesn't*, 112). And also: "All narrative . . . is overlaid with what has been called an Oedipal logic" (125).

145. De Lauretis, *Alice Doesn't*, 121.

146. De Lauretis, *Alice Doesn't*, 143.

147. De Lauretis, *Alice Doesn't*, 149.

148. De Lauretis, *Feminist Studies/Critical Studies*, 12.

149. See for example Brewer, "A Loosening of Tongues," 1157–59.

150. See for example Hélène Cixous, "The Laugh of the Medusa," trans. Keith Cohen and Paula Cohen, *Signs* 1, no. 4 (1976): 875–93.

151. Rosi Braidotti, *Nomadic Subjects: Embodiment and Sexual Difference in Contemporary Feminist Theory* (New York: Columbia University Press, 1994). Traditional, "male" theories consider desire a finite focus on an object to be reached and pos-

sessed. As such, infinite, "female" desire is a perverse mixed form. See Teresa de Lauretis, *The Practice of Love: Lesbian Sexuality and Perverse Desire* (Bloomington: Indiana University Press, 1994).

152. Miller, *Subject to Change*, 14. Miller also speaks of "rematerializing the relations of subjectivity, writing, and literary theory" (16).

153. Braidotti, *Nomadic Subjects*, 6.

154. In this respect we agree with Ruth Page, who says, "It would seem more convincing to argue that if narrative form has anything to do with gender, then this is more prominent when the performance of that story is closely related to gender issues" (Page, "Feminist Narratology?" 52).

155. Thomas Pavel's most important work in this area is *Fictional Worlds* (Cambridge: Harvard University Press, 1986).

156. See for example Doležel's "Narrative Modalities," *Journal of Literary Semantics* 5, no. 1 (1976): 5–15 and "Extensional and Intensional Narrative Worlds," *Poetics* 8 (1979): 193–212. A more recent and encompassing treatment is *Heterocosmica: Fiction and Possible Worlds* (Baltimore: Johns Hopkins University Press, 1998).

157. See especially Marie-Laure Ryan, *Possible Worlds, Artificial Intelligence, and Narrative Theory* (Bloomington: Indiana University Press, 1992).

158. Ruth Ronen, *Possible Worlds in Literary Theory* (Cambridge: Cambridge University Press, 1994).

159. David Herman, "Hypothetical Focalization," *Narrative* 2, no. 3 (1994): 230–53.

160. For the discussion of these three meanings of virtual reality, see Ryan, *Narrative as Virtual Reality*, 25–74. As an example of a theory connecting cybernarratology and modal logic, she presents the views of Pierre Lévy, who sees the transformation of modal operators (for example from "possibility" to "actuality") as a process of virtualization and/or actualization (35–39). Ryan discusses possible worlds theory in *Narrative as Virtual Reality* on pages 99–105.

161. For the discussion of referential speech acts, see John Searle, *Speech Acts: An Essay in the Philosophy of Language* (Cambridge: Cambridge University Press, 1969), 72–96. Susan Lanser deals with this view in "Appendix: Speech Theory and the Status of Fictional Discourse" (*The Narrative Act*, 283–94).

162. This paragraph is based on Ryan, *Narrative as Virtual Reality*, 99–105.

163. See for example the chapter entitled "Lector in Fabula," in Umberto Eco, *The Role of the Reader: Explorations in the Semiotics of Texts* (Bloomington: Indiana University Press, 1979), 200–260.

164. Atte Jongstra, *Het huis M. Memoires van een spreker* (Amsterdam: Contact, 1993).

165. Willem Brakman, *De sloop der dingen* (Amsterdam: Querido, 2000), 118.

166. Brakman, *De sloop der dingen*, 85.

167. Doležel, *Heterocosmica*, 113–32.

168. Doležel, *Heterocosmica*, 121.

169. Claude Bremond already devoted attention to these aspects in the early stages of narratology, but according to Ronen, he still overemphasized the actually selected possibilities in a specific narrative development. See Bremond, *Logique du récit* and "The Logic of Narrative Possibilities," *New Literary History* 11, no. 3 (1980): 387–411.

170. Louis Ferron, *De keisnijder van Fichtenwald* (Amsterdam: Bezige Bÿ, 1976).

171. Herman, "Hypothetical Focalization," 234–35.

172. "The actual world is the world from which I speak and in which I am immersed, while the nonfactual possible worlds are those at which I am looking from the outside" (Ryan, *Narrative as Virtual Reality*, 101).

173. Ryan, *Narrative as Virtual Reality*, 103–5.

174. Salman Rushdie, *Haroun and the Sea of Stories* (London: Granta Books, 1990), 21.

175. See Hans Robert Jauss, *Toward an Aesthetic of Reception*, trans. Timothy Bahti (Minneapolis: University of Minnesota Press, 1982), which contains the seminal essay, "Literary History as a Challenge to Literary Theory" (originally delivered as a lecture in 1967); Wolfgang Iser, *The Implied Reader: Patterns of Communication in Prose Fiction from Bunyan to Beckett*, trans. W. Iser (Baltimore: Johns Hopkins University Press, 1974); and Iser, *The Act of Reading: A Theory of Aesthetic Response*, trans. W. Iser (Baltimore: Johns Hopkins University Press, 1978).

176. Iser here joins Roman Ingarden, who said that a text contains "places of indeterminacy" (*Unbestimmtheitsstellen*) because a description can never match reality in terms of completion and concreteness. A described table cannot be looked at from all sides; a described event is never seen immediately. As a result, many things remain unclear and unspecified in the text. The reader always sees only aspects of the whole. See Roman Ingarden, *The Literary Work of Art*, trans. George G. Grabowicz (Evanston: Northwestern University Press, 1973). The German version was published in 1931.

177. Rimmon-Kenan, *Narrative Fiction*, 117–29.

178. "The very concept of narrative has been broadened, partly under the influence of constructivist theories in the social sciences, to designate a manner of perceiving, organizing, constructing meaning, a mode of cognition different from – but in no way inferior to – logical or discursive thinking" (Rimmon-Kenan, *Narrative Fiction*, 2nd ed., 146).

179. See Elrud Ibsch, "The Cognitive Turn in Narratology," *Poetics Today* 11, no. 2 (1990): 411–18.

180. Gerrig considers such a reading as a trip carrying the reader to another

world on the wings of a narrative script. Upon his or her return, the reader would always be more or less changed. See Richard Gerrig, *Experiencing Narrative Worlds: On the Psychological Activities of Reading* (New Haven: Yale University Press, 1993). Victor Nell considers reading as a form of play absorbing the reader so completely that he or she goes through "cognitive changes." See Victor Nell, *Lost in a Book: The Psychology of Reading for Pleasure* (New Haven: Yale University Press, 1998), 8.

181. "The crucial step in this analysis is to distinguish *text features* from *text effects* . . . . We use the term *text feature* to refer to anything that can be objectively identified in the text. . . . In contrast, *text effects* refer to events in the mind of the reader" (277) (Peter Dixon and Marisa Bortolussi, "Prolegomena for a Science of Psychonarratology," in *New Perspectives on Narrative Perspective*, ed. Willie van Peer and Seymour Chatman [Albany: State University of New York Press, 2001], 275–87).

182. See especially Marvin Minsky, "A Framework for Representing Knowledge," in *Frame Conceptions and Text Understanding*, ed. Dieter Menzing, 1–25(New York: De Gruyter, 1979).

183. Manfred Jahn, "Frames, Preferences, and the Reading of Third-Person Narratives: Towards a Cognitive Narratology," *Poetics Today* 18, no. 4 (1997): 441–68.

184. Nünning, " 'But why *will* you say that I am mad?' "

185. Bal, "Notes on Narrative Embedding," *Poetics Today* 2, no. 2 (1981): 41–59.

186. Jahn uses Stanzel's reflector concept, but what he says about it allows us to equate it with the internal focalizer.

187. For his discussion of this process, Jahn starts from an article by Menakhem Perry, "Literary Dynamics: How the Order of a Text Creates Its Meanings," *Poetics Today* 1, nos. 1–2 (1979): 35–64, 311–61 and from the already mentioned book by Sternberg, *Expositional Modes and Temporal Ordering in Fiction*.

188. See Seymour Chatman's chapter about description in *Coming to Terms*, 22–37. Chatman discusses "The room was dark" on page 30.

189. Flaubert, *Madame Bovary*, 52.

190. Fludernik, *The Fictions of Language*, 72 ff.

191. David Herman, "Scripts, Sequences, and Stories: Elements of a Postclassical Narratology," PMLA 112 (1997): 1046–59.

192. For this definition, Herman uses Dennis Mercadal, *A Dictionary of Artificial Intelligence* (New York: Van Nostrand, 1990).

193. Herman, "Scripts, Sequences, and Stories," 1051.

194. See also Prince, *A Dictionary of Narratology* and especially the essay by Rachel Giora and Yeshayahu Shen, "Degrees of Narrativity and Strategies of Semantic Reduction," *Poetics* 22 (1994): 447–58.

195. Herman, "Scripts, Sequences, and Stories," 1054.

196. See Ansgar Nünning, "Informationsübertragung oder Informationskonstruktion? Grundzüge und Konsequenzen eines konstruktivistischen Modells von Kommunikation," *Humankybernetik* 30, no. 4 (1989): 127–40. The system theorist Niklas Luhmann has also been inspired by scientists who have contributed to the basis of the constructivist paradigm, such as Talcott Parsons and Heinz von Förster. See for example Niklas Luhmann, *Social Systems*, trans. John Bednarz with Dirk Baecker (Stanford: Stanford University Press, 1995).

197. Monika Fludernik, *Towards a "Natural" Narratology* (London and New York: Routledge, 1996).

198. Fludernik suggests that her theory partially parallels the work of Paul Ricœur. See especially the latter's *Time and Narrative*, vols. 1–2, trans. Kathleen McLaughlin and David Pellauer (Chicago: University of Chicago Press, 1984–85); vol. 3, trans. Kathleen Blamey and David Pellauer (Chicago: University of Chicago Press, 1988).

199. For her discussion of this mechanism, Fludernik was inspired by Jonathan Culler's chapter on naturalization in his *Structuralist Poetics* (131–60). Culler's term adds an extra dimension to the meaning of the word "natural" in Fludernik's title.

Bibliography

Aarseth, Espen J. *Cybertext: Perspectives on Ergodic Literature*. Baltimore: Johns Hopkins University Press, 1997.

Adorno, Theodor W. "Notes on Kafka." In *Prisms*. Translated by Samuel and Shierry Weber. Cambridge: MIT Press, 1981.

Bakhtin, M. M. "Discourse in the Novel." In *The Dialogic Imagination: Four Essays*. Edited by Michael Holquist. Translated by Caryl Emerson and Michael Holquist, 259–422. Austin: University of Texas Press, 1981.

———. "Forms of Time and of the Chronotope in the Novel." In *The Dialogic Imagination: Four Essays*. Edited by Michael Holquist. Translated by Caryl Emerson and Michael Holquist Austin, 84–258. Austin: University of Texas Press, 1981.

———. *Problems of Dostoyevsky's Poetics*. Edited and translated by Caryl Emerson. Minneapolis: University of Minnesota Press, 1984.

Bal, Mieke. *Femmes imaginaires: L'ancien testament au risque d'une narratologie critique*. Paris: Nizet, 1986.

———. *Lethal Love: Feminist Literary Readings of Biblical Love Stories*. Bloomington: Indiana University Press, 1987.

———. *Narratology: Introduction to the Theory of Narrative*. 2nd ed. Translated by Christine Van Boheemen. Toronto: University of Toronto Press, 1997.

———. "Notes on Narrative Embedding." *Poetics Today* 2, no. 2, (1981): 41–59.

———. *De theorie van vertellen en verhalen: Inleiding in de narratologie*. Muiderberg: Coutinho, 1990.

Banfield, Ann. *Unspeakable Sentences: Narration and Representation in the Language of Fiction*. Boston: Routledge and Kegan Paul, 1982.

Barthes, Roland. "Introduction to the Structural Analysis of Narratives." In *Image-Music-Text*. Edited by Stephen Heath, 79–124. Glasgow: Fontana/Collins, 1977.

———. *S/Z: An Essay*. Translated by Richard Miller. New York: Hill and Wang, 1974.

Baudrillard, Jean. *The Consumer Society: Myths and Structures*. Thousand Oaks CA: Sage Publications, 1998.

Bertens, Hans. *The Idea of the Postmodern: A History*. London: Routledge, 1995.

Beurskens, Huub. *Suikerpruimen gevolgd door Het lam*. Amsterdam: Meulenhoff, 1997.

Bhabha, Homi K., ed. *Nation and Narration*. London: Routledge, 1989.

Bloom, Harold. *A Map of Misreading*. New York: Oxford University Press, 1975.

Bonaparte, Marie. *The Life and Works of Edgar Allan Poe: A Psychoanalytic Interpretation*. Translated by John Rodker. London: Imago, 1949.

Boon, Louis Paul. *Chapel Road*. Translated by Adrienne Dixon. New York: Hippocrene Books, 1972.

———. *Minuet*. Translated by Adrienne Dixon. New York: Persea Books, 1979.

Booth, Wayne C. *The Company We Keep*. Berkeley: California University Press, 1988.

———. *The Rhetoric of Fiction*. Chicago: University of Chicago Press, 1961.

Bourdieu, Pierre. *Distinction: A Social Critique of the Judgment of Taste*. Translated by Richard Nice. London: Routledge, 1984.

———. *The Rules of Art: Genesis and Structure of the Literary Field*. Translated by Susan Emanuel. Stanford: Stanford University Press, 1995.

Bower, Gordon H., and Daniel G. Morrow. "Mental Models in Narrative Comprehension." *Science* 247 (1990): 44–48.

Braidotti, Rosi. *Nomadic Subjects: Embodiment and Sexual Difference in Contemporary Feminist Theory*. New York: Columbia University Press, 1994.

Brakman , Willem. *Ansichten uit Amerika*. Amsterdam: Querido, 1981.

———. *De sloop der dingen*. Amsterdam: Querido, 2000.

———. *Een weekend in Oostende*. Amsterdam: Querido, 1982.

Bremond, Claude. "The Logic of Narrative Possibilities." *New Literary History* 11, no. 3 (1980): 387–411.

———. *Logique du récit*. Paris: Seuil, 1973.

Brewer, Mária Minich. "A Loosening of Tongues: From Narrative Economy to Women Writing." *Modern Language Notes* 99, no. 5 (1984): 1141–61.

Brooks, Peter. *Reading for the Plot: Design and Intention in Narrative*. Cambridge: Harvard University Press, 1984.

———. *Psychoanalysis and Storytelling*. Oxford: Blackwell, 1994.

Brouwers, Jeroen. *Sunken Red*. Translated by Adrienne Dixon. London: Peter Owen, 1990.

Buchholz, Sabine, Manfred Jahn, and Ansgar Nünning, eds. *Literaturwissenschaftliche Theorien, Modelle und Methoden: Eine Einführung*. Trier: Wissenschaftlicher Verlag, 1998.

Chambers, Ross. *Story and Situation: Narrative Seduction and the Power of Fiction*. Minneapolis: University of Minnesota Press, 1984.

Chatman, Seymour. *Coming to Terms: The Rhetoric of Narrative in Fiction and Film*. Ithaca NY: Cornell University Press, 1990.

———. *Story and Discourse. Narrative Structure in Fiction and Film*. Ithaca NY: Cornell University Press, 1978.

Cixous, Hélène. "The Laugh of the Medusa." Translated by Keith Cohen and Paula Cohen. *Signs* 1, no. 4 (1976): 875–93.

Claus, Hugo. *De Geruchten*. Amsterdam: Bezige Bij, 1996.

Cohan, Steven, and Linda Shires. *Telling Stories: A Theoretical Analysis of Narrative Fiction*. London: Routledge, 1988.

Cohn, Dorrit. "The Encirclement of Narrative: On Franz Stanzel's *Theorie des Erzählens*." *Poetics Today* 2, no. 2 (1981): 157–82.

———. *Transparent Minds: Narrative Modes for Presenting Consciousness in Fiction*. Princeton: Princeton University Press, 1978.

Cohn, Dorrit, and Gérard Genette. "A Narratological Exchange." In *Neverending Stories. Toward a Critical Narratology*. Edited by Ann Fehn, Ingeborg Hoesterey and Maria Tatar, 258–66. Princeton: Princeton University Press, 1992.

Cordesse, Gérard. "Narration et focalisation." *Poétique* 76 (1988): 487–98.

Culler, Jonathan. "Problems in the Theory of Fiction." *Diacritics* 14, no. 1 (1984): 2–11.

———. *Structuralist Poetics: Structuralism, Linguistics and the Study of Literature*. London: Routledge, 1975.

Currie, Mark. *Postmodern Narrative Theory*. London: Macmillan, 1998.

Dällenbach, Lucien. *The Mirror in the Text*. Translated by Jeremy Whiteley with Emma Hughes. Cambridge: Polity Press, 1989.

Davis, Robert Con, ed. *Lacan and Narration: The Psychoanalytic Difference in Narrative Theory*. Baltimore: Johns Hopkins University Press, 1983.

de Lauretis, Teresa. *Alice Doesn't: Feminism, Semiotics, Cinema*. London: Macmillan, 1984.

———, ed. *Feminist Studies/Critical Studies*. London: Macmillan, 1986.

———. *The Practice of Love: Lesbian Sexuality and Perverse Desire*. Bloomington: Indiana University Press, 1994.

Deleuze, Gilles, and Félix Guattari. *Anti-Oedipus: Capitalism and Schizophrenia*. Translated by Robert Hurley, Mark Seem, and Helen R. Lane. Minneapolis: University of Minnesota Press, 1983.

———. "Introduction: Rhizome." In *A Thousand Plateaus: Capitalism and Schizophrenia*. Translated by Brian Massumi, 3–25. Minneapolis: University of Minnesota Press, 1987.

de Man, Paul. *Allegories of Reading: Figural Language in Rousseau, Nietzsche, Rilke, and Proust*. New Haven: Yale University Press, 1979.

———. *Blindness and Insight: Essays in the Rhetoric of Contemporary Criticism*. London: Methuen, 1971.

Derrida, Jacques. "Differance." In *Margins of Philosophy*. Translated by Alan Bass, 1–28. Chicago: University of Chicago Press, 1982.

———. *Speech and Phenomena and Other Essays on Husserl's Theory of Signs*. Translated by David B. Allison. Evanston: Northwestern University Press, 1973.

———. "White Mythology." *New Literary History* 6 (1974): 527–64.

Dickens, Charles. *Great Expectations*. Harmondsworth: Penguin, 1965.

Dixon, Peter, and Marisa Bortolussi. "Prolegomena for a Science of Psychonarratology." In *New Perspectives on Narrative Perspective*. Edited by Willie van Peer and Seymour Chatman, 275–87. Albany: State University of New York Press, 2001.

Doležel, Lubomir. "Extensional and Intensional Narrative Worlds." *Poetics*, 8 (1979): 193–212.

———. *Heterocosmica: Fiction and Possible Worlds*. Baltimore: Johns Hopkins University Press, 1998.

———. "Narrative Modalities." *Journal of Literary Semantics* 5, no. 1 (1976): 5–15.

Ducrot, Oswald, and others. *Qu'est-ce que le structuralisme?* Paris: Seuil, 1968.

Eco, Umberto. "Narrative Structure in Fleming." In *The Poetics of Murder. Detective Fiction and Literary Theory*. Edited by Glenn Most and William W. Stowe, 93–117. San Diego: Harcourt Brace Jovanich, 1983.

———. *The Role of the Reader: Explorations in the Semiotics of Texts*. Bloomington: Indiana University Press, 1979.

Edmiston, William F. "Focalization and the First-Person Narrator: A Revision of the Theory." *Poetics Today* 10, no. 4 (1989): 729–44.

———. *Hindsight and Insight: Focalization in Four Eighteenth-Century French Novels*. University Park: Pennsylvania State University Press, 1991.

Faulkner, William. *As I Lay Dying*. Harmondsworth: Penguin, 1965.

———. "A Rose for Emily." In *Selected Short Stories of William Faulkner*, 49–61. New York: Modern Library, 1961.

Ferron, Louis. *De keisnijder van Fichtenwald*. Amsterdam: Bezige Bij, 1976.

———. *De Walsenkoning: Een duik in het autobiografische diepe*. Amsterdam: Bezige Bij, 1993.

Flaubert, Gustave. *Madame Bovary*. Translated by Geoffrey Wall. Harmondsworth: Penguin, 1992.

Fleming, Ian. "From a View to a Kill." In *For Your Eyes Only*, 7–37. London: Hodder and Stoughton, 1989.

Fludernik, Monika. "Fiction vs. Non-Fiction: Narratological Differentiations." In *Erzählen und Erzähltheorie im 20. Jahrhundert: Festschrift für Wilhelm Füger*. Edited by Jörg Helbig, 85–103. Heidelberg: Carl Winter Universitätsverlag, 2001.

———. *The Fictions of Language and the Languages of Fiction: The Linguistic Representation of Speech and Consciousness*. London: Routledge, 1993.

———. *Towards a "Natural" Narratology*. London: Routledge. 1996.

Forster, E. M. *Aspects of the Novel*. Harmondsworth: Penguin, 1990.

Francese, Joseph. *Narrating Postmodern Time and Space*. Albany: State University of New York Press, 1997.

Friedman, Norman. *Form and Meaning in Fiction*. Athens: University of Georgia Press, 1975.

———. "Point of View in Fiction: The Development of a Critical Concept." PMLA 70 (1955): 1160–84.

Frye, Northrop. *The Great Code: The Bible and Literature*. London: Ark, 1981.

Genette, Gérard. "Discours du récit: Essai de méthode." In *Figures III*, 65–282. Paris: Seuil, 1972.

———. *Fiction and Diction*. Translated by C. Porter. Ithaca NY: Cornell University Press, 1993.

———. *Narrative Discourse*. Translated by Jane E. Lewin. Ithaca: Cornell University Press, 1980.

———. *Narrative Discourse Revisited*. Translated by Jane E. Lewin. Ithaca: Cornell University Press, 1988.

———. *Palimpsests: Literature in the Second Degree*. Translated by Channa Newman and Claude Doubinsky. Lincoln: University of Nebraska Press, 1998.

Gerrig, Richard. *Experiencing Narrative Worlds: On the Psychological Activities of Reading*. New Haven: Yale University Press, 1993.

Gibson, Andrew. *Towards a Postmodern Theory of Narrative*. Edinburgh: Edinburgh University Press, 1996.

Gibson, Walker. "Authors, Speakers, Readers, and Mock Readers." *College English* 11 (1950): 265–69.

Gilbert, Sandra M., and Susan Gubar, *The Madwoman in the Attic: The Woman Writer and the Nineteenth-Century Literary Imagination*. New Haven: Yale University Press, 1979.

———. *No Man's Land: The War of the Words*. New Haven: Yale University Press, 1988.

———. *No Man's Land: The Place of the Woman Writer in the Twentieth Century: Sexchanges*. New Haven: Yale University Press, 1991.

———. *No Man's Land: The Place of the Woman Writer in the Twentieth Century: Letters from the Front*. New Haven: Yale University Press, 1994.

Giora, Rachel, and Yeshayahu Shen. "Degrees of Narrativity and Strategies of Semantic Reduction." *Poetics* 22 (1994): 447–58.

Girard, René. *Deceit, Desire, and the Novel: Self and Other in Literary Structure*. Translated by Yvonne Freccero. Baltimore: Johns Hopkins University Press, 1965.

———. *The Scapegoat*. Translated by Yvonne Freccero. London: Athlone Press, 1986.

———. *Things Hidden Since the Foundation of the World*. Translated by Stephen Bann and Michael Metteer. Stanford: Stanford University Press, 1987.

Greimas, A. J. *On Meaning: Selected Writings in Semiotic Theory*. Translated by Paul J. Perron and Frank H. Collins. Minneapolis: University of Minnesota Press, 1987.

———. *Structural Semantics: An Attempt at Method*. Translated by D. McDowell, R. Schlefier, and A. Velie. Lincoln: University of Nebraska Press, 1983.

Hamon, Philippe. "Pour un statut sémiologique du personage." *Littérature* 6 (1972): 86–100. Revised version in Roland Barthes, and others, *Poétique du récit*, 115–180. Paris: Seuil, 1977.

———. *Texte et idéologie: Valeurs, hiérarchies et évaluations dans l'œuvre littéraire*. Paris: PUF, 1984.

Harvey, David. *The Condition of Postmodernity: An Enquiry into the Origins of Cultural Change*. Oxford: Blackwell, 1989.

Hawkes, David. *Ideology*. London: Routledge, 1996.

Heise, Ursula K. *Chronoschisms: Time, Narrative, and Postmodernism*. Cambridge: Cambridge University Press, 1997.

Herman, David. "Hypothetical Focalization." *Narrative* 2, no. 3 (1994): 230–53.

———, ed. *Narratologies: New Perspectives on Narrative Analysis*. Columbus: Ohio State University Press, 1999.

———. "Scripts, Sequences, and Stories: Elements of a Postclassical Narratology." *PMLA* 112 (1997): 1046–59.

Herman, Luc. *Concepts of Realism*. Columbia: Camden House, 1996.

Ibsch, Elrud. "The Cognitive Turn in Narratology." *Poetics Today* 11, no. 2 (1990): 411–18.

IJlander, Gijs. *Een fabelachtig uitzicht*. Utrecht: Veen, 1990.

Ingarden, Roman. *The Literary Work of Art*. Translated by George G. Grabowicz. Evanston: Northwestern University Press, 1973.

Irigaray, Luce. *This Sex Which Is Not One*. Translated by Catherine Porter with Carolyn Burke. Ithaca NY: Cornell University Press, 1985.

Iser, Wolfgang. *The Act of Reading: A Theory of Aesthetic Response*. Translated by W. Iser. Baltimore: Johns Hopkins University Press, 1978.

———. *The Implied Reader: Patterns of Communication in Prose Fiction from Bunyan to Beckett*. Translated by W. Iser. Baltimore: Johns Hopkins University Press, 1974.

Jahn, Manfred. "Frames, Preferences, and the Reading of Third-Person Narratives: Towards a Cognitive Narratology." *Poetics Today* 18, no. 4 (1997): 441–68.

———. "Windows of Focalization: Deconstructing and Reconstructing a Narratological Concept." *Style* 30, no. 2 (1996): 241–67.

Jakobson, Roman. "Two Aspects of Language and Two Types of Aphasic Disturbances." In Roman Jakobson and Morris Halle, *Fundamentals of Language*, 67–96. The Hague: Mouton, 1971.

James, Henry. *Theory of Fiction*. Edited by James E. Miller Jr. Lincoln: University of Nebraska Press, 1972.

Jameson, Fredric. *Postmodernism, or, The Cultural Logic of Late Capitalism*. Durham NC: Duke University Press, 1991.

Jauss, Hans Robert. *Toward an Aesthetic of Reception*. Translated by Timothy Bahti. Minneapolis: University of Minnesota Press, 1982.

Jongstra, Atte. *Groente*. Amsterdam: Contact, 1991.

———. *Het huis M. Memoires van een spreker*. Amsterdam: Contact, 1993.

Jouve, Vincent. *Poétique des valeurs*. Paris: PUF, 2001.

Joyce, James. *Ulysses*. Edited by Hans Walter Gabler. New York: Vintage Books, 1986.

Juhl, P. D. *Interpretation: An Essay in the Philosophy of Literary Criticism*. Princeton: Princeton University Press, 1980.

Kafka, Franz. "Up in the Gallery." In *The Complete Stories*. Edited by Nahum N. Glatzer. Translated by Willa and Edwin Muir, 401–2. New York: Shocken Books, 1946.

Korthals Altes, Liesbeth. *Le salut par la fiction? Sens, valeurs et narrativité dans "Le Roi des Aulnes" de Michel Tournier*. Amsterdam: Rodopi, 1992.

———. "Le tournant éthique dans la théorie littéraire: impasse ou ouverture." *Etudes littéraires* 31, no. 3 (1999): 39–56.

Krol, Gerrit. *De oudste jongen*. Amsterdam: Querido. 1998.

Labov, William, and Joshua Waletzky. "Narrative Analysis: Oral Versions of Personal Experience." In *Essays on the Verbal and the Visual Arts*. Edited by June Helm, 354–96. Seattle: University of Washington Press, 1967.

Lacan, Jacques. "The Insistence of the Letter in the Unconscious." In *Modern Criticism and Theory*. Edited by David Lodge. Translated by Jan Miel, 79–106. London: Longman, 1988.

Lämmert, Eberhardt. *Bauformen des Erzählens*. Stuttgart: Metzler, 1970.

Landa, José Angel García, and Susana Onega, eds. *Narratology: An Introduction*. London and New York: Longman, 1996.

Landow, George. *Hypertext: The Convergence of Contemporary Critical Theory and Technology*. Baltimore: Johns Hopkins University Press, 1992.

Lanier, Jaron, and Frank Biocca. "An Insider's View of the Future of Virtual Reality." *Journal of Communications* 42, no. 4 (1992): 150–72.

Lanser, Susan Sniader. *Fictions of Authority: Women Writers and Narrative Voice*. Ithaca NY: Cornell University Press, 1992.

———. *The Narrative Act: Point of View in Prose Fiction*. Princeton: Princeton University Press, 1981.

———. "Sexing Narratology: Toward a Gendered Poetics of Narrative Voice." In *Grenzüberschreitungen: Narratologie im Kontext / Transcending Boundaries: Narratology in Context*. Edited by Walter Grünzweig and Andreas Solbach, 167–83. Tübingen: Gunter Narr, 1999.

———. "Sexing the Narrative: Propriety, Desire, and the Engendering of Narratology." *Narrative* 3 (1995): 85–94.

———. "Toward a Feminist Narratology." *Style* 20, no. 3 (1986): 341–63.

Leitch, Vincent B. *Deconstructive Criticism: An Advanced Introduction*. London: Hutchinson, 1983.

Lejeune, Philippe. *Le pacte autobiographique*. Paris: Seuil, 1975.

Lintvelt, Jaap. *Essai de typologie narrative: Le "point de vue."* Paris: José Corti, 1981.

Lowry, Malcolm. *Under the Volcano*. London: Picador, 1967.

Lubbock, Percy. *The Craft of Fiction*. London: Jonathan Cape, 1968.

Luhmann, Niklas. *Social Systems*. Translated by John Bednarz with Dirk Baecker. Stanford: Stanford University Press, 1995.

Lyotard, Jean-François. *The Postmodern Condition: A Report on Knowledge*. Translated by Geoff Bennington and Brian Massumi. Minneapolis: University of Minnesota Press, 1984.

Mann, Thomas. *Der Tod in Venedig*. In *Gesammelte Werke* Vol. VIII. Frankfurt am Main: S. Fischer Verlag, 1960, 444–525.

Margolin, Uri. "Structuralist Approaches to Character in Narrative: The State of the Art." *Semiotica* 75, nos. 1–2 (1989): 1–24.

Martin, Mary Patricia, and James Phelan. "The Lessons of 'Weymouth': Homodiegesis, Unreliability, Ethics and *The Remains of the Day*." In *Narratologies: New Perspectives on Narrative Analysis*. Edited by David Herman, 88–109. Columbus: Ohio State University Press, 1999.

Martin, Wallace. *Recent Theories of Narrative*. Ithaca NY: Cornell University Press, 1986.

McHale, Brian. "Free Indirect Discourse: A Survey of Recent Accounts." *PTL: A Journal for Descriptive Poetics and Theory of Literature* 3 (1978): 249–87.

Mercadal, Dennis. *A Dictionary of Artificial Intelligence*. New York: Van Nostrand, 1990.

Mezei, Kathy, ed. *Ambiguous Discourse: Feminist Narratology and British Women Writers*. Chapel Hill: University of North Carolina Press, 1996.

Miller, J. Hillis. *The Ethics of Reading: Kant, de Man, Eliot, Trollope, James, and Benjamin*. New York: Columbia University Press, 1987.

———. *Fiction and Repetition: Seven English Novels*. Oxford: Basil Blackwell, 1982.

Miller, Nancy K. "Changing the Subject: Authorship, Writing, and the Reader." In *Feminist Studies/Critical Studies*. Edited by Teresa de Lauretis, 102–20. London: Macmillan, 1986.

———. *The Heroine's Text: Readings in the French and English Novel 1722–1782*. New York: Columbia University Press, 1980.

———. *Subject to Change: Reading Feminist Writing*. New York: Columbia University Press, 1988.

Minsky, Marvin. "A Framework for Representing Knowledge." In *Frame Conceptions and Text Understanding*. Edited by Dieter Menzing, 1–25. New York: De Gruyter, 1979.

Modleski, Tania. "Feminism and the Power of Interpretation: Some Critical Readings." In *Feminist Studies/Critical Studies*. Edited by Teresa de Lauretis, 121–38. London: Macmillan, 1986.

Moraru, Christian. *Rewriting: Postmodern Narrative and Cultural Critique in the Age of Cloning*. Albany: State University of New York Press, 2001.

Mulisch, Harry. *Voer voor psychologen: Zelfportret*. Amsterdam: Bezige Bij, 1961.

Müller, Günther. "Erzählzeit und erzählte Zeit." In *Festschrift Paul Kluckhohn und Hermann Schneider*, 195–212. Tübingen: J. C. B. Mohr, 1948.

———. *Morphologische Poetik: Gesammelte Aufsätze*. Tübingen: Max Niemeyer, 1974.

Multatuli. *Max Havelaar, or the Coffee Auctions of the Dutch Trading Company*. Translated by Roy Edwards. London: Penguin Books, 1987.

Murray, Janet. *Hamlet on the Holodeck: The Future of Narrative in Cyberspace*. New York: The Free Press, 1997.

Mutsaers, Charlotte. *Paardejam*. Amsterdam: Meulenhoff, 1996.

———. *Zeepijn*. Amsterdam: Meulenhoff, 1999.

Nash, Christopher, ed. *Narrative in Culture: The Uses of Storytelling in the Sciences, Philosophy and Literature*. London: Routledge, 1990.

Nell, Victor. *Lost in a Book: The Psychology of Reading for Pleasure*. New Haven: Yale University Press, 1998.

Newton, Adam Zachary. *Narrative Ethics*. Cambridge: Harvard University Press, 1995.

Nünning, Ansgar. " 'But why *will* you say that I am mad?' On the Theory, History, and Signals of Unreliable Narration in British Fiction." *Arbeiten aus Anglistik und Amerikanistik* 22, no. 1 (1997): 83–105.

———. "Informationsübertragung oder Informationskonstruktion? Grundzüge und Konsequenzen eines konstruktivistischen Modells von Kommunikation." *Humankybernetik* 30, no. 4 (1989): 127–40.

———. "Renaissance eines anthropomorphisierten Passepartouts oder Nachruf auf ein literaturkritisches Phantom? Überlegungen und Alternativen zum Konzept des 'implied author.' " *Deutsche Vierteljahrsschrift für Literaturwissenschaft und Geistesgeschichte* 67, no. 1 (1993): 1–25.

———. "Unreliable, Compared to What? Towards a Cognitive Theory of Unreliable Narration: Prolegomena and Hypotheses." In *Grenzüberschreitungen: Narratologie im Kontext / Transcending Boundaries: Narratology in Context*. Edited by Walter Grünzweig and Andreas Solbach, 53–73. Tübingen: Gunter Narr Verlag, 1999.

Ohmann, Richard. "Speech Acts and the Definition of Literature." *Philosophy and Rhetoric* 4 (1971): 1–19.

O'Neill, Patrick. *Fictions of Discourse: Reading Narrative Theory*. Toronto: University of Toronto Press, 1994.

Page, Ruth E. "Feminist Narratology? Literary and Linguistic Perspectives on Gender and Narrativity." *Language and Literature* 12, no. 1 (2003): 43–56.

Pascal, Roy. *The Dual Voice: Free Indirect Speech and its Functioning in the Nineteenth Century European Novel*. Manchester: Manchester University Press, 1977.

Pavel, Thomas. *Fictional Worlds*. Cambridge: Harvard University Press, 1986.

Perry, Menakhem. "Literary Dynamics: How the Order of a Text Creates Its Meanings." *Poetics Today* 1, nos. 1–2 (1979): 35–64, 311–61.

Petrey, Sandy. *Speech Acts and Literary Theory*. New York: Routledge, 1990.

Phelan, James. *Narrative as Rhetoric: Technique, Audiences, Ethics, Ideology*. Columbus: Ohio State University, 1996.

———. "Narrative Discourse, Literary Character, and Ideology." In *Reading Narrative: Form, Ethics, Ideology*. Edited by James Phelan, 132–46. Columbus: Ohio State University Press, 1989.

———. *Reading People, Reading Plots: Character, Progression, and the Interpretation of Narrative*. Chicago: University of Chicago Press, 1989.

Poe, Edgar Allan. *The Complete Works of Edgar Allan Poe. Volume II: Tales-Volume I*. Edited by James Harrison. New York: AMS Press, 1965.

———. *Poetry and Tales*. New York: Literary Classics of the United States (Library of America), 1984.

———. *Selected Tales*. Edited by Julian Symons. Oxford and New York: Oxford University Press, 1982.

Pratt, Mary Louise. *Toward a Speech-Act Theory of Literary Discourse*. Bloomington: Indiana University Press, 1977.

Prince, Gerald. *A Dictionary of Narratology*. Lincoln: University of Nebraska Press, 1987.

———."Introduction à l'étude du narrataire." *Poétique* 14 (1973): 178–96.

———. *Narratology. The Form and Functioning of Narrative*. The Hague: Mouton, 1982.

———. "Notes towards a Categorization of Fictional Narratees." *Genre* 4 (1971): 100–105.

———. "On Readers and Listeners in Narrative." *Neophilologus* 55 (1971): 117–22.

Propp, Vladimir. *Morphology of the Folktale*. 2nd ed. Translated by Laurence Scott. Revised by Louis A. Wagner. Austin: University of Texas Press, 1968.

Proust, Marcel. *Remembrance of Things Past: Swann's Way*. Translated by Scott Moncrieff. New York: Knopf, 1982.

Punday, Daniel. *Narrative after Deconstruction*. Albany: State University of New York Press, 2003.

Pynchon, Thomas. *Gravity's Rainbow*. London: Picador, 1975.

Rabinowitz, Peter. *Before Reading: Narrative Conventions and the Politics of Interpretation*. Columbus: Ohio State University Press, 1987.

Reve, Gerard. *Nader tot u*. Amsterdam: Veen, 1993.

———. *Het Boek Van Violet En Dood*. Amsterdam: Veen, 1996.

———. *Het hijgend hert*. Amsterdam: Veen, 1998.

Ricœur, Paul. *Time and Narrative*. Vol. 1. Translated by Kathleen McLaughlin and David Pellauer. Chicago: University of Chicago Press, 1984.

———. *Time and Narrative*. Vol. 2. Translated by Kathleen McLaughlin and David Pellauer. Chicago: University of Chicago Press, 1985.

———. *Time and Narrative*. Vol. 3. Translated by Kathleen Blamey and David Pellauer. Chicago: University of Chicago Press, 1988.

Rimmon-Kenan, Shlomith. *Narrative Fiction: Contemporary Poetics*. London and New York: Routledge, 1983. (Second edition: 2002).

Robinson, Sally. *Engendering the Subject: Gender and Self-Representation in Contemporary Women's Fiction*. Albany: State University of New York Press, 1991.

Roemer, Michael. *Telling Stories: Postmodernism and the Invalidation of Traditional Narrative*. Boston: Rowman and Littlefield, 1995.

Ronen, Ruth. *Possible Worlds in Literary Theory*. Cambridge: Cambridge University Press, 1994.

Rushdie, Salman. *Haroun and the Sea of Stories*. London: Granta Books, 1990.

Ryan, Marie-Laure. "Cyberage Narratology: Computers, Metaphor, and Narrative." In *Narratologies: New Perspectives on Narrative Analysis*. Edited by David Herman, 113–41. Columbus: Ohio State University Press, 1999.

———. "Cyberspace, Virtuality, and the Text." In *Cyberspace Textuality: Computer Technology and Literary Theory*. Edited by Marie-Laure Ryan, 78–107. Bloomington: Indiana University Press, 1999.

———. *Narrative as Virtual Reality: Immersion and Interactivity in Literature and Electronic Media*. Baltimore: Johns Hopkins University Press, 2001.

———. *Possible Worlds, Artificial Intelligence, and Narrative Theory*. Bloomington: Indiana University Press, 1992.

Schweickart, Patrocinio P. "Reading Ourselves: Toward a Feminist Theory of Reading." In *Speaking of Gender*. Edited by Elaine Showalter, 17–44. New York: Routledge, 1989.

Searle, John. *Speech Acts: An Essay in the Philosophy of Language*. Cambridge: Cambridge University Press, 1969.

Soja, Edward. *Postmodern Geographies: The Reassertion of Space in Critical Social Theory*. London: Verso, 1989.

Smart, Barry. *Postmodernity*. London: Routledge, 1993.

Stanzel, Franz K. "A Low-Structuralist at Bay? Further Thoughts on a Theory of Narrative." *Poetics Today* 11, no. 4 (1990): 805–16.

———. *Narrative Situations in the Novel: "Tom Jones," "Moby-Dick," "The Ambassadors," "Ulysses."* Translated by J. Pusack. Bloomington: Indiana University Press, 1971.

———. *A Theory of Narrative*. Translated by Charlotte Goedsche. Cambridge: Cambridge University Press, 1984.

Sternberg, Meir. *Expositional Modes and Temporal Ordering in Fiction*. Baltimore: Johns Hopkins University Press, 1978.

———. "Point of View and the Indirections of Direct Speech." *Language and Style* 15, no. 2 (1982): 67–117.

Todorov, Tzvetan. *Grammaire du Décaméron*. The Hague: Mouton, 1969.

Tomashevsky, Boris. "Thematics." In *Russian Formalist Criticism: Four Essays*. Edited by Lee T. Lemon and Marion J. Reis, 61–95. Lincoln: University of Nebraska Press, 1965.

Turgenev, Ivan. "Asya." In *First Love and Other Stories*. Translated by Richard Freeborn, 100–143. Oxford: Oxford Paperbacks, 1999.

Uspensky, Boris. *A Poetics of Composition: The Structure of the Artistic Text and Typology of a Compositional Form*. Translated by Susan Wittig and Valentina Zavarin. Berkeley: University of California Press, 1973.

Van Boheemen-Saaf, Chr. "Deconstructivisme." In *Vormen van literatuurwetenschap. Moderne richtingen en hun mogelijkheden voor tekstinterpretatie*. Edited by R. T. Segers, 229–47. Groningen: Wolters-Noordhoff, 1985.

van der Heijden, A. F. Th. *Asbestemming. Een requiem*. Amsterdam: Querido, 1994.

van der Voort, Cok. "De analyse van verhalend proza." In *Literatuur en context. Een inleiding in de literatuurwetenschap*. Edited by Peter Zeeman, 24–58. Nijmegen: Sun, 1991.

Vitoux, Pierre. "Le jeu de la focalisation." *Poétique* 51 (1982): 359–68.

Vonnegut, Kurt. *Slaughterhouse-Five*. London: Jonathan Cape, 1970.

Warhol, Robyn R. *Gendered Interventions: Narrative Discourse in the Victorian Novel*. New Brunswick: Rutgers University Press, 1989.

———. "Guilty Cravings: What Feminist Narratology Can Do for Cultural Studies." In *Narratologies: New Perspectives on Narrative Analysis*. Edited by David Herman, 341–55. Columbus: Ohio State University Press, 1999.

White, Hayden. *Metahistory: The Historical Imagination in Nineteenth-Century Europe*. Baltimore: Johns Hopkins University Press, 1973.

Index

In the *Frontiers of Narrative* series:

Story Logic: Problems and Possibilities of Narrative
by David Herman

Handbook of Narrative Analysis
by Luc Herman and Bart Vervaeck

Spaces of the Mind: Narrative and Community in the American West
by Elaine A. Jahner

Talk Fiction: Literature and the Talk Explosion
by Irene Kacandes

Fictional Minds
by Alan Palmer

Narrative across Media: The Languages of Storytelling
edited by Marie-Laure Ryan